The Lost Message of Paul

Steve Chalke

Has the Church misunderstood
the Apostle Paul?

W0009749

First published in Great Britain in 2019

Society for Promoting Christian Knowledge
36 Causton Street
London SW1P 4ST
www.spck.org.uk

British Library Cataloguing-in-Publication Data
A catalogue record for this book is available from the British Library

ISBN 978–0–281–07940–7
eBook ISBN 978–0–281–07941–4

1 3 5 7 9 10 8 6 4 2

Typeset by Manila Typesetting Company
Printed in Great Britain by Jellyfish Print Solutions

eBook by Manila Typesetting Company

Produced on paper from sustainable forests

'This is an exciting and timely book. Accessible and authoritative. A great lay introduction to historical criticism, contextual analysis and the writing of St Paul.'

Robert Beckford, Professor of Theology and Culture in the African Diaspora, Canterbury Christ Church University

'If you've met Steve in flesh and blood, then you know how extraordinarily *alive* he is, how open and free and hopeful and compelling – which brings me to this book. *The Lost Message of Paul* is pulsing and brimming and overflowing with that very same life. Only this time he's homed in on the Apostle Paul and his underrated and overlooked genius, innovation and revolutionary fervour. If you're familiar with the Bible, you will find yourself frequently pausing while reading and thinking, "Wait – what? That's the word, that's the idea, that's what Paul actually said? How come everybody doesn't know this?" And if you are new to the Bible, you'll find yourself saying, "That's what is actually written in the Bible? That's both ancient and yet so fresh and pressing for our world right now. This could change things in all the best possible ways." The research, the stories, the synthesis of then and now – this book is going to set so many people free.'

Rob Bell, author of Love Wins

'Seldom does the same person build an amazing organization and write amazing books. And seldom does an author of an amazing book grapple with a huge body of scholarship and then summarize it in a way that popular audiences can read and enjoy. That's why Steve Chalke is so remarkable. His new book, *The Lost Message of Paul,* is not only well written and fascinating; it is also profoundly bold and revolutionary. In fact, its impact could be of historic importance, if enough of us have the courage to read it and put its message into practice. Highly recommended for all who dare to give life's most important questions a second thought!'

Dr Brian D. McLaren, author of The Great Spiritual Migration

'Some may find the content of *The Lost Message of Paul* troubling, even shocking. Steve Chalke in his inimitable style opens up dense theological debate in an accessible and readable manner. This fascinating book will challenge you to reconsider familiar theological "truths" and may even revolutionize your Christian journey.'

Dr Pauline Muir, lecturer at Goldsmiths, University of London, and member of Oasis Church Waterloo

'In his exploration of Paul's life and teaching, Steve Chalke sets out an expansive and radical vision of inclusion and integration as he invites us to understand Christ through Paul's eyes. This is a bold and compelling book that speaks from beginning to end of the profound good news of God's kingdom. There is joy, liberation and challenge here in equal measure. I thoroughly recommend this book to you.'

Fr Richard Rohr, author of The Universal Christ

'If any biblical figure gets a bad press from Christians, it's St Paul. Steve Chalke does a brilliant job of not just rehabilitating Paul but reminding us that he was an energetic revolutionary. He was far from being a friend of reactionaries, as he is often portrayed today. Steve shows us that Paul's message was radically inclusive and refreshingly modern. Read Steve's book and prepare to have your mind expanded and your spirit stretched as Paul redefines what it means to be a Christian, then and now. Just as when you read St Paul himself, you will not finish this book unchanged.'

Lucy Winkett, Rector of St James's Church,
Piccadilly, London

Steve Chalke is a Baptist minister, author, speaker, justice campaigner, broadcaster, social entrepreneur and former UN Special Advisor on Human Trafficking. In 1985 he founded the Oasis Trust with a vision to build inclusive local communities where everyone is given the opportunity to make a contribution and to achieve their God-given potential. Oasis is now one of the very largest charities in the UK, as well as working in a host of other countries to provide housing, education, healthcare and various other community-building initiatives.

Steve holds an MBE, a number of honorary fellowships and a doctorate from Staffordshire University, all awarded for his work in social inclusion and justice. Steve still leads Oasis and is also the senior minister of Oasis Church Waterloo in central London – a place of inclusion where all are welcome.

Also by Steve Chalke

The Lost Message of Jesus

Intelligent Church: A journey towards Christ-centred community

Change Agents: 25 hard-learned lessons in the art of getting things done

Apprentice: Walking the way of Christ

Different Eyes: The art of living beautifully

Being Human: How to become the person you were meant to be

Radical: Exploring the rise of extremism and the pathway to peace

To the young people of 'The Bridge' on the
Isle of Sheppey and my six grandsons,
Josiah, Reuben, Leo, Ari, Raphael and Rocco

Contents

Contents

Acknowledgements

Throughout this project I have enjoyed the support, feedback and input of a host of friends with degrees and doctorates, expertise and experience in subjects as diverse as theology, psychology, religious studies, youth work, Greco-Roman culture, history, education, church leadership, psychotherapy, neuroscience, ethics, linguistics, sociology, philosophy and common sense. I particularly owe unending thanks to:

Danielle, Jim, David, Sally, Ann, Douglas, Paul, Brian, Clare, Claire, Camila, Joy, Jill, Mark and Esther, as well as all the wonderful volunteers and staff, past and present, of Oasis globally. We are a team.

And, on top of all that, extra special thanks also go to Tony, my editor at SPCK, Judith, my hardworking, forever loyal and extraordinarily resilient PA, and Cornelia, probably the most patient wife in the world.

1

The conversation

I want to start a conversation about Paul the Apostle.

Aside from Jesus, he is – beyond all doubt – the dominant figure in the New Testament; more than half the books it contains were written by, in the name of or about him.

Because of this, across the centuries, Paul has had immeasurable influence on the Church worldwide in all its shapes and sizes, dimensions and denominations. Sadly, as a result, he has very often also shouldered the blame for its worst excesses: its discrimination and dogmatism, its inflexibility and judgementalism, its prejudice and bigotry, its sexism and chauvinism.

But I believe that Paul has been misunderstood. Badly misunderstood.

Too often, his words have been 'borrowed'; lifted out of context and then drummed into the service of ideas and policies, doctrines and behaviours which not only would he never have owned, but also would have strongly opposed.

That is why I chose to write this book and to call it *The Lost Message of Paul*. Rather than forcing our preconceived cultural assumptions on to this extraordinary first-century pioneer, our task is to try to listen as hard as we can to the meaning of his words in terms of their original context and culture. I believe that not only will this liberate them from their incarceration in negativity, it will unearth their revolutionary and positive meaning for our generation as well as for those beyond us.

I grew up in a local church where it was hard to ask honest questions about anything much. The pulpit sat high above all contradiction. But in my twenties I decided I'd rather live a life with questions I might not even find answers for than one filled with questions I wasn't allowed to ask.

That's what led me to begin to ask questions about Paul and to dig into some of the problems that I had with 'the angry Apostle'.

Just last week I had a coffee with someone who told me that she was a member of her local church. During our conversation I happened to tell her that I was writing a book about one of my heroes – the Apostle Paul. She looked horrified. 'Whatever you've got to say, you won't change my mind about him.'

So, here is my confession. The ideas that I present here are not my own. Instead, you will discover as you read that they are taken from the wider world of scholarship; from ancient as well as modern thinkers and writers. They represent a huge body of thought relating to Paul and his message, which – though somehow lost to our society – is, once you have the opportunity to engage with it, literally world-changing.

The conversation

In terms of the study of Paul's life and work, there is a huge gap between the world of scholarship and popular understanding. My task is simply to try to help to bring these insights to a wider audience; to unpack – to make plain – what others have already explored in longer volumes, which although stuffed with pages of uninviting small font and technical language, contain eye-opening information and jaw-dropping wisdom.

I am a leader of a local church. As I often say to our congregation, a sermon should be regarded as great not because everyone in the building agrees with the preacher but because, following its delivery, those present just can't wait to discuss, debate and chew it over with one another on the way home.

In exactly the same way, not everyone will agree with all I have to say here. What is more, you will discover that I don't agree with every scholar I have quoted. In fact, there are some with whom I disagree passionately. With others I sometimes agree and sometimes differ, but with others there is absolutely nothing the depth of whose contribution I can think of adding to, or subtracting from.

However, what I most want to do is express my respect for the contributions of all who, from many traditions and cultures, over the centuries of the history of the Church, have brought their understanding to this dialogue. Whatever my opinion of the content of their work, each has had the courage and commitment to play a part in our ongoing intergenerational conversation, the only means through which any of us can find truth.

That's the point. Although we will not always all agree, our hallmark – the common hallmark of those who seek to follow Jesus – should be to continue to listen to each other, extending grace and patience to one another as we go. After all, our inclusion by God is never on the basis of the correctness of our views, but always because God graciously and mercifully accepts us, mostly in spite of the opinions we adopt. Our acceptance of each other should always reflect this same principle.

Which brings me to one more confession. The way I see things now is not the way I have always seen them. My faith is changing. It is evolving. I hope that it is deepening, developing and maturing. Therefore, for me, rather than placing my primary emphasis on defending immoveable doctrinal positions, the real quest – the real responsibility – is to commit wholeheartedly to the continuous task of grappling with Scripture. For me, this is a lifelong task not driven by any disrespect for or disregard of the Bible but, instead, by the very opposite; by the deepest respect for its collection of inspired texts which have been regarded as sacred by the Church through so many centuries.

So, perhaps it is not so much that I want to start a conversation about Paul the Apostle, as to continue the one that has been running since he first burst on to the stage of history, into the market squares of the Roman Empire, and put his pen to paper.

Here's my contribution. Let's keep talking.

PS. God's personal pronoun is 'spirit' rather than 'he' or 'she'. God is other. But we are confined by our language.

The conversation

Throughout this book I've tried to use terminology that transcends gender when speaking of God, but occasionally – because of the limitations of English – I've failed. Please forgive me.

2

The revolutionary

Howard Thurman was born in 1899 in Florida. In 1953 *Life* magazine ranked him as one of the 12 most important religious leaders in the United States. Years later *Ebony* magazine named him one of the 50 most important figures in African-American history.

Thurman, a theologian and educator, was 30 years older than Martin Luther King, Jr. Through his teaching at Howard University and then Boston, as well as his preaching, he became a trusted intellectual and spiritual advisor not only to King, but to an entire generation of those who would lead the civil rights movement in its struggle for African-American freedom.

Throughout the 1950s and 1960s King quoted, paraphrased and drew on ideas from Thurman in his speeches and sermons. It is said that during the long struggle of the Montgomery bus boycott, King carried in his pocket a copy of Thurman's best-known book. *Jesus and the Disinherited* pictured Jesus as the ally of the dispossessed – from his original small group of followers living under the oppression of the Roman army and the rejection of the Jewish establishment in ancient first-century Palestine, to the African-Americans living under the yoke of slavery and segregation in the twentieth-century USA.

Howard Thurman had been raised by his grandmother, who was born into slavery on a plantation in northern Florida. She was a committed Christian, but never learned to read. 'So,' he said, 'all the years that I was growing I had the job of reading to her every day.' But, he explains, she would never allow him to read any of Paul's letters, except now and then the thirteenth chapter of 1 Corinthians.

It took him years, but one day he finally plucked up the courage to ask his grandmother why. Three or four times a year, she explained, her owner would hold a religious service especially for the plantation's slaves. But the Bible reading would always be the same. Always from Paul's letter to the Ephesians: 'Servants, be obedient to them that are your masters . . .'[1] Then the minister would preach about how the Bible taught that it was God's will that black people were slaves and how, if they were good slaves, God would bless them.

Thurman said his grandmother told him that she had made up her mind right then, that if she ever had the opportunity to learn to read or if freedom eventually came to her, she would never, ever read Paul's words again.

Over the centuries, the writing of Paul has been weaponized. His words have been used to justify cruelty towards and exclusion of black people, people of colour, women, people of other religions, the wrong sort of Christian people (Catholic, Orthodox or Protestant, depending on your point of view), non-believers and of LGBT people, to name but a few. So it is no surprise that countless Christians,

---

[1] Ephesians 6.5 (KJV).

aside from anyone else, feel ambivalent at best towards the 'Apostle' and his words. For too many he is the author of structural social exclusion.

So here is the thing . . .

Warning! Please keep reading at least long enough to give me a chance to explain after you have read this next line.

Although Paul has been presented as the champion of exclusion, I have come to believe that he was, in fact, the opposite. Paul – the real Paul – was the great includer!

The Apostle Paul has been painted as a strange cross between a stern old-time street evangelist and an inaccessible academic theologian. He was neither. I think Paul was a revolutionary who saw a new inclusive world dawning and gave his life to help bring it in. The story is told of a bishop who'd recently written a book on Paul's theology, wryly commenting, 'Everywhere I go to speak about Paul they serve tea and cakes afterwards accompanied by polite conversation. Everywhere Paul went to speak a riot broke out.'

Hold the newspaper in one hand and the Bible in the other. It is the best way of interpreting the world. It's what they used to teach me at theological college. What they were trying to say, in a kind of pre-digital, pre-social media style, was that the Bible provides the best commentary on and practical guide to life.

But for most of the intelligent, thoughtful people I know, this is a ridiculous statement. The Bible seems archaic and irrelevant, and the Apostle Paul, closely connected with half of the New Testament and the author of what are thought to be some of its most draconian (not to mention sometimes incomprehensible) teachings, seems one of the worst offenders. More than that, if we've lost faith in the Bible – or at least in our interpretation of it – we have other narratives that are failing us too.

Whether it is the rhetoric of the left or of the right, both have let us down. Badly. The various idealistic worlds that they offered us have not arrived. Yet they cling for dear life to their broken narratives, just like those helpless and hopeless lost souls left clinging to bits of floating wreckage on a hostile ocean long after the *Titanic* had sunk.

Not only this, but – moving the metaphor on slightly – we have begun to sense that there is a severe storm coming in; that the way of life so many have taken for granted for so long is unsustainable.

We are in crisis. Things feel more polarized, more fragile, more precarious than we have ever known. Our democratic and financial institutions, along with our polar ice caps and local communities, are in danger of collapse. But, worse still, we sense that in all this we are rudderless. Adrift on a sea of confusion without a lifejacket or any sense of direction. Not only has the scientific and technological 'progress' that was meant to save us failed to do so – but, as we are now painfully aware, most of the real progress made has been at someone else's expense.

All the old narratives are dead.

The revolutionary

We need a new story.

And I am crazy enough to believe that's where Paul – the real Paul – can help us.

Our problem is that we've read Paul of Tarsus through the words of other famous men, particularly Augustine of Hippo, Luther of Wittenberg and Calvin of Geneva – all of whom we shall meet along this journey as we seek to rediscover what I think is the long-lost message of Paul. It's time to unlearn our culturally conditioned readings of his words and work hard to allow the real Paul, the first-century thinker, to speak to us instead.

In the West, on one hand, medieval Catholicism slowly distorted Paul's words, turning many of them into the source of a system of control, of shame, fear and crippling Catholic guilt.

Then, in reaction, Martin Luther and John Calvin, the sixteenth-century 'protest-ants', in attempting to 'reform' these abuses, turned the meaning of Paul's words on their heads to power what became a new system of control, of shame, fear and crippling Protestant guilt.

Our task is not to allow the same thing to happen again.

Thirty-plus years ago I founded a charity called Oasis. One of the things we do is to take responsibility for local schools around England. In this process, we've often inherited a tired old building that has slowly 'evolved' over the decades . . . some 1960s classrooms, a 1970s assembly hall, a 1980s kitchen and dining room, a 1990s extension with more classrooms, a gym and a new toilet block. All connected by a tangled web of corridors, an inadequate heating system, uneven floors and leaking roofs.

From this I've learned that sometimes it is best to pull the whole thing down and start again. But I've also learned another lesson: it is far quicker to deconstruct than to build. The bulldozing bit is easy – it's the reconstruction that takes the time, planning, skill and care. What's more, you don't want to throw the baby out with the bathwater. There are some good principles of school building that have been learned over the years. So, although you don't want to repeat the same old mistakes, you do want to benefit from hard lessons won as well as from good new methods and research.

The way I see it, it is time to start again with Paul. His writing is a hidden treasure. Hidden because it's been discoloured, encrusted and buried in the dirt and grime of Church history and scholarship over the centuries, and then used, sometimes unintentionally, sometimes not, to construct some extraordinarily repressive and controlling structures.

The meaning that we load language with can be very personal. Even simple words, such as 'father', 'mother', 'school', 'health', 'home' or 'work', can convey very different emotion and meaning for different people. But rarely is this recognized. Instead, we assume when using them that their meaning is plain and obvious. In truth, however, words and phrases used by another person can set us free or act as prison cells from which we cannot escape. They can relax and soothe us, or put us on edge. Inspire and excite us, or oppress and deflate us. Create space for us or hem us in.

First-century words and phrases are often far too tarnished and discoloured by their use over the centuries to be easily understood in the twenty-first century. Terms like justification, law, judgement, salvation, holiness, wrath, righteousness, heaven and hell can all end up, in their decontextualized form, sounding pretty frightening, not to mention causing huge levels of confusion and pain. In fact, I guess you know people – lots of people – who though once counting themselves within the Church, now regard themselves as outside it. And, likewise, many others who have never even considered joining.

The result of all this? Paul's voice has ended up being misheard, misunderstood, misinterpreted, misused, misjudged, and therefore sometimes written off altogether as too stern, too misogynistic and too disciplinarian. It has been lost.

It is time to let him speak again.

3

Longing

There are 27 books in the New Testament. Thirteen of them were either written by Paul or written in his name by another author strongly influenced by his thought. On top of this, he also features as the central figure of the Acts of the Apostles. That amounts to just over half of the entire New Testament.

There is an almost universal consensus that Paul himself wrote the seven letters that we know as Romans, 1 and 2 Corinthians, Galatians, Philippians, 1 Thessalonians and Philemon. The scholars disagree with one another over Ephesians, Colossians and 2 Thessalonians because of questions about content, style and vocabulary. There is widespread consensus that what we call the three pastoral letters – 1 and 2 Timothy and Titus – were written by others, perhaps even after his death, in his name.[1]

---

[1]   Some early Church leaders also credited Paul with the authorship of the anonymous Epistle to the Hebrews, but this was rejected as early as Origen of Alexandria.

   Many scholars challenge the authenticity of 2 Thessalonians because to them it looks like a deliberate attempt to rewrite 1 Thessalonians. They suggest that 2 Thessalonians quotes from and follows the format of 1 Thessalonians while offering a different plan for when the 'end' will come. Others dispute whether there is any contradiction between these two texts. Colossians and Ephesians present a different kind of question. Both seem to differ from the

14

None of this is sinister. Instead, it's rather like the fact that although loyal students of Rembrandt, inspired and influenced by his life and work, did their best to paint in his exact style and colours, scholars can still distinguish, through thoughtful research, original Rembrandts from those painted by his followers. But – while not ignoring the others, especially where it is clear that they are seeking to amplify principles that Paul sets out elsewhere – for the purposes of this book I will focus primarily on those letters that are undisputed.

Because of the sheer volume and influence of Paul's work, to try to understand the development of the Church without reference to him is a bit like trying to understand the development of modern music without any reference to Elvis . . . or the Beatles, the Stones, Dylan, Michael Jackson and U2, all put together. Some people even go so far as to claim that Christianity, as we have come to practise it, should more accurately be labelled 'Paulianity'. No one, however, can doubt for a moment that Paul's influence on the whole way in which we think of what it is to follow Jesus is huge.

---

undisputed letters of Paul in their style and vocabulary, which leads many scholars to suggest that they come from a different writer.

There is general consensus, however, that the three pastoral letters were written in Paul's name after his death. The technical term for this is pseudepigraphical. They present a more elaborate set of church offices and services and new concerns about doctrine and practice, while vocabulary, style and even key Pauline concepts are either ignored or changed to represent the Church as a far more rigid hierarchy. All six of these disputed letters are sometimes termed Deutero-Pauline, i.e. written in Paul's name by another author strongly influenced by Paul's thought.

Paul, or to give him his Hebrew birth name Saul, was born around AD 6, to Jewish parents in the city of Tarsus, in modern south-eastern Turkey, 20 kilometres inland from the Mediterranean Sea. He was perhaps a decade younger than Jesus. Around seventy years earlier, Pompey – one of Rome's great military leaders – had marched into Tarsus and made it the capital of the Roman province of Cilicia – so as well as being Jewish, Paul was born a citizen of the Empire.[2]

It is often argued that Paul took hold of the simple, grace-filled, generous message of Jesus and twisted it into a legalistic system of exclusion and control – a misogynist, homophobic cult – and that what we've somehow got to do is get back to the simple message of Jesus. I disagree. I see things very differently.

It is true that Saul was brought up as a legalist. A strict Jew. A Pharisee. But as Acts 9 tells us, on that now famous Damascus road, this ultra-legalistic, fiercely nationalistic, religious conservative, on a mission to destroy the infant Church, experienced 'a light from heaven flashing around him, blinding him'. We are then informed that 'as he fell to the ground he heard a voice calling to him, "Saul, Saul, why do you persecute me?"' And that, on enquiring who was speaking to him, he received the response 'I am Jesus . . . now get up and go into the city, and you will be told what you must do.'

Of course, the exact details of what happened are contested. Historians, theologians and psychologists have

---

[2] Paul was most probably one of Saul's Roman names.

been arguing for many years about the exact nature of this encounter. Was it psychological or physical? Was this a literal blinding searchlight from the sky? Was anyone else aware of it? Acts tells us that the people with him heard a sound, but doesn't confirm whether they could recognize it as a human voice. So, was Saul's whole experience internal?

These are impossible questions to answer. However, what is indisputable is the outcome. Whatever happened on that road, Saul was transformed by it. Until that point his considerable energy and passion had been totally dedicated to preserving and pursuing Israel's traditions. That's why he was so engaged in the violent persecution of the followers of 'the Way' (as the followers of Jesus were known); they were peddling a dangerous heresy. Just when, in the face of Roman pressure, Israel needed to keep its sense of identity and purpose clear and strong, these weak-minded renegades were diluting and eroding it.

But, from that moment on, Saul was an unreserved devotee of Jesus. He was mesmerized by him. As far as we know he was in his late twenties at this point, and for the rest of his life he would devote all his energy, dedication and ambition to this new story.

So he spends the rest of his life travelling (he covers about ten thousand miles), often locked up and beaten up, but constantly writing, teaching and – most importantly – building small cross-cultural revolutionary cell groups committed to a different worldview, all centred on his understanding of the risen Christ.

Saul – or Paul, which clearly became his preference[3] – was an energy-packed, creative, innovative, strategic negotiator, global thinker and thought leader. Far from subverting Jesus' message, he truly grasped it and spent the rest of his life grappling with what it actually meant when applied to the broad canvas of the non-Jewish world.

Jesus' audience was primarily Jewish. He had insisted, however, that his followers should take his message 'into all the world', teaching them about his revolutionary way of being human.[4] This, of course, was to prove a huge challenge. But cometh the moment, cometh the leader. Enter Paul.

It was this challenge that took Paul into areas of thinking that Jesus had not encountered, or on which he had left no specific teaching. This accounts for the huge amount of time he spends talking about topics that Jesus never even mentioned.

Paul's task was to discover how to apply Jesus' life-transforming and liberating message to communities for whom the cultural trappings of Judaism were completely foreign. Themes like circumcision and food laws seem remote and hair-splitting to us, but, far from being a diversion from the core of Jesus' liberating message, this was frontline stuff for Paul. His was the gigantic task

---

[3] It is often assumed that Saul's name was changed when he became a follower of Jesus, but that is not the case. Luke continues to use the name Saul for him even when he has become an accepted teacher within the Church. Then, in Acts 13.9, Luke indicates that the names were interchangeable: 'Saul, who also is called Paul'.

[4] See Mark 16.15; Matthew 28.19–20; Acts 1.7–8.

of negotiating and thinking his way through it all, and then seeking to apply Jesus' revolutionary values to new cross-cultural situations.

Thanks to his strategic awareness, he recognized that these cell groups had to be integrated expressions of the teaching and example of Jesus, genuine peace communities – because, if not, Jesus' message would forever be a cause of division and segregation rather than human unity. In addition, he faced a second challenge which complicated everything. He had to achieve this new understanding of Jesus as the Messiah for the whole world at the same time as working with the first followers of Christ, who were all Jewish; for these first followers of Jesus, little was more important or sacred than food laws and the rite of circumcision.

So Paul wrote:

> To the Jews I became like a Jew, to win the Jews. To those under the law I became like one under the law . . . so as to win those under the law. To those not having the law I became like one not having the law . . . so as to win those not having the law.[5]

And the record left behind in the Bible's account of his life and work tells us that he approached this task with an enthusiasm that was irrepressible and a drive that was to change the world.

---

[5] 1 Corinthians 9.20–21.

4

Air

My eldest grandson loves sharks. All sharks. When he was three I bought a blow-up plastic shark for him to enjoy in a swimming pool on our family summer holiday. It arrived in the post. He couldn't wait to open the package, but when he did he was extremely disappointed. The shark didn't look very shark-like at all. Instead it was flat and shaped like the box it came in.

I managed to curb his disappointment by explaining that all we had to do was blow air into it for long enough and it would soon be authentically shark-shaped. He suggested we start and watched eagerly as I blew. First the dorsal fin and then the tail appeared. He was fascinated by this and gave me a running commentary. But he had a problem. He could see right through the transparent plastic 'skin' of the shark and it troubled him.

In the end his curiosity was too much to contain. 'Grandpa,' he said, 'what's happening?'

'I'm filling it with air and that's what's slowly giving it shape.'

There was a long silence. 'What's air?' he enquired.

'Air is what I'm blowing in.'

Air

'Where does it come from?'

'Out of my lungs.'

'What are lungs?' That was confusing because we had to spend the next few minutes talking lungs before returning to the story of air.

'Air', I eventually explained, 'is all around you. You can't see it but it's what I've been blowing into the shark, and it's what we all breathe every day. It's what keeps us all alive. We depend on the air.' My little grandson had lived quite happily for three years, totally dependent on air, without ever being aware of its existence.

The culture we inhabit is like the air that we breathe. Even if we are aware of it, we tend to take it for granted and forget about it. We absorb it without noticing it. We rarely stop to ask questions about it, test it or analyse it.

The experts have various complex names for this – a grand narrative, a framing script, a controlling cultural construct – but in the end it all boils down to the same thing. We all live inside some sort of big story. And, in the West, a core part of that dominant story is capitalism. Even though many of us do our best to keep our eyes open, to resist accepting its assumptions blindly without filtering them and to live 'counter-culturally', its 'air' is all around us, we are immersed in it, and we take many of its implications for granted.[1]

---

[1] For more on 'framing narratives', see Neil Postman, *The End of Education* (London: Vintage, 1996).

Equally, Paul lived inside a particular framing story; it was the air that he breathed. And in 1977, a theologian by the name of Ed Sanders opened our eyes in a new way to what this story was. He wrote a book called *Paul and Palestinian Judaism*, which was much like an atom bomb being dropped into the Western Church's understanding of Paul. And its impact grew slowly into what is now called by theologians the 'New Perspective on Paul'.[2]

What Sanders sought to do was to answer the question about the kind of cultural story Paul lived in. What was the cultural air that he breathed? What did he take for granted? What were the unwritten assumptions that he made about life and that sat behind everything he said? Sanders claimed that the basic problem facing New Testament scholarship was that it had not taken history seriously enough, and so had misunderstood what Paul was saying to his original audience and therefore what his teaching is saying to us today.

The problem is that there is always a time-lag between the developing edge of new theological understanding and teaching as delivered in a local church. Over the years I've seen this played out time and time again; the gap can be a big one. But, by anyone's schedule, it's time we all got to grips with Paul's culture.

The story that Paul lived in is what we call Second Temple Judaism. This is the oxygen that he, like all other first-century Jews, breathed.

---

[2] Advocates of the New Perspective include scholars such as Tom Wright, James Dunn, Wayne Meeks and many others.

Why is this important? Because a text without a context becomes a pretext. And that has been the whole problem with the tales of exclusion and rejection, damnation and segregation that the writing of Paul has been used to fuel.

The story of Judaism is the story about how God chose the people of Israel and worked with them across the centuries. Its beginnings are recorded for us in the book of Genesis, with the account of a man called Abraham and God's promise to him, not only to bless him with many descendants but through them to bless all the peoples of the earth.

It's a wonderful story. But it's one that goes wrong. And, to get to the point, much later the people of Israel end up, believe it or not, as slaves in Egypt – the superpower of the day – for a period of around four hundred years. Yet, from the depths of their despair, they cry out to God for freedom. And eventually, via another famous character, Moses, God answers their prayer.

They are rescued through the event that is to become known as the exodus. They're set free from slavery and from Egypt. They are redeemed. They are saved; saved as a whole people, rather than as individuals. And this extra-ordinary piece of history becomes the foundation of their understanding of themselves and of their relationship with God.

Their escape – or rather their rescue – from Egypt only intensified the Ancient Jews' shatterproof trust in their covenant relationship with the God of all creation. The God of all creation had made unbreakable covenantal promises to them. The God of all creation had acted on those responsibilities and could therefore be relied on in the future. The God of all creation would not fail them.

This is what Paul believed and, indeed, this is what people of the Jewish faith still believe. Even today, if you were to try to convince a Jew that by praying a certain prayer she might be 'saved', she would find your words incomprehensible. Though too polite to say it, she would be thinking: *We are saved, we are redeemed, it's already happened and it will happen again. We are the people who know God's grace.*

So, what about the Second Temple bit?

Well, redeemed through the exodus, though it takes another generation, the people of Israel finally end up in what they call 'the Promised Land', and there settle down to enjoy their new life of freedom. Over time they establish a monarchy. The best known of their kings is David, who is followed by his son Solomon, who commands a temple to be built.

The first Temple.

This Temple houses God's 'Shekinah'. *Shekinah* is a Hebrew word meaning 'dwelling' or 'settling' and denotes the divine presence of God. In fact, back in their journey across the desert, the Jews carried with them a kind of travelling temple – a huge tent which they called the Tabernacle – where they had also believed God's Shekinah was present.

So far, so good. But then things go wrong again.

The monarchy becomes corrupt. Leadership breaks down. Unity is lost. The north and south of the country fall out with each other and divide into two separate entities: Israel (the north) and Judah (the south). The latest super-power – Assyria – overwhelms the north. Later it falls to Babylonia, led by the tyrant Nebuchadnezzar, who then besieges Jerusalem, which results in its destruction – including the demolition of the Temple – in 587 BC. Judah's king, Zedekiah, is captured. His sons are executed in front of him. He is then blinded and deported, along with many others, to the city of Babylon. The independent kingdom of Judah is ended and suffers the ignominy of becoming a Babylonian province.

Eventually, however, in the way that it is with empires, Babylon itself falls to the Persian king, Cyrus the Great. And, under his administration, the exiled Judeans are permitted to gradually return to Judah from around 538 BC. According to the biblical book of Ezra, the wall of the city is rebuilt and construction of the second Temple in Jerusalem begins around 520 BC. Second Temple Judaism is born!

But there was still a problem.

Although back in their own land, the Jews were not really free and the second Temple was unfinished. In fact, it was never finished. Herod – a puppet 'king' – was still building it during Jesus' lifetime. Nor did it ever enjoy – in popular opinion – God's Shekinah presence, because, although the Jewish people were back in their own land, they felt that they were really still in exile. Still waiting. Living under the boots of a succession of foreign powers who ruled their precious land and robbed them of freedom.

Between 336 and 323 BC, Alexander the Great conquered much of the eastern Mediterranean world, including what had once been the kingdom of Judah and the city of Jerusalem, as well as Egypt and much of Persia. After he died, these lands were divided up and ruled by his generals and those who followed them. Among the rival groups were the Seleucids and the Ptolemies who, between them, at different times, controlled life in Palestine (both the old southern and northern kingdoms), though happily both chose to respect Jewish culture and protect Jewish institutions.

This policy, however, was deliberately and cruelly reversed by the Seleucid king Antiochus IV, whose nickname was Epiphanes.[3] Although his exact reasoning is disputed, around 168 BC he took the unprecedented step of banning the practice of the Jewish religion. He made a declaration that outlawed study of the law of Moses, including the observance of the Sabbath and the practice of circumcision. And, to top things off, he commanded the Jews to worship Zeus, set up of a statue of the Greek god in the Temple and sacrificed a pig to it (the 'abomination of desolation' spoken of in the prophecy of Daniel).[4]

This deliberate provocation made traditional Jews' blood boil. Under the command of a local hero named Judas Maccabeus, the result was a successful revolt against Antiochus' troops.

---

[3] 'Epiphanes' means 'a god manifest'.
[4] The story is preserved in the books of 1 and 2 Maccabees (part of the Catholic Bible and the Protestant Apocrypha).

The Maccabean rebels set up their own government and, in an event still remembered by Jews today in the celebration of Hanukkah, purified the Temple. Known as the Hasmonean dynasty, the Maccabean family then held on to rulership for the next one hundred years until eventually the Roman general Pompey – the same Pompey who overran Tarsus – successfully invaded Jerusalem in 63 BC, bringing the whole land under Roman control. However, as a 'client kingdom' of Rome, the Hasmoneans retained their position until 37 BC when Herod the Great – designated 'King of the Jews' by the Roman Senate – became king of Israel.

Once again, this time under the Roman boot rather than that of the Greeks, the Jewish people felt trapped. They didn't feel free to be themselves, or to practise their faith as they chose. So they waited; impatient for God, whom they were in covenant relationship with and in whom they had absolute trust, to redeem them again just as had happened in the past. Their prayer was simple: 'Lord, step in and do it again. Do it again.'

Isaiah, one of Judah's sages, once prophesied:

> On this mountain the LORD Almighty will prepare
> a feast of rich food for all peoples,
> a banquet of aged wine –
> the best of meats and the finest of wines.
> On this mountain he will destroy
> the shroud that enfolds all peoples,
> the sheet that covers all nations;
> he will swallow up death forever.
> The Sovereign LORD will wipe away the tears
> from all faces;

> he will remove his people's disgrace
> from all the earth.
> The LORD has spoken.[5]

Every Second Temple Jew clung to this passage, along with others from various books in the Hebrew Bible, now contained in our Old Testament, as they waited impatiently for their 'messiah' – another liberator in the mould of Moses – to arrive.

No Jew believed in a set of ahistorical, theological concepts about an otherworldly salvation. Instead, they all believed that they were living in a 'real-time' drama, one which would reach its climax when their long-awaited messiah figure finally arrived to wage war on their enemies and set them free. And this salvation – this rescue – was never about being set free from an inner sense of private angst, but was rather a release from the reality of social enslavement through a physical event that would turn around human history in the here and now.

More than that, they believed that they were actors, all active participants, rather than simply passive audience members in this great unfolding drama.

That's why when Jesus rode into Jerusalem on a donkey, at the beginning of the week that was to end in his death, the people chanted 'Hosanna', which means 'save us, liberate us'. They sang it because they dared to believe, in that moment, that he was the Messiah they had long hoped for. They had placed their hope in others – such as Judas

---

[5]   Isaiah 25.6–8.

Maccabeus – in the past. This time they pinned their nation-alist hopes on Jesus; then, tragically from their perspec-tive, they saw those hopes crushed again. Why? Because instead of freeing them from Roman control, Jesus failed to deliver and then suffered the ultimate humiliation: exe-cution on a cross just a few days later.

That's Second Temple Judaism with its particular set of longings and expectations.

And, in a nutshell, that's Paul's framing story.

5

A new world

No narrative, no theology, is of theoretical and abstract interest only. All our beliefs matter. For us and for others. Now and for the next generations. They shape us. They shape our world. They shape the lives of others.

Saul's encounter on the road to Damascus changed his story. But rather than destroying it, his experience completed it. It brought it alive. It brought him alive. But the question remains: why exactly was Saul hounding the followers of Jesus in the first place? The answer is not quite what you might expect.

Saul's decision to seek permission to hunt down the followers of Jesus was not because of their belief in a messiah. He also believed in – and longed for – the coming of a Jewish messiah. His problem was a different one. His problem was that Jesus was the wrong kind of messiah.

Jesus was dead. And a dead messiah was no messiah.

How could a dead liberator be a liberator? How could a dead messiah take on the imperial army and win freedom for Israel? It was simply intolerable for a zealous Jew like Saul that a would-be messiah could have died a criminal's death. How could the holy end up full of holes? In fact, years later, he acknowledges this very point. A crucified messiah is, he admits, a 'stumbling block' or 'scandal' for the Jewish people.[1]

This is the reason why Saul feels that he has to snuff out the fledgling movement, which is diluting Judaism, and doing so at the very moment when its distinctiveness has to be maintained. The followers of the Way have to be destroyed before they can do too much damage.

But on the road to Damascus Saul hears the voice of Jesus. And through this encounter – whatever form it takes – Saul recognizes that Jesus is alive. For him this has huge implications. From that moment on, with the same boundless energy he has brought to his task of exterminating the Church, he spends the rest of his life telling this new story about Jesus, the unlikely Messiah.

For Paul this commitment turned into a particularly punishing business. Over the coming years he would undertake three enormous journeys, covering thousands of miles on the primitive, precarious and perilous transport systems of the day to enthuse others across the Empire with what he had discovered. What's more, wherever he travelled, he would always ensure that he was not a burden by insisting on working to earn his own living.[2] But his message wasn't always well received, and enduring riots, attacks and imprisonments became part of his life. While coping with this, all the time he was also writing to the

---

[1] 1 Corinthians 1.23 (NIV and Aramaic Bible in Plain English).

[2] Paul, Luke tells us, was a tentmaker by trade.

other cell groups that he had already established, in order to help encourage and direct them.

Yet, throughout it all, he remains strategically aware. As a Roman citizen, although Paul is free to travel the whole Empire, he deliberately chooses to head west rather than east. The reason? His goal is to reach the very heart of the imperial system: Rome itself. There is, he believes, a new emperor in town, his name is Jesus and everybody needs to know it.

Saul's narrative had always been in conflict with the great imperial story of his day. Augustus, who had died only some 20 years beforehand, was the first emperor of the Roman Empire. He had controlled imperial Rome from 27 BC until his death in AD 14 and, besides anything else, had built an extraordinary PR machine.

Under Augustus' leadership, Rome had been transformed, it was proclaimed, from a struggling republic into the greatest and most famous empire of them all. And as its founder and sole leader, Augustus had developed what he termed his 'gospel' for the people; the 'good news' articulated in an inscription found at Myra, in Lycia: 'Divine Augustus Caesar, son of god, imperator of land and sea, the benefactor and saviour of the whole world has brought you peace.'[3]

Rome's writers and poets – Horace and Ovid, Livy and Virgil – as well as many others, told this story in terms of

---

[3] Quoted in Brian D. McLaren, *The Secret Message of Jesus* (Nashville: Thomas Nelson, 2006), p. 10.

being the climax of human history. It pictured Augustus, the adopted son of the deified Julius Caesar, as bringing justice not only to Rome, but also to the whole world; of ushering in an era of prosperity – the still famous 'Pax Romana' or 'Roman Peace'. This was the narrative that was enthusiastically 'sold' to the people via the social media of the day, from imperial architecture, monuments and statues to coins, plays and poems. You couldn't miss it.

But Saul always saw through the hype to the reality. He recognized it for what it was: nothing more than a parody of the true story. And now that story, the story of Second Temple Judaism, had reached its climax through Jesus, the long-awaited but equally improbable Jewish Messiah – who was also the true Lord of all. But this king, unlike Caesar, Paul has come to understand, does not rule through acts of violence and subjugation. Instead he chooses to bring true liberation of all men and women through his self-sacrifice.

It is a big mistake to regard Paul as a Christian. Paul wasn't a Christian, he was a Jew. He never threw away his Jewish heritage; he never abandoned it. He simply came to believe that Jesus, the Jewish Messiah, was the Messiah for the whole world – not just for the Jews.

Paul's writing is filled with references to the Jewish prophets, to King David, to Abraham and Moses. Why would he do that if he had abandoned Judaism? Paul was still living in the Second Temple Jewish story; he had simply come to believe that Jesus was its fulfilment.

So he writes to his friends in the city of Colossae:

The Son is the image of the invisible God, the firstborn over all creation. For in him all things were created: things in heaven and on earth, visible and invisible, whether thrones or powers or rulers or authorities; all things have been created through him and for him. He is before all things, and in him all things hold together.[4]

But, in Paul's mind, this was not about two rivals – Caesar and Jesus – vying for the top position. It was about a different order of thinking. It was about liberation rather than control. Liberation *from* the pursuit of power and self-interest rather than *through* the pursuit of power and self-interest. Liberation not *with* the sword, but *from* the sword.

A new world had been born.

If Saul stood before us today, he would ask the same questions of the imperial systems we have placed our trust in. Have they liberated or enslaved us? Has our supposed 'progress' set us free? How is our concept of a global village developing? Have all 'benefited' from our globalized world – or are some disillusioned and disenfranchised by it? Which, of course, poses some even deeper questions for us.

Is the child that we have given birth to behaving like a beast? Does our version of globalization beget corporations and multinationals that view the world as a single market in which they are free, indeed duty bound, to allocate and reallocate their resources, to shift production and to market goods for efficiency and for their own sustainability

---

[4] Colossians 1.15–17.

and continuous growth? Does it concentrate economic power and the unequal distribution of economic gains as the global super-wealthy pull away from the rest?

Would we have to admit that, driven largely by unfettered capitalism, our version of globalism has produced social dislocation? That it has eroded customs, political processes and ideas; that it has endangered health? That it has turned lush meadows into barren deserts; that it has led to the disintegration of indigenous cultures and the loss of sovereignty? That it offers no answer to the fact that broken economies, drought and poor harvests, as well as war zones, produce mass migration, which is often not just the logical choice but perhaps the only choice for those whose loss is the greatest?

Would we have to confess that we long for a generation of leaders across the world who are capable of thinking selflessly about the needs of the whole earth and all its people from an integrated global perspective?

Not so long ago I was invited to talk with senior executives of a leading multinational financial institution. We discussed the ever-growing problem they had with staff retention. They explained that the average age of their staff was just 28, and that their challenge was to address the issue of why 'so much talent' was leaving their employment. This issue is one which, from my conversations with other large financial organizations, I know to be commonplace.

As we talked, a young Harvard-trained graduate – a staff member – sat in the room observing the conversation. I asked whether she could relate to the trend we were discussing. Her response was that not only did it sum up her view of things, but it was also the common view of all her young colleagues. 'We will work here to gain experience – but leave here to give our lives to something more satisfying and fulfilling, although less well paid.'

For Paul, his new-found faith in Christ was never a passport to turn his back on the world or on any of its people. That was never his position. Tribalism had no place in his thinking. The creator and redeemer God of Israel, Paul had now come to believe, could be relied on to put the whole world to rights and create justice for all in line with his ancient promises.

It is not until the fifth century, about AD 420, that the cross of Jesus begins to appear as a symbol of Christianity. One of the big reasons for this was obviously the threat of persecution. But if you visit the catacombs in Rome, you will notice that all the early images painted by the Christians are images of deliverance. Of Daniel in the lion's den. Of the three young men in the fiery furnace. Of the exodus. Why? Because for all the early Christians, just as for Paul, Jesus was the liberator, the Messiah. And the movement he inaugurated was the new exodus; but this time for the whole world.

Paul doesn't believe in some disembodied theology. He doesn't believe that faith is an assent to a set of ethereal beliefs. For him faith is a way of living. It is a way of being.

Too often we make the mistake of believing that Christianity is about intellect. That it is somehow about believing the right stuff, about having orthodox beliefs that can be written down and stated clearly without hesitation or deviation. But, for Paul, being a follower of Christ is about changing society, it's about being in a story. It is a societal revolution.

It surprises some, but, in his writing, Paul only ever mentions the birth of Jesus once, in a single line in his letter to his friends in Galatia.[5] For him it is the Easter story that is the central, world-changing, life-transforming moment. He would have agreed with the words of a great theologian of another age, Karl Barth, who put it this way: 'The resurrection of Jesus was like a boulder crashing into the pool of history.'[6]

Paul has come to believe that Jesus is the Messiah because he has done what Isaiah spoke of. He has 'swallowed up death'. Because of this Paul is convinced that the new world is being born and that through Jesus the rest of the Isaiah passage will be fulfilled: 'a feast of rich food for all peoples, a banquet of aged wine – the best of meats and the finest of wines'. He believes that 'The Sovereign LORD will wipe away the tears from all faces; he will remove his people's disgrace from all the earth.'[7] For Paul, Jesus is the beginning of a new creation; a new liberation which is for all the people of the whole world, not just as recipients but also as participants.

---

[5] Galatians 4.4: 'But when the set time had fully come, God sent his Son, born of a woman, born under the law . . .'

[6] Karl Barth, *The Word of God and the Word of Man* (San Francisco: Harper, 1957), p. 63.

[7] Isaiah 25.6–8.

Our problem is that, as we will discover later, the focus of attention in much of the Western Church has shifted since the Middle Ages from the larger biblical framework which is clear in Paul's letters, and has been recast around the much more self-centred discussion of how we as individuals can be 'put right with God' and 'go to heaven'.

But it's time to follow Paul in lifting our story out of this lingering medieval framework, and bolt it firmly back into the biblical narrative of how God is renewing the whole creation and seeking our part in that great mission.

After his Damascus road experience, we know that Paul completed his journey to the city, where he spent some time with the followers of 'the Way' and began to talk about the revolution that had taken place in his life. The result was a precursor of things to come. Those who had once been his supporters now tried to kill him. So he was smuggled out and dispatched to Jerusalem.

There, although some members of the church were afraid of him – and who can blame them – Barnabas, one of their leaders, believed in him and began to act as his sponsor. As a result, Paul soon found himself given the opportunity to explain publically the reasons for his turnaround, which led some of the traditional Jewish faction once more to make an attempt on his life. This time, the church decided that the best thing was to pack him off back to his cosmopolitan home town of Tarsus for a while.

So Paul disappeared, and we are not sure for how long. But at some point Barnabas went to look for him, found him and took him to the city of Antioch where they spent the next year together; during this period Paul no doubt learned as well as taught about the revolutionary new way in which he saw the world. It was the church there that recognized his global passion and gift, and commissioned him to head off to Cyprus with his mentor Barnabas.

This erstwhile ferociously nationalistic, deeply conservative and merciless persecutor of the followers of the Way has re-emerged having rethought his entire worldview in the light of Jesus' death and resurrection.

Paul the global leader is born!

6

Perspective

We have made a category error.

We've chopped life up. Aristotle was a philosopher, Pythagoras was a mathematician, Ptolemy was an astronomer, Cicero a lawyer and Paul a religious leader.

We love separating, categorizing and labelling life's components. But life is not like that. Aristotle, Pythagoras, Ptolemy, Cicero and Paul: each was a world-class polymath, a cross-disciplinary genius.

Paul was not primarily a religious writer. He was writing about life; about philosophy, about ethics, about culture, about politics, about economics and sociology as well as theology.

Preachers often act as though their opinions are beyond question; as if their pulpit, or stage, is – metaphorically as well as literally – six feet above all contradiction. But, if this was ever true, it is not now. Paul is not the private property of the Church. It does not have a monopoly on the interpretation of his thought and its meaning. He is studied around the world by historians and philosophers, archaeologists and political analysts, sociologists and anthropologists, psychologists and psychotherapists, linguists and strategists, as well as theologians. More than that, scholarship is diverse, cross-pollinating, always advancing and, in the case of the archaeologists, literally digging up new understanding with each passing year.

Old-time preachers could get away with yanking a few words or a couple of verses out of Paul's overall thought (or anyone else's for that matter) and using them as a prop for their own pre-developed ideas. It still happens. We all know how anyone can take a phrase from a politician or celebrity, out of context, and then 'spin' it to fit their own purposes. But we have a name for that now; we call it fake news.

There is a big word that biblical scholars use to help us detect and deal with all this: hermeneutics, the theory of interpretation. Rather than ask, 'What does this Bible passage, verse or story mean for me?' hermeneutics insists that the first question always has to be, what did it mean for its original audience, its initial hearers or its first readers? And to answer that question we have to engage with questions about the culture or framing story in which the statement sits.

So, what was going on when Paul wrote his letter to the Romans or the Corinthians? What was happening in civic life? What was concerning the people who lived in these cities? What were their hopes and aspirations? What was going on in Paul's life? It's only as we grapple with these questions that we can possibly understand what he was saying to his original hearers.

The mistakes we make with respect to such matters can be very costly. Take, for instance, this piece of advice from Paul to the young followers of Jesus in the city of Corinth:

> Because of the present crisis, I think that it is good for a man to remain as he is. Are you pledged to a woman? Do not seek to be released. Are you free from such a commitment? Do not look for a wife . . . But those who marry will face many troubles in this life, and I want to spare you this.[1]

Do a quick search on the internet and you'll discover that the vast majority of articles written by church leaders about this passage are attempts to try to rehabilitate Paul's seemingly anti-sex, anti-marriage view of life – maybe because the writers are mostly married!

But it gets murkier. This anti-sex, anti-marriage understanding of Paul's words has also played its part in the development of Roman Catholic leadership policy concerning compulsory celibacy. Through the Church's first centuries, clergy continued to get married if they chose to. But in 1075 Pope Gregory VII issued a decree that effectively barred married priests. Fifty years later this was formalized by the First Lateran Council, which was held in 1123. Ever since, celibacy has been required of Roman Catholic priests.

I'll leave it to you to reflect on some of the issues that this has contributed to; from the chronic lack of applicants now coming forward for the Roman Catholic

---

[1] 1 Corinthians 7.26–29.

priesthood, to the number of sexual scandals that have dogged that wing of the Church historically and continue to bite today.

But what if the Church has read Paul wrong? What if the context in which he wrote those verses was completely different? What if Paul really wasn't anti-sex or anti-marriage, was never committed to a view that the best way for all, because the end of the world was imminent, was celibacy? What if Paul's concern was about something much more here and now?

In fact, that's exactly what Paul himself claims. 'Because of the present crisis, I think . . .' he writes. The question is, what was that present crisis?

We now know that ensuring regular supplies of food was a constant concern in Ancient Roman cities. In Corinth, 'so critical was the need to import food, especially grain, the city had its own official . . . who was in charge of the acquisition of adequate supplies', says the Greco-Roman historian Donald Engels in his book *Roman Corinth: An alternative for the classical city.*[2]

We also know, from Luke, writing in Acts 18.1–18, that Paul spent about eighteen months living in the city, working hard to set up a local church there. It is generally agreed that he arrived there 'about March 50 and stayed there until about September 51' and, having left them, he then wrote the letter we call First Corinthians

[2] D. F. Engels, *Roman Corinth: An alternative for the classical city* (Chicago: University of Chicago Press, 1990), p. 58.

to his friends there, some eighteen months or two years later in 53 or 54.[3]

We also know from various ancient historians that grain shortages in parts of the Roman Empire led to a series of severe famines in the middle of the first century, during the reign of the Emperor Claudius.[4] This is confirmed by Luke in Acts 11.28. In fact, it is believed that Corinth was probably severely affected by the famine of AD 51; the famine that the Roman historian Tacitus refers to as a 'calamity', and that Suetonius, another late first-century historian, also writes of. So, as the theologian Raymond Collins explains, 'Paul may simply be giving the unmarried Christians of Corinth a bit of practical advice in the midst of life's difficulties.'[5]

It makes perfect sense that the terrible famine Paul experienced while he was there, and realized could so easily recur, would have had a huge impact on his perspective, and influenced the practical advice he gave to his friends still living there.

Without doubt, following his Damascus road transformation, Paul would have viewed this 'present crisis' as yet more evidence of the unravelling of the power structures which held the current world order in place. But, it seems more than likely that, rather than being anti-sex or

---

[3] David Prior, *The Message of 1 Corinthians* (Leicester: IVP, 1985), p. 14.

[4] Bruce W. Winter, *After Paul Left Corinth: The influence of secular ethics and social change* (Grand Rapids: W. B. Eerdmans, 2001), pp. 215–32.

[5] Raymond F. Collins, *First Corinthians*. Sacra Pagina, ed. Daniel J. Harrington, vol. 7 (Collegeville: Liturgical Press, 1999), p. 293.

anti-marriage, he simply understood that in the middle of the first century AD (long before contraceptives), in a famine-stricken city, more marriages meant more mouths to feed.

Which leads us to another hermeneutical principle.

All Paul's letters are occasional. Every one is written to a particular audience. Each of them (with the possible exception of the letter to the Romans) is addressed to people he knows well, and is written on the occasion that he has something important to say to them, or because they have contacted him with a specific problem they are facing.

That means that Paul says different things to different churches in different situations at different times. So, to decontextualize a specific point that he makes to a particular church and then to try to turn it into a universal principle – applicable at all times, in all places, to all people – is to make a dangerous error, no matter how many preachers endorse it.

Some years ago I went through a period of being responsible for leading two churches. They were in entirely different communities (about five miles apart) and their members didn't know each other very well at all. I would regularly write to the leaders of both. But my advice to each was completely different. Looking back, I've often thought that if anyone ever got hold of those old emails and tried to construct a cohesive theology based on them, whatever they wrote would end up misrepresenting me badly, but worse still, confusing themselves terribly.

Reading each of Paul's letters in the light of the specific cultural contexts into which it was first written makes a huge practical difference to understanding them. What was clear to their original readers is very often not clear to us.

Breaking out of our assumptions – digging deeper and getting to grips with the cultural references, allegories and metaphors of Paul's world – is therefore a vital foundation if we are to understand his writing for what it is. Only when we do this can we get out of the text what was actually there in the first place. Whenever we fail to recognize the cultural distance between the biblical world and our contemporary settings, we simply bring our modern Western bias to the text, which inevitably leads us to make all sorts of false assumptions. The result is that we load Paul with our 'stuff', turning his writing into little more than an echo chamber for our own preconceived thoughts.

Take, for instance, the famous Church reformer Martin Luther, the sixteenth-century German monk, priest and scholar. In October 1517 he took his stand against organized religion of his day by nailing his 95 theses to the door of the Castle Church in Wittenberg (which served as the town noticeboard), as well as delivering them to his area bishop. The boldness of this action kick-started what we now call the Reformation: the re-formation of much of the Western Church.

Luther had come to believe that the established Church, with its excesses of power and control, just didn't fit with the life of Jesus or the needs of the world in which he was called to live and serve. From this starting point he reimagined faith, salvation and the shape of church, all based on his understanding of the work of Paul and especially his letter to the Romans. But, even in the moment that Luther made his brave protest, he also made some big mistakes.

Luther misread Paul, and what Paul taught about Jews and Judaism, as a direct equivalent to his own struggle against medieval Catholicism. In doing so, he created as many problems as he solved – some of which we are still battling with today. For instance, few doubt that his reading and interpretation of the New Testament and what it meant for the Jewish people was at least a contributory factor to the Holocaust, the Nazis' attempt to wipe the Jewish people from the face of the earth.

In his younger years Luther defended the Jewish people. But he seems to have expected them to convert en masse to his version of Christianity. When they didn't, his attitude slowly hardened against them, eventually growing into real fury.

All this reached a head in 1543 when, in his late fifties, Luther wrote *On the Jews and their Lies*, a 65,000-word anti-Semitic book in which he denounced the Jews and urged their persecution. In it, he sets out at considerable length his views concerning Jews and Judaism. To quote him, this 'base, whoring people, that is, no people of God, and their boast of lineage, circumcision, and law must be accounted as filth'.[6]

---

[6] Martin Luther, *On the Jews and their Lies* (1543), Chapter 4.

He goes on to call for Jewish synagogues and schools to be burnt down, their prayer books and religious writings to be destroyed, their rabbis to be forbidden to teach and preach, and their property and money to be confiscated – to be given back only to those who truly convert. They should, Luther claims, be shown no mercy or kindness, afforded no legal protection, and drafted into forced labour or expelled from Germany for all time. Even more shockingly, he appears to go as far as advocating their murder, writing, 'We are at fault in not slaying them.'

It should, therefore, be no surprise that four hundred years later Luther was to become a Nazi favourite, idolized as a German hero especially for his anti-Jewish writing. The Third Reich even reprinted and displayed *On the Jews and their Lies* during the Nuremberg rallies. For them it was perfect fuel to stoke their violently anti-Semitic fervour.

We will look at some of the other problems that Luther's reading of Paul has created for the Church and wider society a little later on. But let it be recorded here that bad theology often costs lives.

We must learn the lesson and do all we can to resist the temptation to read our own situations back into Paul. Instead we have to do the hard work of getting into his world and allowing him to challenge us. Luther failed to recognize that Paul was not a sixteenth-century Reformation thinker; later Europeans failed to grasp, as they tried to exclude the mystical nature of faith, that Paul was not an eighteenth-century Enlightenment thinker. What we all – including me – have to be very careful not to do is to turn Paul into a twenty-first-century post-modern thinker.

Paul was a first-century, Second Temple Jewish follower of Jesus. It takes huge discipline, but it's our task to enter Paul's world instead of trying to push him into ours. If we fail to do this we appoint ourselves ventriloquists and turn Paul into our dummy.

We all know the stories of the pain caused by the mis-reading of Paul through the centuries. We know how his words have been used to justify some of the most inhu-mane, brutal and repressive episodes in human history: to sanction crusades and inquisitions, to approve witch-hunts across Europe and North America, to portray African people as cursed by God and therefore to justify the enslavement of millions, to legitimize apartheid as well as anti-Semitism, to keep women subservient to men, to incite Islamophobia, to oppress gay people, to abuse the environment and more.

We can't just keep reading our own pre-existing theology back into Paul and then claiming his authority for it. We have to wrestle with the text rather than assume that Paul agrees with us – and that means we have to acknowledge that we all come to Paul's writing with our prejudices, produced by our contexts and cultures, our hopes and fears. This, of course, means that we have to recognize that everything we say, even when we say it's final, is actually provisional.

If we respect the Bible, we've got to work harder at it together – and that's only going to happen through open, honest enquiry and questioning. And, in the process, it is vital to keep listening to the voices and opinions of others – without maligning, slandering and misrepresenting those who disagree with us. There should be no question that cannot be asked, that's too dangerous to discuss.

7

A legal error

Trying to understand Paul's teaching without understanding the worldview of Second Temple Judaism is a little bit
like trying to grasp the plot of a long and complex film
by watching the final half hour. Without a deeper grasp
of the storyline, it's almost inevitable that you will fall into
the trap of making some huge misassumptions and reach-
ing some wrong conclusions.

'We maintain that a person is justified by faith apart
from the works of the law', Paul explains to his friends in
Rome.[1] Little wonder, then, that at first sight he appears
to be saying that the only way anyone is counted as 'just'
by God is by 'faith' rather than by any attempt to fulfil
'the works of the law', by which, contextually, Paul means
the law of Moses.

But, as popular as it is, the view that Paul had somehow
come to believe that the Jewish law was dead – that the moral
teaching of the Old Testament had been obliterated – and
that the only thing that mattered now was 'faith in Christ', is
illogical. It just can't be what he meant.

---

[1] Romans 3.28.

Even a casual glance through Paul's writing reveals a very different message. For instance, 'put off your old self' with 'its deceitful desires' and 'put on the new self, created to be like God', he tells the Ephesian church.[2] That habits such as lying, murdering, cheating or the abuse of other people are incompatible with living well, are all key tenets of the Ten Commandments. So it's clearly not these 'works of the law' that Paul has in mind. Instead, he is thinking about something else altogether.

The Apostle sets out what's really on his mind most fully in his letter to his friends in Galatia. Following the story-line of chapter 2, it is clear that there was an influential group of Jewish Christians within the church who did not like the implications of Paul's liberal approach to the inclusion of Gentiles. They were still insisting that all followers of Christ – Gentiles as well as Jews – were required to observe *all* the traditional rites of the Jewish religion, including circumcision and the food laws. But Paul sees things very differently. As far as he is concerned, all these old boundary markers or badges of Judaism – the fences that divide Jew from non-Jew – have been swept away by Jesus. As he makes very clear: 'Neither circumcision nor uncircumcision means anything.'[3]

Which brings us all the way back to Ed Sanders and *Paul and Palestinian Judaism*, the book which turned our understanding of Paul and his message on its head. In the generation since, a huge number of scholars, inspired by Sanders' insight, have continued to research, discuss and

---

[2] Ephesians 4.22–24.

[3] Galatians 6.15.

debate the issues that his work raised. Whole libraries of books and articles of New Testament theology have not only been published but then continuously revised to keep up with our advancing thinking and evidence. And the work of writers like James Dunn, Tom Wright and count-less others[4] – just like me in this book – represents noth-ing more than the ripples and aftershocks of that huge detonation.

This is by no means to say that all these thinkers are say-ing exactly the same thing. In fact, it has been suggested that a plural title of 'New Perspectives on Paul' might far more accurately describe what is going on. What, however, everyone agrees on is that the historic Lutheran perspec-tives on Paul, Judaism, faith and works were fundamen-tally misleading.

The problem, as I see it, is that some New Perspective writers enjoy deconstructing what's old rather than build-ing what's new. Others want to keep most of what's old but play around with the thought of a new extension or two. Still more love tampering with the architecture, but from a purely technical point of view; they delight in the science of it all but haven't quite got the courage to com-mit to the major rebuild that they all know someone has to carry out eventually.

---

[4] James 'Jimmy' Dunn is a leading British New Testament scholar who was for many years Professor of Divinity in the Department of Theology at the University of Durham. He is credited with coining the phrase 'New Perspective on Paul' during his 1982 Manson Memorial Lecture. Tom Wright is an English Pauline theologian and retired Anglican bishop. In academia, he also publishes under the name N. T. Wright. Tom is one of the most prolific 'New Perspective on Paul' writers.

Like I've already said, however, rather than criticizing bits of the Reformation floor plan, deconstructing some of its walls, patching up the roof, adding an extension or two and hoping it doesn't leak, or just playing with design plans, in my view it's time for us all to admit that the building we have now isn't fit for purpose. It is time to go back to the drawing board and start again, not for the sake of the academic exercise but because we want to build something that is healthy to live in and that provides us the space and resources we need to get on with the job we are employed to do.

If we are wise, of course, what we build will have a continuity as well as a discontinuity with what has gone before, learning from the past and at the same time looking to the future. But, whatever its design, it must be built again on the foundation that is the vision of the two greatest revolutionaries I believe the world has ever seen: Jesus of Nazareth and his loyal and courageous follower, Paul of Tarsus.

So let's explore in a little more depth the epicentre of the 'New Perspective' explosion.

Most informed Christians know that Luther – the father of the Reformation and the Protestant Church – had a problem with the New Testament book of James. He didn't like it; he called it an 'epistle of straw' and campaigned to have it removed from the Bible. But why?

The answer is also common knowledge. James's message just didn't fit with Luther's thesis, which – based on his understanding of Paul's letter to the Romans – was that salvation is 'by faith alone'. Annoyingly, James taught the opposite, that 'a person is justified by works, and not by faith alone'.[5] No wonder Luther wanted him silenced.

For us, this raises a much, much bigger question. If the main foundation of the Reformation is built on a doctrine – an assumption – that doesn't fit with the text of at least one of the books of the New Testament, is that doctrine correct, or is it mistaken? An epistle of straw or a doctrine of straw? If all the facts don't fit the explanation we've been given for the last five hundred years – is it time to head back to the drawing board?

Sanders argued exactly this: Luther's core assumption was a huge mistake![6] Indeed, so explosive was Sanders' writing that he struggled to find anyone to print it – and was turned down several times – before securing a brave enough publisher.

But, back in 1963, more than a decade before Sanders' famous book appeared, Krister Stendahl – a scholar whose speciality was Lutheran theology – published a paper in which he argued that Luther's understanding of the Apostle Paul's worldview did not fit the facts. It was, he said, based more on a set of mistaken assumptions about Paul's beliefs than a careful reading and interpretation of his writings. As Stendahl suggested, the problem was that the father of the Reformation, and others who followed him, all made the same mistake, that of 'imposing modern

---

5   James 2.24.
6   In fact, Sanders wasn't the first to do so – but he was the first to really bring this giant issue to the attention of the wider world of scholarship.

Western ideas on the Bible, and especially on the works of Paul'.[7]

In a nutshell, according to the historic Protestant view – based on Luther's idea of *sola fide*, or justification 'by faith alone' – Paul is understood to be arguing that 'good works' don't count; they just don't factor in salvation. It is only 'faith' that makes any difference. But, said Stendahl, we must lift Paul's letters out of this misleading framework and instead interpret them based on an understanding of first-century Judaism, in its own terms. If we don't immerse ourselves in the cultural assumptions and values behind the text, we will never understand it correctly. It is too easy to take Western cultural assumptions for granted when interpreting the Bible, an ancient document produced in a very different culture.

Sanders picked up on this and, through his study of Jewish writings and Paul's letters, argued that the traditional Lutheran understanding of the theology of Judaism and Paul was fundamentally flawed. Rather than being opposed to Jewish law, said Sanders, Paul's problem was simply with observances such as circumcision, dietary laws, and the keeping of special days – all of which had become boundary markers that most Jews used to set themselves apart from other nations.

Paul, he said, was simply dismissing the common Jewish view that following these traditional Israelite customs

---

[7] Krister Stendahl, 'Paul and the Introspective Conscience of the West', *Harvard Theological Review* (1963), quoted in James Allman, 'Gaining Perspective on the New Perspective on Paul', *Bibliotheca Sacra* 170:677 (January 2013), 51.

makes a person better off in God's eyes. In illustration, Sanders pointed out Paul's reminder to his readers in Rome that, just as Genesis says, before the Torah (the Jewish law) was ever given, 'Abraham believed God, and it was credited to him as righteousness.'[8]

Paul, insisted Sanders, was never questioning good works in general – indeed it is clear from his letters that they are very important. He spends a great deal of time talking about lifestyle. For instance, in his letter to the followers of Jesus in the city of Colossae he writes:

> rid yourselves of all such things as these: anger, rage, malice, slander, and filthy language from your lips. Do not lie to each other, since you have taken off your old self with its practices . . . clothe yourselves with compassion, kindness, humility, gentleness and patience. Bear with each other and forgive one another if any of you has a grievance against someone. Forgive as the Lord forgave you. And over all these virtues put on love, which binds them all together in perfect unity.[9]

The Jewish people of Paul's time, as Sanders showed, never taught a legalistic salvation through their 'works'. Instead, they believed that they were 'saved' because they had been chosen by God. This was absolutely nothing to do with them, and absolutely everything to do with God. Historically this had been through the famous exodus from Egypt and, although things had taken a difficult turn since – and the Romans were now in control of their country – they knew on the basis of their history that

---

[8] Romans 4.3, quoting Genesis 15.6: 'Abraham believed God, and it was credited to him as righteousness.'

[9] Colossians 3.8–9, 12–14.

God would be faithful to them and that they would be rescued again in the future. They could trust God. God was
faithful. They were God's chosen people. They were in an
ancient, unbreakable and everlasting covenant with God.

If you had asked any first-century Jew – including Saul –
whether he was saved, he would have replied, 'Of course.'
And, if you had followed it up with 'So, what did you do
to win this?' he would have shrugged his shoulders, smiled
and answered, 'I was born Jewish!'

So, for Paul, just like all other Jews, keeping the law
was simply a way of living for people who were already
redeemed. Practising the Sabbath or the rite of circumcision was simply a way of expressing gratitude for what was
already true, not a method of trying to do enough to make
themselves acceptable. In fact, although this comes as a
shock to some who have been taught that Christianity is
the only religion built on grace, and that all other religions
are attempts to work their way to God, the very concept
of grace is rooted in the Old Testament's word – *hesed* –
which means God's loving-kindness, undeserved faithfulness and benevolence. Judaism is not, and never was,
driven by 'works' or 'effort'!

Judaism was always a religion of grace; it remains a religion
of grace.[10] If this were not so, it would be like God saying,
'Well, look. For a couple of thousand years I've tried this
law stuff, but lately I've realized it doesn't work; people

---

[10] See James D. G. Dunn and Alan M. Suggate, *The Justice of God: A fresh look
at the old doctrine of justification by faith* (Grand Rapids: W. B. Eerdmans,
1994), pp. 7–8.

just can't do it. So, I've changed my mind. I'm abandoning plan A and working on an entirely new idea.' Where would that leave God's insight, 'never-changingness' or eternal nature?

The problem is that Luther seems to have never understood this. Instead he viewed first-century Jews as early fifteenth- and sixteenth-century Catholics. If he had read Paul more carefully, he'd have seen that what the Apostle was writing about was not the whole law, but simply the Jewish purity laws, the food laws, the Sabbath regulations and the practice of circumcision. And it was not even these practices themselves, but rather that many traditional Jews had turned them into boundary markers; badges that had slowly become more important in themselves than what they originally stood for. The message had become, 'If you get circumcised, if you keep the Sabbath and all the Jewish food regulations, then you're in. If not you're out.'

Although Judaism itself was built on grace, these Jews had somehow managed to erect boundaries that were now keeping others out. And this was also true of some of the Jews who became the first followers of 'the Way'. They celebrated the fact that they were 'in', but they built fences to keep others out. At its core, Paul's whole message is about removing those boundaries because Christ is Messiah for the whole world.

Paul really didn't believe that there was anything wrong with Judaism at all. He was a Jew and through his lifetime would have identified himself exactly that way. What is different is that, because of his experience on the Damascus road and his subsequent reflection on it, he comes to believe that through Jesus, all the benefits that the Jews have always enjoyed have now been extended to the whole world.

Today we still have boundary markers. In the local church that I grew up as part of, you had to say the 'sinner's prayer' to be 'in'. That was the proof that you were 'born again' – a real Christian rather than a fake one. In others, it is more about whether you have been 'filled with the Spirit' – the evidence of which is that you 'speak in tongues'. In other churches, it's about being careful not to challenge the leader or to ask too many awkward questions. For others it's different altogether. It is about regular attendance, being at mass, or confession, or about being christened, or not being divorced or a practising gay or gender non-binary or . . .

Boundary markers are alive and well in the twenty-first century.

But for Paul the only boundary marker is being human.

8

Faithful

The story of Anjezë Bojaxhiu.

Not *a story about* Anjezë Bojaxhiu. *The story of* Anjezë Bojaxhiu.

During her lifelong service to the poorest of the poor, Anjezë, or Teresa as she was much better known, became an icon of Christian faith in action; her extraordinary compassion for the sick, the dying and thousands of others whom nobody else was prepared to care for has been recognized and is acclaimed across the globe.

But, after her death in 1997, a collection of Teresa's private letters were put together which revealed another, until then, secret dimension to her story. She had spent almost 50 years of her life feeling completely disconnected from God and often doubting God's very existence.

Back in 1946, after 17 years working as a teacher in Calcutta, Mother Teresa, then 36, went on retreat to the Himalayan foothills. On the journey there, she says that she felt Christ calling her to abandon the safety of her role at the school and, instead, go to work in the slums of the city, dealing directly with the poorest of the poor – the sick, the dying, beggars and street children. She said that she heard the voice of Jesus himself challenging her to 'Come be my light.'

Two years later, in 1948, Teresa was finally given permission by her seniors to embark on what would become her lifetime vocation – among the poor and dying. She wrote, 'My soul at present is in perfect peace and joy.' But within two months of beginning her new work, she wrote to a close friend to confess that she was struggling: 'What tortures of loneliness . . . I wonder how long will my heart suffer this?'

A whole five years later, in 1953, she wrote to another friend: 'Please pray especially for me . . . that our Lord may show Himself – for there is such terrible darkness within me, as if everything was dead. It has been like this more or less from the time I started the work.' But, as her later letters reveal, and although she found a way to accept this absence, except for a break of a few weeks in 1958, it never lifted again for the rest of her life.

Teresa's letters – more than 40 of them, written over almost a half-century – were finally published as a book, *Come Be My Light*, in 2008.[1] Put together by her own order, the Missionaries of Charity, they are filled with brutal honesty about the depth and intensity of her struggle with faith, about what she describes as the 'dryness', 'darkness', 'loneliness' and 'torture' she is undergoing, and about 'The smile', which she explains is 'a mask', 'a cloak that covers everything'.

---

[1] Mother Teresa, *Come Be My Light: The revealing private writings of the Nobel Peace Prize winner*, ed. Brian Kolodiejchuk (London: Ebury, 2008).

So, why were these letters published?

Some of Teresa's critics have seen them as clear evidence that she was essentially a fraud; her deception to use a religion in which she did not really believe as a way to win support for her work. In my view this is to misunderstand her – and her honesty – completely. My own journey through life leads me to think very differently. As the editor of Teresa's letters, a member of her own order, explains, the book is 'a written ministry of [Teresa's] interior life'. He even goes so far as to suggest that it might be 'remembered as just as important as her ministry to the poor'.

The doctrine of *sola fide* (Latin for 'by faith alone'), often also referred to as the doctrine of justification by faith alone, has been the cornerstone of Protestantism since Martin Luther first announced it. 'This one and firm rock, which we call the doctrine of justification,' Luther insisted, 'is the chief article of the whole Christian doctrine, which comprehends the understanding of all godliness.'[2]

Sola fide asserts that God's pardon for guilty sinners is granted to and received through faith alone, excluding all works. It was developed by Luther in opposition to the abuses and power control systems he encountered in Catholicism. By faith we are saved. And to this day *sola fide* distinguishes many Protestant churches from the Catholic Church and Orthodox churches.

---

[2] Martin Luther, 'Commentary on Galatians', quoted in Herbert Bouman, 'The Doctrine of Justification in the Lutheran Confessions', *Concordia Theological Monthly* 26:11 (November 1955), p. 801.

For many people, 'faith' rather than 'good works' is what it takes to get across the line – to be counted as belonging, to 'getting in'. God has decided who will be 'saved' – and the answer is those who have 'faith'. But, the problem then is, how much faith is enough to get you safely 'in'? How much doubt is too much doubt and will keep you 'out'?

The way that Luther saw it – as do all who have since followed or imbibed his ideas – 'works' are the futile human efforts we make in order to try to meet God's 'out of the ball park' standards. Paul was the great champion who argued against the doomed idea that humans could ever merit salvation from God via their 'good works', and replaced it with the good news that faith was enough.

It's strange. On one hand, Luther rightly recognized that being accepted by God is all about God's undeserved grace for us, rather than what we do. But then, having made this huge contribution, he misunderstood the nature of 'faith' – which ironically he turned back into a work. If you are saved 'by faith alone' then it all boils down to your ability to believe; to muster the right thoughts, enough of the right thoughts, and with the right intensity.

The result of all this: salvation anxiety – exactly what the whole system was designed to replace. Which is, paradoxically, why so many churchgoing people – Protestant as well as Catholic – are riddled with guilt or worry. It is not that 'faith alone' isn't enough. It is that it is too much. It asks of people more than they can sustain. It leaves many of them broken, crushed and confused.

By contrast, Sanders, and over the last forty years a huge number of other theologians, linguists, sociologists and historians, are categorical: Luther and, following him, all the other Reformation thinkers – including John Calvin – made a giant mistake. Although they chose to translate the little New Testament Greek word *pistis* (πίστις) as 'faith' in the sense of 'belief' in God or Christ, it is far more accurately translated 'faithfulness'.

And, although on first hearing this might all seem rather boringly technical, in fact it changes absolutely everything!

If *pistis* is 'faithfulness', it is of a different nature from 'faith'. It is a firm commitment to a narrative or story in which you live – whatever you may feel, or believe, at any particular moment in time. Take, for instance, a husband and wife's commitments to be faithful to one another.

A long time ago now I stood in front of a congregation in south London and made some big commitments to Cornelia, who through this process was to become my wife:

> I call upon these persons here present
> To witness that I Stephen John Chalke
> Do take you Cornelia Reeves
> to be my lawful wedded wife,
> to have and to hold,
> from this day forward;
> for better, for worse,
> for richer, for poorer,
> in sickness and in health,

to love and to cherish,
until we are parted by death, and to this end I give
you my word.

And Cornelia made exactly the same commitments to me.

Over the years, I've learned that sometimes all this has been
easier than at others. Sometimes our feelings have helped
us, sometimes they have not. Sometimes circumstances
and opportunities have worked in our favour, sometimes
they've been against us. Sometimes faithfulness has been
about the sheer pleasure, joy and fulfilment of the experience. Sometimes, in the face of the mundane nature of life,
doubt and temptation, it's been mostly about just hanging
on and digging in.

So *pistis*, understood as faithfulness, implies and requires
lots of effort. Faithfulness, it turns out, is a risky commitment to a way of being and behaving, in the face of endless
natural fears and uncertainties. In fact, sometimes faithfulness – as I confessed earlier – is about nothing more than
hanging on to a story and doing your best to live in it. It
is not about the consistency, intensity, strength or concentration of our feelings. It is not about a state of cast-iron
certainty or stability, beyond the reach of all questioning
or hesitation.

Faithfulness embraces doubt as part of the journey. It
learns that struggle and setback are not its enemy, but an
instrument that helps strengthen it. In fact, living faithfully to anything would be a practical impossibility if this
were the case – because our feelings are never static, they
fluctuate; they ebb and flow like the tide. Choosing to live

faithfully to anything means engaging with your doubts, rather than ignoring them, because living 'intentionally' is a demanding route to take through life.

Faithfulness is hard; it's demanding; it requires resilience and honesty – perhaps this is one reason why so many drift. But it is only through faithfulness that we thrive.

The problem with the word 'faith' is that it always leads us in the direction of 'belief', in the sense of an intellectual assent to a set of theories or doctrines, whereas 'faithfulness' is instead about a life lived to a commitment made. *Pistis* is more about action and behaviour than 'cerebral' acceptance. In other words, living faithfully is a choice made in the face of doubt and setback. A commitment to live intentionally.

Perhaps it helps to ask how *pistis* as faithfulness sits with the theology of the book of James – the one that Luther felt he had to dispense with. The truth is that when we replace 'faith' with 'faithfulness', the problem that Luther had with James's writing disappears completely. James's concern is with all those who, in his day, were trying to reduce *pistis* to an intellectual assent or subscription to a 'belief' without any intent to live 'faithfully' to it. This is why he is adamant that *pistis* without works is no *pistis* at all – it is dead. In our terms – this is New Perspective thinking!

If Luther had grasped that *pistis* means 'faithfulness' in the sense of dogged trust rather than 'faith' in the sense of merely 'believing' he would have never coined his misleading slogan, 'by faith alone'. Because, as James also bluntly insists, belief without works leaves you in no better a place than a demon.[3]

We are 'saved' – we will talk more about what that word means later – by God's grace and God's grace alone. It is all about God and nothing to do with us. And then we are called to live 'faithfully' to that great truth – that we are all 'in'!

So the question is 'in what'? Paul's answer: 'God's people'. We are all chosen. Therefore, living in line – in sync – with this is the best way of being human, the most fulfilling way of being human.

Put differently, the gospel is not about 'inviting Jesus into your heart'. Instead it is about Jesus 'inviting us into his heart'!

And that, of course, is actually the point of the story of Anjezë Bojaxhiu's life. The woman who believed a story and then chose to live faithfully within it. The members of Teresa's order initially fought against the publication of her letters, arguing that they wanted them to be destroyed in order to protect her reputation. It was only as the Vatican stepped in that they were saved. This proved to be a wonderful decision – for, far from being an embarrassment, they have become a source of strength for others as they speak of genuine faithfulness.

Whatever Teresa's feelings, fears, doubts or state of unbelief, her commitment to the narrative she inhabited

---

[3] James 2.19.

never wavered. For Teresa, 'faithfulness' to her story – even though, for her, 'faith' in terms of her feelings was always elusive – was enough.

That's *pistis*!

9

Think like a Hebrew

Imagine someone who lives in your city and who has recently, for the first time in her life, started attending a local church. One Sunday its leader suggests that everyone make the decision to read a short passage of Paul's letter to the Romans every day over the coming few weeks – because it is the most detailed setting out of the Apostle's theology that we have. 'Why don't you commit to reading it on your phone, maybe on the bus or train, on your way to work each morning?'

What the leader hasn't told them is that:

- Paul was writing roughly two thousand years ago in an ancient language filled with cultural references, allegories and metaphors which are unknown to us.
- Paul was a Second Temple Jew and he is writing from that specific worldview. However, he's a Second Temple Jew whose thinking had been radically re-engineered, though not superseded, by his encounter with Christ. It is essential to develop a working understanding of his inner worldview in order to grasp his argument.
- Paul was writing to a multi-ethnic local church audience.
- A section of Paul's audience, though steeped in Jewish thought, had chosen to follow Jesus as the true Messiah. However, unlike him, some of this group still chose to

cling to a number of their old nationalistic and religious prejudices.

- Others were followers of Christ from pagan Roman backgrounds who now sought equality with their Jewish counterparts, but were being marginalized by those traditional Jews who refused to accept them unless they adopted a number of Jewish religious ritual practices including circumcision.
- Paul was seeking to address and engage both these groups at the same time. In fact, he was writing his letter to the Romans specifically to adjust and settle their 'culture war'.
- Understanding context is central to understanding any author's intent. Therefore, in order to understand Romans, you first have to get to grips with all these issues.

So, a question: in your opinion, what would be the chances of the new enthusiastic twenty-first-century individual, reading the Bible casually on the bus on the way to work, getting to grips with this in any helpful or meaningful way?

Even for those of us who have been schooled in the Bible and local church for decades, the problem is that too many of our ideas about faith, salvation, the kingdom of God, justification, judgement, salvation and so on, have been shaped and coloured by worldviews very different from that of Paul, the first-century revolutionary. Put simply, this means that if we really want to understand what Paul had to say in terms that are relevant to our culture, it's time for us to take the responsibility of learning to read him, in his original context, far more seriously.

Which brings us right back to that word: *pistis*. I believe that it is far more accurately translated as 'faithfulness' than 'faith'. But, of course, for all those who agree, there are plenty who don't; who are convinced we should stick to the old reading of 'faith' and the worldview it represents.

This is no small matter, because the idea of 'faith' or of 'faithfulness' dominates the entire New Testament. Which means that the decision we make regarding what we believe will therefore shape our very definition of what it is to be Christian.

So, how do we know who is right? How can you trust what I am writing? Does *pistis* denote faith or faithfulness? And how can we be sure?

Have you heard of that book *Men Are from Mars, Women Are from Venus?* I know all about its shortcomings and tendency to stereotype male and female but, in spite of this, when my wife Cornelia and I finally read it, about fifteen years after we were married, it still felt as if scales were falling from our eyes. We are all unique, and every relationship different, but it showed us how we approached and 'read' countless situations we'd encountered throughout our marriage entirely differently from each other. If only we had read John Gray's book a decade earlier, it would have saved us huge amounts of, to put it politely, misunderstanding.[1]

---

[1] John Gray, *Men Are from Mars, Women Are from Venus* (London: HarperCollins, 1992).

The documents that make up the Bible are all written from the perspective of Eastern – Hebraic – thought. Eastern thinking is not the same as Western thinking. But, for those of us bathed in Western thought, it is very hard for us to interpret these writings through any other lens than that of Western philosophy. It is just the way we see things. The result: some serious mistranslations, misinterpretations, misunderstandings and misrepresentations of the text.

Paul's thought was bathed in the Jewish tradition of Torah. Although he became the 'Apostle to the Gentiles',[2] this was not because he was a Greek thinker, but because he was a Jewish thinker who became convinced that Jesus was the Jewish Messiah and the Jewish Messiah was the Messiah for the whole world.

'Paul's theology was essentially Hebraic,' writes Marvin Wilson in his book *Our Father Abraham: Jewish roots of the Christian faith.*[3] Rather than reading Paul through the eyes of what we call Hellenism (Greek thought and culture), it is essential to remember that Paul, although he understood and walked in the Greco-Roman world, was first and last a Hebrew to the core.

Paul was proud of being a Jew;[4] in his words, 'a Hebrew of Hebrews . . . a Pharisee'.[5] And, as a faithful Jew, he believed

---

[2] Romans 11.13.

[3] Marvin R. Wilson, *Our Father Abraham: Jewish roots of the Christian faith* (Grand Rapids: W. B. Eerdmans, 1989), p. 8.

[4] 2 Corinthians 11.22.

[5] Philippians 3.5.

that his responsibility was to be the careful interpreter of Hebrew Scripture. For him, to choose to follow Jesus was not a break with his Judaism, but its full flowering.

It is an important point: the Bible – the whole Bible, including Paul's writing – is born out of, and only fully understood in terms of, its Hebraic cultural environment. To ignore this is to subvert its message. So, in order to understand Paul, it's our task to focus on the language and thought-patterns of the Hebrew people.

And when we do that, it changes everything!

Ancient Hebrew is primarily a language of senses rather than concepts. Its words express concrete or material things, movements and actions which strike the senses and create an emotional response. It uses words that are expressions of things that can be seen, touched, smelled, tasted or heard. Only secondarily, and in metaphor, can they be used to denote abstract ideas.

This is the way in which the whole of the Old Testament is written, and it's the thought world in which Jesus operated. Therefore, if we are ever going to better understand the texts and ideas that informed Paul's worldview, it's essential that we learn at least the basics of the philosophy of the ancient Hebrews.

Here is an important principle: everyone is entitled to their own opinion, but not to their own set of facts.

Take just one simple example. In Psalm 1.3, speaking of a person who does not 'walk in step with the wicked', the writer goes on to comment: 'That person is like a tree planted by streams of water, which yields its fruit in season, and whose leaf does not wither.'

Right here, in this passage, we have a collection of concrete words expressing abstract thoughts: 'a tree' (for one who is upright and just), 'streams of water' (for grace), 'fruit' (for good character), 'an unwithering leaf' (for well-being and prosperity), and 'walking' (for living well).

The Bible's very first book, Genesis, introduces what will become a central theme within Judaism. It explains that both Enoch and Noah 'walked with God'. And from then on that is what Judaism was; a way of walking the road of life and doing it well. As the book of Isaiah puts it: 'This is the way; walk in it.'[6] It's why Micah tells us that a person who lives well acts justly, loves mercy and 'walks' humbly with God.[7]

All of which creates an extraordinarily new dynamic to Jesus' famous words 'I am the way', not to mention a subversive clarity around the reason why the early followers of Jesus designated their faith as 'the Way'. You can read about this, for instance, in Acts 9. Here, when Saul was still looking to wipe out the followers of Jesus, he went, we are told, to the High Priest in Jerusalem to ask for letters to the synagogues in Damascus. His goal was as ruthless as it was simple: to take prisoner any and everyone he found there who belonged to 'the Way'.

---

[6] Isaiah 30.21.
[7] Micah 6.8.

For the Hebrew people, religion was never simply a system of ethics, a code of conduct, an ideology, a set of beliefs or a creed. Hebrews understood their daily life of faith in tangible terms. It was an ongoing journey or pilgrimage; the way in which they chose to walk.

But, in huge contrast to this Eastern concrete approach, Western philosophy uses abstract language to express itself; concepts and ideas that cannot be seen, touched, smelled, tasted or heard.

This, of course, raises a big question – one which, if we don't deal with it now, you are guaranteed to raise later. If the Hebrew language never uses abstract thought, how come there are lots of examples of abstract thought in the Old Testament? Take, for instance, Psalm 103.8: 'The LORD is compassionate and gracious, slow to anger, abounding in love.'

What are the abstract words 'compassionate', 'gracious', 'anger' and 'love' doing here? The answer is simple. Each one is an abstract English word that has been used to translate and replace an original material Hebrew word. Bible translators often translate in this way, because the original Hebrew makes no sense when literally translated into English.

To demonstrate this, let's take one of the abstract English words used in Psalm 103.8 – 'anger'. 'Anger' is a translation of the Hebrew word אַף (*aph*), which literally means 'nose'. A very concrete word. But the sentence 'The LORD is compassionate and gracious, slow to nose, abounding in love' would be a very strange one; it would have made little sense to an English reader!

In fact, of the 270 times אַף appears in the *Tanakh*,[8] in most translations, on more than two hundred of these occasions it is translated into English as 'anger' or 'angry', rather than 'nose'.

So the question is, what's the connection?

Well, when someone is angry, they breathe harder and their nostrils begin to flare. That's why Hebrew sees anger as 'the flaring of the nostrils', and why the linguists translate 'nose' as 'anger' in Psalm 103.8.

But this raises another equally important principle of translation, which once again is fundamental to understanding Paul. Context! Nose is best translated as 'anger' here in Psalm 103, but elsewhere, as part of a different paragraph, it might also mean a literal nose – for instance in Psalm 115.6: 'They have ears, but cannot hear, noses, but cannot smell.'

So, back to *pistis*, which of course isn't a Hebrew word. Instead, it is a Greek word, used by Paul and others to translate a Hebrew idea. Which is why the real litmus test of whether *pistis* means 'faith' or 'faithfulness' in Paul's writing is simply to ask about its history – its etymology – and which Hebrew word or words it is translating.

First things first. When the early followers of Christ received the letters of Paul, no one sat there and worried,

---

[8] The Hebrew Bible is also known as the *Tanakh*, which is an acronym of the first Hebrew letter of each of the Masoretic Text's three traditional subdivisions: Torah ('Teaching', also known as the Five Books of Moses), Nevi'im ('Prophets') and Ketuvim ('Writings'). It is, of course, also the textual source for the Christian Old Testament.

'What does he mean by this strange word *pistis*?', as if he'd just invented it and it needed explanation. Paul's letters were not written to academics with hours to spend in the reference section of a theological library, but to ordinary busy people, in terms that they could easily relate to.

In Greek mythology, Pistis was the goddess – the personi-fication – of trust, honesty, goodness, reliability and loyalty or fidelity. And, because of this, in Greek rhetoric, it came to take on the metaphorical meaning of the impact or out-come of (as opposed to the clever or persuasive presentation of) the truth. So, aside from any other consideration, our Western evolution of *pistis* as 'faith' to mean assent to a con-cept, belief or doctrine as opposed to its practical outcomes is in stark contrast to its usage in Greek culture.

More than that, it's worth noting that the Roman name for the Greek goddess Pistis was none other than Fides. And *fides* is the Latin word from which our English word 'faith' – which is thought to date from around 1200 – is derived.

The deepest question, however, is around the full content of the Hebrew idea that *pistis* was used to translate. In fact, there are a number of Hebrew words, used in the *Tanakh*, which are related to faith or believing in God. We'll look briefly at just one – although research into any and all yields the same sort of outcome – exactly in line with what we've already discovered about the 'concreteness' of the Hebrew language.

The Hebrew verb *aman* (אָמַן) – often translated 'to believe' – is used 110 times in the Old Testament. So, in Genesis God said to Abram, 'Look up at the heavens and count the stars – if indeed you can count them . . . So shall your off-spring be.' The passage concludes, 'Abram believed (*aman*) the LORD, and he credited it to him as righteousness.'[9]

Although this is usually translated, as it is here, to mean that Abram believed God's promise, *aman* actually means much more than just knowing something to be true. At a deeper level it means to support, to be permanent, to be trustworthy, true, certain, steadfast and faithful. But, digging even deeper, once again we discover that these definitions of *aman* are all derivative of its literal, material, concrete original meaning, which is 'to support with the arm', 'to carry a child', or 'to nurse'. In other words, the use of *aman* means that Abram put his money where his mouth was – he threw himself into living in and working for this story, hook, line and sinker.

By the way, it's no coincidence at all that this word is the verb form of a word we all know very well: 'amen'. When we say 'amen', what we are declaring literally is 'we support this, we are committed to this with all that we are – we will carry this'.

Any serious reading of *pistis* that even begins to do justice to its Hebraic background and roots must recognize that, given all this context, it can only mean faithfulness (or faith in the sense of faithfulness and reliability); nothing else even begins to fit.

Pistis rendered as faith, in the sense of belief – the ability to hold to a particular set of intellectual positions – is robbed

---

[9]   Genesis 15.5–6.

of all its ethical value and implications. It is reduced to a meaningless badge of merit – another boundary marker – that every word of Paul's writing battles against. Indeed, the way I see it, because the word faith is so frequently misunderstood in this way, the core of the New Testament's message has been misidentified, and its full ethical power and relevance to daily life remains untapped.

In fact, this should be clear to anyone who critically engages with the New Testament. Take the use of the word *pistis* in Paul's letter to the Galatians: 'But the fruit of the Spirit is love, joy, peace, forbearance, kindness, goodness, *faithfulness (pistis)*, gentleness and self-control.'[10]

This discussion also raises other helpful and thought-provoking suggestions for the translation of *pistis* – such as obedience and loyalty. The theologian Matthew Bates has another suggestion. He argues that there are specific contexts, especially in Paul's writing and the Gospels, in which the only reasonable rendering of *pistis* is 'allegiance', the proper attitude of loyal subjects to their sovereign ruler. Instead of Martin Luther's 'faith alone', he says, Christians should speak about salvation by 'allegiance alone'.

If the word faith didn't exist – or went on an extended holiday – and we had to use a different word – we couldn't do better than to replace it with trust, loyalty or allegiance.

I think of my own experience of life and leadership. People often interview me these days about the growth of Oasis. They ask me about how they can set up a charity or

---

[10] Galatians 5.22–23.

business and achieve scale. My first answer is don't! My second response is that if you must, then you really must. But I say, 'Remember this – it will cost you everything. It will be wonderful but it will also be terrible, because what it takes for any enterprise to succeed is for at least one person to be irrationally committed to its success.'

Faithfulness is about purposeful persistence and perspiration rather than great moments of inspiration. I remember a whole period, between about 1998 and 2003, when life for me was just about clinging on to the commitments I had made in the face of what seemed to be the brick walls of resistance placed in front of me. Faithfulness, I've learned, is often about the ability to just hang on, keep on and not give up, no matter where your thoughts might be taking you.

I understand that some might be fearful that simply in saying these things I am somehow dismantling the building blocks of their 'faith'. I know that the fear of losing an old and trusted worldview that has long supplied a sense of plausibility can be challenging and disorientating. But it is only the pursuit of the truth that, in the end, sets us free.

Biblical 'faith' is not intellectual assent to a concept, a commitment to a set of doctrines and theories, or a mystical sense of peace and well-being. Instead it is a risky commitment to a radical way of living; a call to action, a way of walking, a summons to loyalty and allegiance. This, and only this, is *pistis*.

Whenever Paul, the Jew, speaks of 'faith', he always has in mind faithful obedience and loyalty to walking through life in the way of Christ – and the good works that naturally flow from it. His constant emphasis on ethical behaviour, on putting off the old habits of life and putting on the new, is central to his understanding of an appropriate response of faithfulness to already being counted 'in'.

Jesus is the Messiah for the whole world.

10

What if?

Luther centred his whole 'protest' against the medieval Catholic Church on a number of central creeds – each one a Latin term. The two best known are still often quoted today: *sola gratia* (grace alone) and *sola fide* (faith alone).[1]

The last time I heard someone pronounce in tones of certainty that we are 'saved by grace through faith alone' was just two days ago. Of course, such a notion stems from passages in Paul's writing like this one: 'For it is by grace you have been saved, through faith – and this is not from yourselves, it is the gift of God – not by works, so that no one can boast.'[2]

But the problem is, when you really stop to think about it, that traditional – as we call it – understanding of these words reveals more than one circle that is difficult to square.

For starters . . . how exactly can we be saved by grace through faith? We are either saved by grace, or saved by

---

[1] Luther's work was based on five basic tenets or *solas* – *sola Scriptura* (Scripture alone), *sola gratia* (grace alone), *sola fide* (faith alone), *solus Christus* (Christ alone) and *soli Deo gloria* (glory to God alone).

[2] Ephesians 2.8–9.

faith. It can't be both – because they are not just different, they are mutually exclusive.

Grace is a free gift – there is nothing that the recipient can do to deserve it. It is nothing to do with her merit or effort. On the other hand, faith is very different. As we've already explored, faith has everything to do with our own ability and effort – it is, in the end, a 'work'.

Grace through our faith? Surely it's about one or the other. Grace or our faith? It is either a free gift or a big effort.

But there's another issue. If, as Paul then suggests, this 'faith . . . is not from yourselves, it is the gift of God', things get even more complicated. Faith, from an old Protestant point of view, becomes something that you are either born with – good news for you – or not – very bad news for you. But there is nothing you can do about it. You either have it or you don't. You are either 'saved' or not. And all this is preordained: decided beforehand. A gift, or not, from God. You are born 'in', or you are born 'out'.[3]

But if this is true, then why is Paul bothering to do all that writing, preaching, teaching and travelling in the first place? The dice have already been rolled. You can't change it. Like it or lump it, accept your destiny. Just suck it up.

It is a muddle!

---

[3] This worldview was really developed by another sixteenth-century reformer, John Calvin, and taken up by his followers and successors; it is now known as 'reformed theology'.

But what if it is not only that *pistis* means faithfulness? What if the faithfulness that Paul is talking about in those verses from Ephesians 2 is God's faithfulness rather than ours? What if, rather than reading this statement the way that it has been translated so often, in context it should actually read: 'For it is by grace you have been saved, through Christ's faithfulness – this is not from yourselves, it is the gift of God – not by works, so that no one can boast.'

Not only does it suddenly make sense, but it leads us on to another piece of Paul's core language: the Greek phrase *pistis Christou*, which he uses half a dozen times in his writing.[4]

Martin Luther, John Calvin and countless others following them have chosen to translate *pistis Christou* as 'faith in Christ', and then to hang their whole doctrinal approach on it. We are saved, it is taught, by putting our 'faith in Christ'. But I put it to you that this translation was a giant mistake; that it is at the very heart of the muddle we have been in for the last five hundred years, and that it is time to sort it out!

If, as we've discovered, the Greek word *pistis* implies 'faithfulness' in the sense of faithful obedience, loyalty, allegiance and trustworthiness, rather than 'faith' in the sense of an ability to commit immoveably to a particular set of doctrinal positions and beliefs, what does this mean for *pistis Christou*?

As a child I was taught that I would be 'saved' through my 'faith in Christ'. If I believed, I would inherit eternal life, but, of course, the dark side was that, if not I would face

---

4   Romans 3.22, 26; Galatians 2.16; 3.22; Ephesians 3.12; Philemon 3.9.

the consequences: eternal separation from God. Well, the thing is this – I did believe. But the problem was that many of the kids that were in Sunday school with me, or later those in the church youth group I attended, didn't. Or, to state it more clearly, sometimes, as hard as they tried, they just couldn't.

This same approach is still very much alive, well and sadly continuing to condemn millions. Just a couple of months ago I attended a funeral, where the vicar giving the sermon chose to use the occasion to inform all those in the congregation who were not Christians, who were there grieving the loss of their dear friend, that in their present unbelieving state, their eternal destiny would be destruction.

Back to *pistis Christou*. It might surprise you to know that until the time of the Protestant Reformation, virtually all translations of the New Testament chose to translate this famous Pauline phrase as 'the faith *of* Christ', in the sense of the faithfulness exercised by Christ, rather than 'faith *in* Christ', in the sense of our personal belief levels in Christ.

For instance, the famous translation of the Bible into Latin, the Vulgate – largely the result of the labours of the early Church Father Jerome, who in AD 382 was commissioned for his task by the then leader of the Church, Pope Damasus I, chose to translate Romans 3.21–22 as: 'But now, without the law, the justice of God is made manifest, being witnessed by the law and the prophets. Even the justice of God, by faith of Jesus Christ . . .'[5]

---

[5] As Latin began to replace Greek as the common language in the western Roman Empire, by the end of the fourth century AD the need for a Bible in

Some will point out that this rendering of *pistis Christou* in the English version of the Latin Vulgate comes from the Catholic Douay-Rheims translation which was published in France after Luther's death. Thus they might argue that it was produced to combat Luther's views, and therefore is biased in favour of Catholic rather than Protestant doctrine.

None of this, however, can be said of William Tyndale's English translation. All agree that it promoted many of Luther's anti-Catholic ideas. In fact, many scholars suggest that it was even partly inspired when in 1522 Tyndale acquired a copy of Luther's German New Testament.

Tyndale, who would eventually pay with his life for his work, was a highly gifted linguist who had studied at Oxford. Fluent in French, Greek, Hebrew, German, Italian, Latin and Spanish as well as English, he painstakingly began his translation of the Bible into English by using a Greek text compiled by Erasmus from several early manuscripts.[6] But he also consulted Erasmus' Latin New Testament, Luther's Protestant German version and the Vulgate.

To this faithful linguist all that mattered was the goal of accurately translating the Bible into the language of the ordinary people, so that everyone could have access to

---

Latin became essential. Pope Damasus I chose Jerome for this task because of his linguistic command of Greek, Hebrew and Latin. The resulting translation is known as the Vulgate.

[6] Desiderius Erasmus (*c.* 1466–1536) was one of Renaissance Europe's most famous and influential scholars, and defined the humanist movement in northern Europe. He penned several editions of the New Testament in Greek and Latin, which helped fuel both the Protestant Reformation and the Catholic Counter-Reformation.

it for themselves rather than rely on a priest. According to Foxe, in his famous Book of Martyrs, Tyndale himself explained that his reason for creating his translation was to 'cause the boy that driveth the plow to know more of the Scriptures than thou [the clergy of the day]'.[7]

However, having been refused permission by the Catholic Church to produce this new text in England, Tyndale was forced to flee to the Continent, where he published his first complete edition of the New Testament in 1526. It was from there that he began to smuggle copies of his work back to England.

Tyndale's scholarship was to produce a radical translation of the New Testament, which infuriated the Catholic Church. He felt, for instance, that the Greek word ἐκκλησία (*ekklesia*) should more accurately be translated 'congregation' than 'church'. This, of course, had the effect of undermining the centralized structure of the Church. He chose to translate the Greek word πρεσβύτερος (*presbuteros*) as 'elder' rather than 'priest', which stripped away the Church's clerical power. He was clear that the Greek word μετανοεῖτε (*metanoeite*) should be translated 'repent' instead of 'do penance', so lending his weight to the views of reformers like Luther who had taken issue with this practice.

Thomas More, the committed Catholic whom King Henry VIII had made Lord Chancellor in 1529,[8] saw Tyndale's

---

[7] Foxe tells Tyndale's story in Chapter 12 of his Book of Martyrs.

[8] Thomas More (1478–1535) is venerated by the Catholic Church as Saint Thomas More. An English lawyer, author and statesman, More was a councillor to Henry VIII, and Lord High Chancellor of England from October 1529 to 16 May 1532. He opposed the king's separation from the Catholic

New Testament as part of the Protestant threat to the stability of Church and society, and put all his energy into vigorously suppressing it. Not only did he condemn and ban it, but he had Tyndale hunted down until he was eventually captured in Antwerp in 1535. Then, having been tried on a charge of heresy in 1536, according to Foxe, Tyndale – the faithful and fearless Bible translator – found himself condemned to death by being strangled and then burned at the stake, where his last words were, 'Lord! Open the King of England's eyes.'

In the light of all this, how Tyndale chose to translate Romans 3.21–22 is of huge significance. This is his text:

> Now verely is ye rigtewesnes that cometh of God declared without the fulfillinge of ye lawe havinge witnes yet of ye lawe and of the Prophetes. The rightewesnes no dout which is good before God cometh by *ye fayth of Iesus Christ* . . . (emphasis added)[9]

Even though Tyndale backed many aspects of Luther's understanding and was willing to give his life for this commitment, he just could not bring himself to translate *pistis Christou* as 'faith in Christ'.

As the Reformation took hold across Europe, however, other Protestant translators had no such qualms. Almost as one they turned their backs on the former way of understanding *pistis Christou* and instead began to translate it

---

Church, and eventually refused to acknowledge Henry as Supreme Head of the Church of England or the annulment of the king's marriage to Catherine of Aragon. This led to his conviction for treason and his execution by beheading.

[9] <https://www.biblestudytools.com/tyn/romans/>

in line with Luther's understanding. The result is that by the twentieth century this reading – 'faith in Christ' – was taken for granted and today has become the unquestioned basis of the whole approach of hundreds of thousands of local churches around the world.

The modern gospel message is clear to all: 'Believe and you will be saved! But, because God is love, we are granted free will, which means that if you turn your back on God, your wish will be granted and beyond death you will spend eternity in hell!' To most people outside the Western Protestant bubble, this is not so much 'God is love', but more like 'God is volatile'.

Luther's stance was, of course, in many ways driven by the cultural assumptions we've already explored, through which he and the other reformers made the mistake of reading their own sixteenth-century situation, circumstances and battle with the Roman Catholic Church of the day back into Paul's first-century world and words. But, in England, where the break from Rome was initially much more about political independence from Rome than doctrine, in the text of the translation sponsored by King James I (every inch an anti-Catholic monarch) – published in 1611 (almost a hundred years after Luther introduced his *pistis Christou* innovation) – Romans 3.21–22 still reads like this:

> But now the righteousness of God without the law is mani-
> fested, being witnessed by the law and the prophets; Even the
> righteousness of God which is *by faith of Jesus Christ* . . .

More than that, King James's Authorized Version (which is still loved and used by millions around the world) renders

Paul's words to the followers of Christ in Galatia this way: 'The life which I now live in the flesh I live *by the faith of the Son of God*, who loved me, and gave himself for me.'[10] And whereas the New International Version of Philippians 3.9 reads 'and be found in him, not having a righteousness of my own that comes from the law, but that which is *through faith in Christ*', the King James Version reads, 'And be found in him, not having mine own righteousness, which is of the law, but that which is *through the faith of Christ*'.

It wasn't until the 1980s – the heyday of the likes of Wham!, Whitney Houston, Madonna, Tina Turner, Lionel Richie, Michael Jackson and Diana Ross – that Richard Hays wrote his seminal book *The Faith of Jesus Christ*.[11] In it, he insisted that the only way to read Paul's phrase *pistis Christou* authentically is in line with the old traditional reading of 'the faith or faithfulness *of* Jesus Christ'.

Hays was categorical, arguing that to speak as though the 'work' called faith is the thing that we really have to do to please God, is to betray a fundamental misconception. According to Hays, Paul's primary emphasis, exactly in line with that of William Tyndale, is on Christ's faithfulness rather than our struggling human faith. Christ's allegiance to his divine mission is the source of our acceptance by God; and the recognition of this great redemptive truth calls each one of us to a life lived in faithfulness to it.

---

[10] Galatians 2.20.
[11] Richard Hays, *The Faith of Jesus Christ* (Grand Rapids: W. B. Eerdmans, 1983).

Richard Hays' views have now been built on by many other 'New Perspective' thinkers but, at the same time, there are those who worry that pressing this 'faithfulness of Christ' interpretation of Paul's famous phrase corrodes what they regard as the absolute necessity of human faith. For them, the sixteenth-century notion that salvation comes through the ability to have and hold 'faith in Christ' has become the central pillar of their understanding of Scripture.

So, how do we resolve this? Whose *pistis* is Paul talking about? Are we saved by grace through Christ's faithfulness? Or, are we saved by grace through *our* faith or faithfulness? It makes all the difference in the world.

First, whatever our personal judgement on this issue, it's worth reflecting that, as a matter of historical record, this 'revolutionary' *new* perspective on Paul's thought – centred on the 'faithfulness of Christ' – is the same understanding that's been held throughout history by the Eastern Church and, it turns out, the same as that of the old pre-Reformation writers. So, the 'novel' understanding of *pistis Christou* (as 'faith in Christ') is the one that was introduced by the sixteenth-century European reformers.

Warning! For all those not interested in the technicalities of Greek grammar, I am sorry about the next 180 words or so. For those of you who are, enjoy . . .

It's very clear from the two-word Greek phrase *pistis Christou* that it contains no linking preposition such as the English 'in' or 'of'. So where does the 'in' or 'of' come from and who decides which one is right? First, some facts:

- The relationship of the two Greek words that make up the phrase *pistis Christou* is determined by their nature – and *Christou* is a genitive.
- Genitives can be either subjective or objective.
- What is known as an objective translation of *Christou* makes Christ the object of faith, which means that the phrase would read 'faith in Christ'.
- What is known as a subjective translation of *Christou* sees Christ as the one possessing faith, and so *pistis Christou* would read 'the faith or faithfulness of Christ'.

The question that we are left asking is this. On what grounds does one expert come to render the phrase as '[your] faith *in* Christ' (an objective genitive translation), another as 'the faithfulness (faith) *of* Christ' (a subjective genitive translation), while still others waver between the two possibilities, depending on the exact verse involved?

If you are prepared to put the time in, you can read those on both ends of the argument, as well as others with various in-between stances. And you will discover that all argue their position is the right one on the basis that their opponents have made the rookie error of mistaking a subjective genitive for an objective genitive, or vice versa!

The way I see it, however, not only is this all very confusing, but in truth it misses the real hermeneutical point by a mile. Anyone who makes absolutist statements based on what they claim to be the technicalities of the Greek language is, in fact, simply being disingenuous. The issue is not technical – which is exactly why different linguists reach different conclusions. In truth, each writer's decisions have been determined not by some obscure formula which governs Greek grammar but instead by their wider understanding of, and pre-existing assumptions about, the overarching narrative and context of Paul's writing.

Don Carson, an anti-'New Perspective' writer, acknowledges this. 'At the level of mere grammar,' he agrees, 'the Greek expression (which does not use prepositions akin to English "in" or "of") could be read either way.' But, having acknowledged that 'the issues, frankly, are complex', he insists that 'although the theme of Jesus being faithful and obedient to His heavenly Father is quite a strong one in the New Testament . . . it is far from obvious that the theme is found in the half-dozen "faith in/faithfulness of Jesus Christ passages."'[12]

So although some might think that the translation of this highly contentious Greek phrase is a dry technical task to be left in the hands of professional linguists, it turns out that this is very far from the case.

The idea that it is the 'faithfulness of Christ' as opposed to the old concept of 'faith in Christ' which is the basis of salvation would be nothing short of a revolution. It would turn our understanding of the message of the Bible upside down. It would stand Luther's sixteenth-century idea on its head. It would be a paradigm shift. Not just the latest development in business as usual; not some helpful new extension to the old Reformation building. It would be, at one and the same time, a return to the ancient pathway, and a brand-new beginning.

---

[12] D. A. Carson, '"Faith" and "Faithfulness"'. https://www.ligonier.org/learn/articles/faith-and-faithfulness/

11

Aha!

As we know, a text without a context is a pretext.

Jane Austen's novels are famous, and famously entertaining – but informed readers also understand that her plots are written to explore the dependence of women on marriage in the pursuit of favourable social standing and economic security at the end of the eighteenth century in the UK.

Austen's writing is designed to critique the way of life that the British landed gentry regarded as normal. No serious critic or scholar would ever dream of trying to analyse the meaning of her work by lifting single words or phrases out of their context. This kind of narrow approach to linguistics would hinder rather than help good interpretation. Any thoughtful analysis of Austen's text requires a much deeper and wider view than that.

Likewise, whenever we yank a phrase, a verse or a sentence out of Paul's thought and then use it to help support a pre-assumed argument that we hold dear, we make a huge mistake. Instead we have to do the hard work of getting into Paul's world and thinking. To the extent that we don't or won't do this, we will always – as we've seen – run the risk of reading our situation back into Paul's world rather than reading his understanding into our world.

Paul was neither a sixteenth-century Catholic nor Protestant thinker; neither a twentieth-century conservative
nor liberal thinker, neither a twenty-first-century evangelical nor progressive thinker. To say it again, Paul was a
first-century, Second Temple Jewish thinker and follower
of Jesus.

But, as we go about this listening task, there is another
principle about Greek words – or any words for that
matter – that we need to appreciate. Neither Hebrew nor
Greek words had permanently fixed meanings, any more
than English words do. So it can be highly misleading to
attempt to understand the meaning of any sentence in
terms of a kind of mathematical process, which looks
up suitable dictionary meanings for each of the individual words that make it up, and then adds them together
to determine the correct result. Meaning is not found in
the word by itself. Words are building blocks of bigger
concepts, which means that claims to be able to unearth
whole worldviews from individual words or phrases or
grammatical rules are misleading. To put it differently, the
fundamental semantic unit is not the word, the phrase or
often even the sentence.

Words often acquire their meaning from the context in
which they are deployed. The real meanings associated
with language are often the result of much larger slices of
written or spoken material or cultural narratives. A phrase,
sentence or paragraph, even a whole text, can take on a
meaning that is very different from the sum of its parts.

To illustrate this, we all know that the term 'hot dog' is not
usually the sum of the meanings of the two words 'hot'

and 'dog' that make it up, although we also know that in some contexts it is. A hot dog in the context of a story about a group of friends at a football match is a completely different thing from a hot dog in the context of a story about a family pet which is left in the car in a heatwave on a midsummer's day. That's why it is vital to think about word study within the wider context of an analysis of the whole text as well as the framework of the author's life, worldview and work.

So, back to the technicalities of Greek grammar for a moment, and to the question of whether the genitive *Christou* in the phrase *pistis Christou* is, in fact, subjective or objective. The truth is that this can only ever be finally determined by the larger cultural context in which the phrase sits.

This particular phrase of Paul's, just like all others, requires deeper careful study around the broad shape of his wider worldview and theology, before any accurate judgement on its meaning can be reached. Only this approach is capable of providing us with a reliable lens through which to read any of his specific words. Which is why the Hebrew background we have looked at is so important.

Should *pistis Christou* be translated as 'faith in Christ' or the 'faithfulness of Christ'? For my part, I believe passionately that the only translation that does justice to, rather than ignoring, the whole framework in which Paul was thinking, living and working is the 'faithfulness of Christ'. As Tom Wright puts it bluntly, 'When Paul speaks in Galatians and Romans of *pistis Christou*, he normally intends to denote the faithfulness of the Messiah to the purposes of God rather than the faith by which Jew and Gentile alike believe the gospel . . . .'[1]

In other words, according to Wright, Paul is not writing about the human struggle to muster or maintain faith *in* Christ the Messiah, but rather about the faith *of* Christ the Messiah. Neither is he referring to Christ's faith in the sense of 'belief' or assent to a set of doctrinal views, but rather to his actual faithfulness to God's purpose for the way he lived his life. By using this phrase Paul is speaking of Christ's willingness to live out a life of real service, sacrifice and love, whatever the cost. Jesus was excluded and executed for his unwillingness to be intimidated into following any other pathway through life than that of living faithfully to his calling.

This understanding, if correct, is a liberation. A liberation that puts the emphasis firmly on Christ's faithfulness to his father's plan as the source of our acceptance by God, rather than on the ups and downs of our faltering faith. No more salvation angst!

In his commentary on Romans, John Stott explains of chapter 3 that the six tightly packed verses (21–26) which we began to explore in the last chapter are 'the centre and heart' of the whole letter, and may possibly be 'the most important single paragraph ever written'. According to Martin Luther, they are 'the chief point . . . of the whole Bible'. So now let's take a deeper look at how

---

[1] N. T. Wright, *Paul: Fresh perspectives* (London: SPCK, 2005), p. 47.

both *pistis* and *pistis Christou* work in this highly significant context.

Romans 3.21–22, in the latest edition of the New International Version (NIV) of the Bible, reads like this: 'But now apart from the law the righteousness of God has been made known, to which the Law and the Prophets testify. This righteousness is given through faith in Jesus Christ . . .'

As we've seen, however, from Jerome, William Tyndale and the King James Authorized Version to Ed Sanders, Richard Hays, Tom Wright and countless other contemporary scholars, it is suggested that it should be read this way: 'But now apart from the law the righteousness of God has been made known, to which the Law and the Prophets testify. This righteousness is given through the faith/faithfulness of Jesus Christ . . .'

It is completely different! It turns everything on its head. If John Stott and Martin Luther are right – and this passage is the centre of the New Testament – the whole meaning and message of the Church is entirely dependent on how you translate this phrase. One way it is one thing, the other way it is something else altogether.

So now, the extraordinary thing.

If you take a look at a copy of the NIV (either at the latest paper version or online), you'll notice the little superscript letter by the phrase 'faith in'. It looks like this: 'faith in [a] Jesus Christ'. And it has a footnote attached to it, which reads as follows: 'Or *through the faithfulness of* Jesus Christ' (emphasis original).

Well, the Christian gospel is either one thing or the other, but it can't be both!

I'm sure, however, that there are some who will want to point out that I have – in all the translations I've quoted – left the last clause of the sentence off. So here it is. Using the NIV's alternative wording it actually reads like this: 'This righteousness is given through the faithfulness of Jesus Christ *to all who believe*.'[2]

So, does this change it all back again? Even if we are saved by the *faithfulness of* Christ rather than our own *faith in* Christ, is Paul trying to say that, in the end, you either choose to *believe* it or face God's anger and final rejection? The only way to answer this question, as ever, is to enter Paul's world and so allow him to speak to us instead of trying to push our own pre-existing ideas back into his before claiming his authority for them.

Read in context, Paul's words here are addressed to those Jews within the Corinth congregation who still hang on to the belief that it is only those who sign up to and keep the Jewish food laws and the rite of circumcision that are gold-standard members of the church. 'No,' says Paul. Every member of the church community is 'in' on exactly the same basis as every other member. The Church is made up of all who 'believe' (the word Paul uses is *pisteuontas*, a derivative of *pistis*); all those who choose to live faithfully to the way of Christ. There is no difference between Jew and Gentile; the 'works' of Judaism count for nothing. Everyone

---

[2] Romans 3.22–24.

gets the same deal on exactly the same basis – the faithfulness of Christ and the grace that is theirs as a result.[3]

Paul's intention here – set in the context of his whole letter – was to provide some practical, pastoral advice about church life, on one hand to a Jewish faction within the local congregation that looked down on Gentile members, and on the other to that Gentile group who were often made to feel inferior or even altogether unacceptable.

It is, therefore, a very serious error to mistake Paul's words for the draft text of an evangelistic tract to be handed out to anyone outside the church. Paul's words are not a statement about the fate of anyone beyond death (church member or not), or of their final exclusion in hell. To jump to such a conclusion is a little like putting two and two together to make 48.[4]

A paraphrase of Paul's words (vv. 21–22) might read this way:

> Dear Jewish church members, quite apart from your badges and boundary markers – food laws and circumcision – God's deliverance and justice has been made known. In fact, it is this to which all our Hebrew scriptures point. All this is given through the faithfulness of Jesus Christ to you all, absolutely everyone whether you are a Jew or a Gentile.

---

[3] The same context is true of Galatians 2.15–16, which uses the word *pistis* and its derivatives three times.

[4] We will explore this in much more detail in Chapters 16–20.

Aha!

So, as Paul goes straight on to explain in verses 22–24:

> There is no difference between Jew and Gentile, for all have sinned and fall short of the glory of God, and all are justified freely by his undeserved by his grace through the redemption that came by Christ Jesus.

I remember the terrible internal struggles I endured in the first years after I became a Christian about whether my faith was 'real faith', 'saving faith', or all my own effort. Was I really a Christian or just a fake? Was I the real thing, a true 'spirit-filled', 'born-again' believer, or not? Did I have enough 'faith'? Healing faith; nation-shaping, life-changing, problem-solving faith? And what would become of me eternally, if it wasn't the right kind of faith?

The tragedy is that, over the many years I've been serving as a pastor, I've heard too many horror stories of ill-informed Christians, and even of church leaders, telling those struggling with hard and painful situations in their lives that their suffering is because of their absence of faith; that their illnesses are caused because they don't have enough faith or the right kind of faith. That they are not praying hard enough or in the right way. That their prayers are not answered because of the sin of their lack of faith. Surely you, like me, have heard these stories and they have left you feeling that this is nothing short of abuse.

But, once you understand the phrase *pistis Christou* to be about Christ's faithfulness, then the amount or quality of our faith is no longer a factor. What is important is that God's faithfulness always stands firm, even if and when

102

we find ourselves faithless. And this lifts a monumental burden from the shoulders of humanity.

When you hear truth, it resonates. It chimes. It rings. It creates one of those 'Aha!' moments. At one and the same time it is both radical and yet simple. It is life-changing. It is transformational.

In the rush to the analysis of Greek grammatical terminology, it's too easy to miss what is in front of our noses.

Biblical faith is Hebrew faith – and Hebrew faith cannot ever be belief in a set of concepts, it has to be earthed. It must always be faithfulness. Just as James always wants to remind us, 'the idea of faith without works is dead'.

Israel's whole relationship with Yahweh was built around the ancient Jewish theme of covenant faithfulness; God has to be faithful and true to the Jewish people – God has redeemed them in the past and can be trusted to do so again.

The Jewish people never believed that their salvation was anything to do with them; instead it was absolutely everything to do with God. For Paul, just like all other Jews, living faithfully was simply the way of responding, for people who were already redeemed, which demonstrated gratitude for what had already happened to them.

Paul's understanding of all this, as a Second Temple Jewish thinker, is clear. But through his experience on the Damascus road he came to see that Jesus was the Jewish Messiah – who through his faithfulness to his Father's plan was also the Messiah for the whole world (for Jews and Gentiles alike) and indeed for the entire cosmos.

Through Christ's faithfulness, what was once true for the Jewish people is now true for the whole of humanity. And that's what Paul means by his claim that 'Jesus Christ is Lord'. Nothing more, but nothing less![5]

The Revolution has begun.

---

[5] Philippians 2.11.

12

Oxymoron

'For the wrath of God', states Paul in Romans 1.18, 'is being revealed from heaven against all the godlessness and wickedness of people, who suppress the truth by their wickedness.'

Yikes!

The wrath of God; what an ominous-sounding phrase – and one which makes all that talk of 'God's faithfulness' instantly sound like an oxymoron. As Bible-thumping, churchgoing Ned Flanders thundered to his wayward neighbour, Homer Simpson, 'I don't judge you. I leave that to a wrathful, angry God to do.'

But before we get into all that, first a small recap and then a short update.

The small recap:

The way I see it, Martin Luther's great breakthrough was that he recognized salvation was all about grace – about God, not about our effort or works. But then he went and misunderstood faith, which ironically he turned back into a giant effort or work.

Now the short update:

In Luther's wake, within a few years, arrived another famous reformer, John Calvin, a brilliant – extremely serious and extraordinarily focused – French lawyer, who spent much of his working life as an exile in Geneva. Although Luther, the German monk, did much of the spadework, laying the foundations of this new 'reforming' movement with its innovative ideas about God and the Church, it was Calvin, the lawyer, who was to become its most towering figure. His relentless rigour – aided by the explosion of printing – meant that his understanding of God was imposed on the Western world. We still live with its legacy today.

Calvin, following Luther, believed not only that salvation was all about grace, but also that we are 'saved by our faith'. However, thanks on one hand to his decision to accept Luther's basic premise, and on the other to his logical and legal mind, he faced a huge problem.

Calvin's logic drove him to see that, on the face of it, salvation by grace (which he wanted to retain at the centre of his system) and salvation by faith were incompatible with each other. He had to find a way of resolving the impossible problem. If it was all by the grace of God, and also by our faith, then our ability to have faith must be a gift of God's grace. Therefore, he reasoned, that grace must logically be limited to people God chooses and withheld from those God doesn't. It's what his followers went on to refer to as 'limited atonement'. Some of us are chosen and so are saved (we are 'in' because grace is irresistible). Some of us are not (we are 'out' because atonement is limited).

Oxymoron

But what do you do with the moral dilemma that this creates, that of people born simply to be eternally damned? The answer: think like a lawyer. Calvin (unconsciously or not) effectively replaced Jesus' image of God as a loving parent with that of God as a stern, courtroom judge – just like the ones he knew and respected, whose job it was to make cold, pitiless and impersonal, although fair, decisions about those who were unfortunate enough to appear before their bench.

I believe that – as we will see – the results of this giant mistake have been catastrophic, not only when it comes to our perception of God's nature, but also to the deep sense of guilt and unworthiness that so many practising or former Protestant churchpeople live their whole lives under.

Now, back to the story.

I grew up in a home where we never went away on a summer holiday. My parents were poor and so, along with my brother and two sisters, we'd spend the long summer break from school at home, where my very creative mum found all sorts of inventive ways to keep us entertained.

One of them was that each year she would buy us a huge jigsaw puzzle, consisting of one or two thousand pieces. But these were jigsaw puzzles with a difference. My mum always got them from the second-hand shop at the top of our little street, and they usually came in an old paper bag, with no box and, most confusingly, no lid with the picture on it.

It's very difficult to piece a jigsaw together when you don't know what the overall picture is. It would always take us the whole summer. And, in the process, I'd come across various bits that I just couldn't place anywhere. It was so frustrating. Each day I'd end up looking at those same pieces, turning them round and round and wondering where they fitted. And each day I'd fail.

Somehow though, every year – over the last few days of the long summer holiday – that puzzle would miraculously come together. It took me years to realize that this was primarily due to our mother's nightly interventions after we'd gone to bed, perhaps with the help of the picture we never knew existed. But what I remember most was that invariably – when we finally got to see the finished picture – you could count on three truths:

One. There were always a few gaps in the picture – caused by missing bits of jigsaw that we just didn't have!

Two. Most of the pieces that all summer I'd not been able to fit in or understand, had now found their place.

Three. Very frustratingly, some of the pieces that I'd spent the whole summer trying painstakingly to place didn't belong at all. They'd somehow ended up mixed into our puzzle, at the second-hand shop, by accident.

That's exactly the problem with the term 'the wrath of God'. It's like a piece of jigsaw that we don't know what to do with. It is very awkward. The question is: does it fit at all? And, if so, where and how does it fit into the big picture that the Bible presents us with?

Here's the thing. Over the last few centuries the Bible translators have chosen to translate as 'wrath' or 'anger' a whole range of Old Testament Hebrew and New Testament Greek words with various shades of meaning. And that – as you might expect – has created several serious problems. We've all played Chinese whispers often enough to know that the translation business can be tricky at the best of times.

First, our words 'wrath' and 'anger' – which are used as interchangeable replacements for one another in different English Bible translations – both represent rather blunt, one-size-fits-all solutions which fail to do justice to the nuances of the array of original words they have replaced. English dictionaries define 'wrath' as 'extreme anger', before going on to add terms like rage, fury, annoyance, indignation, outrage, vengeance, hot temper and bad temper – all behaviours which often imply a selfish, malicious or vindictive mood.

Next, the Greek terms for 'wrath' and 'anger' which are used in the New Testament are themselves only attempts, once again, to do justice to the Hebrew words and thought which sit, unseen – and unknown to modern audiences – behind them.

Lastly, unfortunately, both the English words 'wrath' and 'anger' have different emotional, spiritual and psychological loads for each individual reader. They often carry extremely negative connotations, undertones, associations and inferences which are personal to every reader, though frequently held unconsciously.

And, I put it to you, all this creates a giant problem, which is why we think that the piece of the picture of God we've labelled 'wrath' just doesn't fit.

Let's start with the Old Testament. There is an array of Hebrew words which all get translated as anger or wrath, even though each one has a specific and different meaning. However, a survey of them reveals that typically they depict God's wrath in terms of a father's discipline towards his children, or a broken-hearted husband's yearning for an unfaithful wife, or a king's yearning for his wayward people. In fact, surprisingly, the Old Testament even presents God's wrath as a motivating attribute in prompting people to respond to God's overtures of grace. Which, once you stop to think about it, raises all sorts of questions about the way we have understood and applied this word.

So, let's take a look at those original Hebrew words and their roots.

For instance, *chemah* (הֵמָה) is very often rendered 'hot displeasure' or 'anger', although in fact it is more accurately defined as meaning hot, fever, or gripped with passion. The point is that it is not only when you are angry that you become hot and red in the face. For instance, you blush and become hot when you're embarrassed. So, *chemah* can mean embarrassment.

Or you might feel *chemah* when you've been betrayed. Is this anger, or a deep and burning sense of hurt? If a woman discovers that the husband she loves has been cheating on her, or a man feels betrayed by the woman he is utterly committed to, what do they feel? You may choose to call it anger; I think it is more complex than that. It is about the agony of rejection; the suffering of a broken heart. Perhaps God's heart – the heart of the loving parent, husband or king – is wrung with pain when we choose to turn our backs on God.

Then we have *'ebrah* (אֶבְרָה), which means outburst of passion, and *qetseph* (קֶצֶף), which means literally a splinter, but when translated metaphorically means to be displeased, to fret or to burst out. And *kaac* (כַּעַס), which means to be grieved, hurt, sorrowful or troubled.

The Hebrew word *aph* (אַף), which we have already come across, and literally means 'nose', can in a freer sense imply rapid breathing in passion. But it too, as we've seen, is often translated simply as anger. And then, among others, there is *ragaz* (רָגַז), meaning to be emotionally agitated, excited or perturbed, to tremble or quiver.[1]

Although God has been so often painted as frightening and ferocious, the obvious impact of a deeper understanding of such Hebrew words is that we recognize that these have been the traits of the god of our theological assumptions, rather than the God of reality. Far from being driven into a red-hot rage by our sin, the Bible reveals to us a passionate God who is taken aback, troubled, pained and broken with sorrow by our rebellion and rejection of his ways.

---

[1] *The Brown-Driver-Briggs Hebrew and English Lexicon* (Peabody, MA: Hendrickson, 1991), p. 919.

Then we come to the New Testament, where the two leading Greek words which are translated into English as wrath or anger are *thumos* (θυμός) and *orge* (ὀργή). Both have been regularly read as articulating the heat of God's anger against human sin as well as those who commit it. It is often presented as fact that *thumos* speaks of God's wrath poured out in the heat of the moment, whereas *orge* has more to do with God's considered and ongoing angry response to our sin. So, for instance, Strong's Concordance confidently states that *orge* can be defined as anger, wrath, passion; as punishment or vengeance.

But, once again, digging a bit deeper to take a look at the root meanings of these words reveals that *thumos* can indicate any kind of emotional response or outburst of emotion – rather than necessarily an angry one.

In the works of Homer, the legendary Ancient Greek poet and author of the *Iliad and* the *Odyssey*,[2] *thumos* is simply used to denote emotion or desire; so when one of Homer's heroes is under emotional stress, we read about how they will sometimes choose to externalize their *thumos*, whatever it is.

---

[2] Although it is generally accepted that the poems were originally composed at some point around the late eighth or early seventh century BC, modern scholarly opinion then divides into two main groups. One holds that most of the *Iliad* and the *Odyssey* are the works of a single poet: Homer. The other regards the 'Homeric' poems, as we now have them, as the result of a long process of working and reworking by many contributors – specifically as the plays were performed in public, slowly evolving and developing through this process. In this view, rather than a person, the name 'Homer' is a label for an entire tradition – although there must have been an original author.

And then, in his book *Phaedrus*, the fourth-century BC Greek philosopher Plato depicts *logos* (knowledge) as a charioteer driving and guiding the two horses *eros* (erotic love) and *thumos* (spiritedness). Later, he picks up this same theme when, in the *Republic*, he argues that *thumos* is one of the three core constituent parts of the human psyche, which are:

- *epithumia* (our appetites), our desires;
- *thumos* (our passion), our emotional response to pain, suffering, injustice, attraction, etc.;
- *nous* (our intellect or reason), which is, or should be, the controlling part that subjugates our appetites with the help of *thumos*.

Likewise, rather than necessarily referring to anger, *orge*, which comes from the verb *orago*, simply implies a longer-term and more sustained feeling.

It is highly informative, therefore, that, in his letter to the church in Ephesus, where Paul writes 'Be angry (*orge*),[3] and yet do not sin', all agree that he is quoting King David who in Psalm 4 pens the phrase 'Be angry (*ragaz*),[4] and do not sin.'[5] But, whereas in the 1984 edition of the New International Version, Psalm 4.4 reads, 'In your anger, do not sin', the 2011 edition of the very same version – with its updated understanding of Ancient Greek – has changed the words to 'Tremble and do not sin'. What's more, the New American Standard Version agrees, while

---

[3] The actual word Paul uses is *orgizesthe*, which is a derivative of *orge*.

[4] Once again, the actual word used is a derivative of *ragaz*.

[5] Ephesians 4.26–27; Psalm 4.4.

the Good News translation gives us 'Tremble with fear and stop sinning'.

The real irony here is that, once again, none of this is new. The old King James Version of 1611 always read: 'Stand in awe, and sin not'. So there it is in black and white!

Ragaz really does simply mean any emotion that causes you to tremble or quiver, to catch your breath, to be taken aback, to shudder, rather than necessarily referring to a response of anger. No one knows that better than Paul, the Second Temple Jewish thinker, and that is the meaning that he imports into his usage of *orge*.

Some years ago I had the opportunity to ask Rabbi Jonathan Sacks, one of the UK's senior Jewish leaders, about the concept of God's anger. I will never forget his answer. 'It is perhaps better, and far more accurate,' he said, 'to understand God's anger as his anguish – a dimension of his love, but never an emotion in opposition to it.'

I remember sharing this story of Jonathan Sacks' amazing insight with another rabbi friend of mine. He smiled at me, with one of those kind but knowing smiles, and then said, 'Well, if you are going to take the Hebrew Bible and build it into your Christian understanding of life, it probably makes sense to ask a Hebrew what the words you are reading might actually mean.'

But of course, even to those who read no Hebrew, all this should be obvious – because the most profound theological truth expressed in the whole canon of Scripture is that 'God is love'.[6] It is not that God approves of love. Love is not a quality that God possesses. It is the divine essence itself – God's essential being. Indeed, the Bible never makes assertions about God's anger, power or judgement independently of God's love. God's 'anger' (as we call it) is nothing more than an aspect of this love, and to understand it any differently must therefore be to misunderstand it.

My critics will of course respond that surely, if God is love, God must also experience anger at injustice. But this misses the point. As the great theologian Karl Barth once explained, if God exhibits characteristics of anger, judgement and the like, they are never more than 'repetitions and amplifications of the one statement that God loves'.[7] If we forget this – if we ever talk about God's anger outside of the context of God's love – we make a great mistake.

If God is love, then every action and reaction dealing with humanity flows out of love. This is why we make a tremendous mistake whenever we juxtapose God's love with God's 'wrath'. But to speak of God's love in the same breath as God's anguish, as an expression of love, makes all the sense in the world. The expressions 'wrath' and 'anger' are too loose. Both terms carry overtones of vindictive and malicious behaviour. God is always redemptive.

The attempt to explain that God is love *but* that God is also wrathful is wrongheaded and nonsensical. There

---

[6] 1 John 4.8.

[7] Karl Barth, *Church Dogmatics*, Vol. 2 (London: Continuum International, 2000), p. 284.

is no 'but'. God's love, and what we have come to refer to as God's anger, are part of the same whole which consists completely of love. Although he is not always consistent in his understanding of this, as David grasps in Psalm 145.17: 'The LORD is righteous in *all* his ways and faithful in *all* he does' (emphasis added). God's anger, it turns out, is nothing more or less than a dimension of deep love.[8]

Jesus taught his followers to pray: 'Our Father, who is in heaven . . .' Jesus encouraged us to think of God primarily as a parent rather than a judge.

Any of us who have known the joy of raising children have also known the struggle of coping with and responding to their moods and rebellions – and yet no well-adjusted parent, who truly loves their child, ever seeks retribution for bad behaviour and wrongs done to them. For a loving parent, anger (better termed anguish or frustration) is never violent or destructive. Instead, genuine love drives parents to serve their children devotedly and unselfishly, to overlook and forgive shortcomings, often without any apology, let alone thanks.

Now imagine why Paul might have written these words: 'I am convinced that nothing can ever separate us from God's love . . . Neither death nor life, neither angels nor demons . . . not even the powers of hell can separate us from God's love.'[9]

---

[8] See Psalm 145.9: 'The LORD is good to all; he has compassion on all he has made', but then in verse 20: 'The LORD watches over all who love him, but all the wicked he will destroy.'

[9] Romans 8.38, 39.

It is only in the light of perceiving God, in the way that Jesus taught us, as the perfect parent that we begin to see that the divine response to our rebellion is always more accurately described as anguish than as anger or wrath. It is passionate love for us that causes God to tremble, to be plunged into sorrow. When love endures the pain of rejection it hurts.

But how do we know that all this is the correct reading of a New Testament mindset? Because, as 1 John exclaims, 'God is love', before going on to explain, 'There is no fear in love, but perfect love drives out fear, because fear has to do with punishment.'

13

The double whammy

If all the foregoing is true, then where did this overwhelming sense of our human guilt and unworthiness originate, the idea that so riddles the lives of countless churchgoers, while at the same time driving others from its doors?

Although it comes as a huge shock to most Western churchgoers, here it is:

The Eastern half of the Church – what we know today as the Orthodox Church – never did, and still does not, accept the theological construct we take for granted and call 'original sin'. So where does it come from?

Original sin is an idea developed by Augustine of Hippo in the early fifth century, in the Latin-speaking Western Church, and perfected much later by John Calvin.[1] '[Augustine's] impact on Western Christian thought', wrote Oxford historian and theologian Diarmaid MacCulloch, 'can hardly be overstated; only . . . Paul of Tarsus has been

---

[1] Augustine (354–430) was a Roman African, early Christian theologian and philosopher whose writings influenced the development of Western Christianity and Western philosophy. He became the Bishop of Hippo in North Africa and is viewed as one of the most important Church Fathers in Western Christianity. Among his most important books are *The City of God*, *On Christian Doctrine* and *Confessions*.

more influential, and Westerners have generally seen Paul through Augustine's eyes.'[2] And that, in my view, sits at the root of the problem of our sense that we somehow live under the wrath and judgement of God.

As a young man, Augustine – a North African, from modern-day Algeria – who would go on to become one of the Church's all-time most influential thinkers, was heavily influenced by a movement known as Manichaeism. Manichaeism was the teaching of Mani, a third-century Iranian, who grew up in one of the many Jewish/Christian sects that were common at that time. Manichaeism thrived between the third and seventh centuries and, at its height, was widespread.

One of Manichaeism's core concepts was that each one of us has a 'divine spark' which is trapped in our physical bodies, and which is constantly trying to escape to be reunited with God, from where it first came. This is part of the cosmic struggle between a good, spiritual world of light, and an evil, material world of darkness. But, through the ongoing process of human history, light is being gradually removed from the world of matter and returned to the world of light, from where it first came. It's a deeply pessimistic view of humanity.

On becoming a Christian in Milan at the age of 32, some of the thinking in which he was steeped as a young man played a role in shaping Augustine's developing approach to theology, especially in his formulation of the doctrine

[2] Diarmaid MacCulloch, *A History of Christianity: The first three thousand years* (London: Penguin, 2010), p. 319.

of original sin.[3] As he put it: 'the deliberate sin of the first man is the cause of Original Sin', which he understood to have infected and polluted us all.[4]

In Augustine's first book, *Confessions* – a kind of autobiography of his early years – he tells a story of how, as a boy, he once stole some pears. He did this, he says, not because he was hungry, or even because he wanted the pears (he gave them away). He did it because he knew it was wrong and he wanted to enjoy the pleasure of stealing. Later in the same book he revisits his story of the pears and uses it as an illustration of all sin; we have a delight in doing the wrong thing just because it is wrong. It's irrational, it's absurd, but it is our way of choosing to assert ourselves against God.

Centuries later, John Calvin, who quotes Augustine more than a thousand times in his writing, picked up on this theme. Those who followed him slowly codified his extensive teaching into what was to become known as the Five Points of Calvinism, still widely influential today, and known to us by an acronym: TULIP.[5]

---

[3] Developing an idea first put forward by an influential Christian leader and writer, Irenaeus, in the second century.

[4] Augustine, *De Nuptiis et Concupiscentia* (On Marriage and Concupiscence), II.26.43.

[5] There is huge ongoing debate around whether, in their enthusiasm to embrace Calvin's teaching and to codify it, successive generations of 'Calvinists' fell into the trap of going further than his original theology had done. TULIP stands for: Total Depravity (also known as Total Inability and Original Sin); Unconditional Election; Limited Atonement (also known as Particular Atonement); Irresistible Grace; and Perseverance of the Saints (also known as Once Saved Always Saved). These teach that God by sovereign grace predestines people into salvation; that Jesus died only for those predestined; that God regenerates individuals where they are then able and

The double whammy

The first point – the very beginning of Calvin's theology – represented by the T of TULIP, stands for 'Total Depravity'. This teaches that the condition of original sin is the state into which every human being is born; a problem which it lays at the feet of the first man, Adam, who disobeyed God by eating the forbidden fruit from the tree of knowledge of good and evil and, by consequence, transmitted his sin and guilt by heredity to the entire human race.

The result is that we all enter the world with a 'fallen nature'. We are all enslaved by original sin – it is inherent in us all. We are born, condemned already.

This means that our guilt as human beings – as far as God is concerned – is rooted, not first in our individual sins or actual self-centred attitudes and behaviours, but in our connection with Adam. Adam's guilt is credited by God not just to Adam himself, but to us all. We are all deserving of the same punishment – death – before we take our first breath. We are all Adam's descendants. We are all born already 'morally ruined'. There is no island – no vestige – of goodness left in us.

We are all placed under the wrath and judgement of God from the moment of our birth. We are not sinners because we sin; rather, we sin because we are sinners. It's our original sin that manifests itself throughout our lives in actual sins: the actions, thoughts and feelings we choose that violate God's moral commands of which we are also guilty. It's a double whammy.

---

want to choose God; and that it is impossible for those who are redeemed to lose their salvation.

I see things differently. I do not believe that God perceives any of us as totally depraved. As Martin Luther King once put it, there is some bad in the best of us, but there is also good in the worst of us.

In my view, original sin is a deeply pessimistic view of humanity and a deeply flawed theory. I believe that the Bible starts with original goodness rather than original sin.

It's not just that the Bible's story starts with Genesis 1 ('God saw all that he had made, and it was very good') rather than Genesis 3 (the story of Adam, Eve, the snake and what we have come to term 'the fall'). In my view, the concept of original sin is a defective theological construct, which does not sit comfortably with the flow of the biblical narrative.

We all know how the traditional reading of the Adam and Eve story goes. It's the tale of the first man and first woman; they enjoy a beautiful garden, God establishes some boundaries for them, satan tempts them, they eat the apple, they get kicked out, and we are all stained and born into the guilt of original sin as a result. But here are three facts you might not know.

One. There is no satan in the story of Adam and Eve. In fact, we know that the concept of the devil doesn't really develop in Hebrew thought for hundreds of years after this story was first written down.[6]

Two. Not only does the word 'sin' not appear within the story; the beginnings of the concept of the theory of original

---

6 Perhaps the result of the Hebrews' engagement with Zoroastrianism.

sin were first put forward by the influential Christian leader and writer, Irenaeus, in the second century after Jesus, and were, as we've seen, later to be adapted – many would say twisted – by Augustine in the fifth century and finalized by Calvin the lawyer in the sixteenth century.[7] As Harry Williams, a Cambridge theologian of a previous generation, once quipped, 'St Augustine took the worst out of St Paul, and Calvin took the worst out of St Augustine.'

Three. The theory of original sin has never been taken up as an authentic interpretation of the Adam and Eve story by any Jewish teacher, either before or since Jesus. Instead, they have always seen this foundational story from the Hebrew Bible quite differently. The truth is that the vast majority of biblical scholars now understand that the story of Adam and Eve is a myth – a kind of profound fable rather than an historical narrative, much like similar stories in the literature we have from other ancient civilizations.

It is a myth that is packed with wisdom: about a man formed from the dust and given the task of tending paradise (a garden of innocence), about a woman created to be the man's companion, and about a talking snake who tempts them into eating fruit from the magical 'Tree of Knowledge of Good and Evil', which has been declared off-limits by the God who created it all.

Rather than a tale of human depravity, Jewish theology has always interpreted the story of Adam and Eve as one

---

[7] Irenaeus sees the sin as an act of immaturity; as a stumble rather than a fall from grace. So, although they both spoke about 'original sin', the outcomes are far more hopeful in Irenaeus than in Augustine.

of growing up. Rules can't create morality. Only the knowledge of good and evil, of right and wrong, of choice, can do that. This is the birthplace of all true morality. The story is not about the fall of humanity, or the coming of sin. Instead it is about the loss of innocence; the journey of humankind, as well as that of every individual, into moral responsibility.

Having been enticed by the seductive appeal of the snake's deception, the first man and woman learn the huge price of surrendering to their appetites. Their act of immaturity has giant ramifications. It leads to their loss of innocence, their awareness of their nakedness, their discovery of their inability to hide from their creator, and their banishment from paradise into a world where they will from now on have to deal with the responsibility of what it is to know the moral difference between good and evil, and the implications of choosing between them.

So it is that, together, Adam and Eve leave their garden of innocence as moral adults – free moral agents – to work out what it means to live well and to do good. The story speaks to all humanity. It teaches us a great truth: that our moral freedom – our human autonomy which comes with the knowledge of right and wrong – is a daily challenge as well as an ongoing opportunity.

Yet, even in this new demanding existence, 'East of Eden' as Genesis puts it, the God who made them and delights in them will not abandon them. In spite of their stumble, they are still representatives of God whose indelible image remains in them. Although their moral accountability for – as well as the continuing consequences of – their own short-sighted decisions will inevitably distort life for them, the God of love will not, cannot, give up on them.

For me, therefore, those who search this story for some universal principle that the whole human race is enslaved to original sin – that the God of creation sees us all as objects of inherited depravity, wrath and guilt, or creatures under divine condemnation – is entirely wrongheaded and misses the whole point of the profound and practical wisdom it was written to offer us. Seeing God's primary and first response to humanity as one of condemnation because of our supposed total depravity is neither true nor biblical, but the invention of a misguided theological system. God is not wrath; God is love.

And, as I reflect on my own experience and understanding of God, my relationship with God – although, over the years, I've had many people (most of them, sadly, Church people) pronounce God's wrath over me, and I've certainly felt the impact of their disapproval and rejection – yet, from God, I have only ever experienced forgiveness, love and undeserved grace.

I recognize that my own pathway through life has been, and still is, every bit as much in deficit of God's best as any of those ancients whom, I am told, incurred God's wrath as the result of their wrongdoing. But my experience tells me something different. It tells me that God never stops pouring out grace and mercy, love and forgiveness, compassion and delight.

Frustration born of love is not the same emotion as fury born of anger.

14

True

God is love.

Once you understand that, everything else cascades from it. Every other category or concept in Paul's thinking – the righteousness of God, the cross, the judgement seat of Christ, justification, anger – is defined by it, as we will discover.

When my children were young, I would warn them not to do things that I knew might hurt or harm them. But what I never said was, 'If you disobey me, I'll reject and punish you for ever.' My purpose and, hopefully, most of the time my tone was different: 'I love you and I don't want to see you hurt or injured.'

And, when those wonderful, though sometimes stubborn, sometimes self-centred, young and immature children of mine broke those boundaries, as was inevitably the case, my response was usually – I am glad to be able to report – motivated by my love. But, when it wasn't – whenever my anger got the better of me outside the context of my love – it always left me filled with regret and having to apologize to them for *my* immature behaviour.

So how can it be that our view of God is that the message for us is, 'Look, I love you and want the best for you, but don't mess with me, because if you choose to disobey me and the guidelines I have given you, I'll make sure that you pay for it – for ever.'

That's not love – it's megalomania.

Instead, perhaps God, who is the definition of love, might say, 'I love you and want the best for you. I don't want to see you hurt or injured. I know that when you choose to live outside guidelines I've given you, life will be a mess. But, count on this, I'm always there. My love for you will never fail.'

God showers all humanity with unwavering, unconditional, parental – fatherly and motherly – love. But we live in a consequential universe, and wrongdoing has its consequences. Which is why God is filled with anguish and frustration at our selfish and short-sighted decisions.

There are important clues to all this, even in the Old Testament. For example, take a look at Psalm 7.14–16:

> Whoever is pregnant with evil
>   conceives trouble and gives birth to disillusionment.
> Whoever digs a hole and scoops it out
>   falls into the pit they have made.
> The trouble they cause recoils on them;
>   their violence comes down on their own heads.

We dig a pit, and sooner or later we fall in. We create trouble, and sooner or later it returns to haunt us. We employ violence, and sooner or later it rebounds on us. Wrongdoing has consequences – here and now. Or, to put the same thing slightly differently, sin is its own punishment.

As Jesus explained, 'Love your enemies, do good to them . . . and you will be children of the Most High, because he is kind to the ungrateful and wicked. Be merciful, just as your Father is merciful.'[1] God, the Father, is kind and merciful . . . even to the evil and ungrateful! We are punished *by* our sins rather than *for* our sins.

A few years ago, I was taking part in a live debate on BBC Radio 5 Live. As we chatted about the Church, the presenter chipped in with an observation not untypical of the sort of thing many of us have probably had thrown at our feet: 'Why is God so miserable? Why is the Bible so full of "don't do this and don't do that"? Don't desire what other people have got. Don't lie. Don't steal. Don't commit adultery. It's all so negative.'

I interrupted her. 'Where does it say that? I've never read that. I must have missed that bit. Where does God say, "Don't commit adultery"?'

'You know very well it's in the Bible,' she retorted. 'It's one of the Ten Commandments.'

'Oh,' I exclaimed, 'now I know what you're talking about. It's just that I didn't recognize it at first because of the tone of voice you were using.'

'What do you mean?' she said.

'You're absolutely right,' I replied. 'The Bible does say that we shouldn't commit adultery, but not in the way

---

[1] Luke 6.35–36.

you've read it. You see, just before God gives the people of Israel the Ten Commandments, he is introduced as the God who loves them. God is for them, not against them. He wants the best for them.

'God didn't come up with a list of all the things that human beings like doing and then outlaw them, just to spoil our fun. Instead, this is God saying, "I love you. I'm on your side." In fact the text of the Ten Commandments begins, "I am the Lord your God, who brought you out of Egypt, out of the land of slavery." I got you out of slavery, God is saying. I'm the best deal you've got going for you. Trust me. I've proved that I'm on your side. So don't steal. Don't lie. Don't abandon me. Don't commit adultery. Because if you do it will unleash destructive powers that you will come to regret, that will slowly overshadow and overwhelm you, your families, your community and your society. Just don't do it."'

The presenter looked at me in astonishment. 'No one has ever explained it to me in that way,' she said quietly. 'That makes so much sense.'

In the light of this, let's take another look at those words of Paul – the ones that I quoted at the start of Chapter 12 – from Romans 1.18: 'The wrath of God is being revealed from heaven against all the godlessness and wickedness of people, who suppress the truth by their wickedness.' What is often not recognized is that, having made this point, Paul goes on to explain exactly how God's anger is revealed; this anguish, the outworking of deep love.

Verse 24 reads: 'Therefore God "gave them over" in the sinful desires of their hearts to sexual impurity for the degrading of their bodies with one another.'

Verse 26 reads: 'Because of this, God 'gave them over' to shameful lusts. Even their women exchanged natural sexual relations for unnatural ones.'

Verse 28 reads: 'Furthermore, just as they did not think it worthwhile to retain the knowledge of God, so God 'gave them over' to a depraved mind, so that they do what ought not to be done.'

God, though wracked with the pain of anguish, because love never imposes itself, 'gives them over'. God gives these people up to their own sinful ways. God doesn't punish them or harm them in any way. Why would God do that? Instead, trembling with sorrow, God simply lets them go the way they have chosen and weeps as they punish themselves by their short-sighted and wrong decisions. They reap what they have sown. But none of this means that God gives up on them.

This is what Paul is so keen to impress on his Corinthian audience:

> Love is patient,
> love is kind.
> It does not envy,
> it does not boast,
> it is not proud.
> It does not dishonour others,
> it is not self-seeking,
> it is not easily angered,

it keeps no record of wrongs.
Love does not delight in evil but rejoices with the truth.
It always protects, always trusts, always hopes, always perseveres.
Love never fails . . .
And now these three remain: faith, hope and love. But the greatest of these is love. [2]

Paul is emphatic: 'Love never fails.'

Is this true or not? Has Paul just got carried away with himself in a rash and flowery flourish which he later regrets, or are his words carefully chosen?

His words are either true, or irresponsibly misleading. 'Never' either means never, or it doesn't. The tragedy is that over the centuries the Church has time and again failed to communicate, or even to understand, what it is clear that Paul believes to be at the core of his message.

Perhaps some of the most disastrous examples of this failure are the Church's historic creeds, which, forged over the centuries, have universally failed to explicitly set out the sublimely simple yet profound biblical statement found in 1 John 4.8 – 'God is love.' As a result, the fact that the God of the universe not only claims to love but is wholly defined *as* love has become one of the world's best-kept secrets.

In 1741, in Enfield, Connecticut, USA, the renowned preacher, theologian and Puritan revivalist, Jonathan Edwards (1703–58), delivered one of the most famous

---

[2]   1 Corinthians 13.

sermons in the history of the Church. He called it 'Sinners in the Hands of an Angry God':

> The God that holds you over the pit of hell, much as one holds a spider or some loathsome insect over the fire, abhors you and is dreadfully provoked: his wrath towards you burns like fire; he looks upon you as worthy of nothing else, but to be cast into the fire; he is of purer eyes than to bear to have you in his sight; you are ten thousand times more abominable in his eyes than the most hateful venomous serpent is in ours.
>
> You have offended him infinitely more than ever a stubborn rebel did his prince; and yet it is nothing but his hand that holds you from falling into the fire every moment.
>
> It is to be ascribed to nothing else that you did not go to hell the last night; that you were suffered to awake again in this world, after you closed your eyes to sleep. And there is no other reason to be given, why you have not dropped into hell since you arose in the morning, but that God's hand has held you up. There is no other reason to be given why you have not gone to hell, since you have sat here in the house of God, provoking his pure eyes by your sinful wicked manner of attending his solemn worship.
>
> Yea, there is nothing else that is to be given as a reason why you do not this very moment drop down into hell.

This grim sermon delivered to a packed auditorium must have been almost unbearable to listen to. But here we are, almost three centuries later, and humanity is still mesmerized and terrified by a vision of the God of the Bible who is presented as angry and retributive.

Preaching like Edwards' has over the last few hundred years been all too representative of the portrayal of 'the gospel' by whole sections of the Church and therefore, by implication, of any popular understanding of the message of Jesus. And although today, for the most part, the worst of this ferocious rhetoric is a thing of the past, the angry echoes of such portrayals are still heard in many a sermon across the world today.

People still believe and teach that the Christian God is a God of conditional love rather than undeserved grace; a God whose strapline is something like 'Turn from your sin and place your faith in Christ who died in your place on the cross, or you'll pay for it for ever.' Still today countless people, including Christians, struggle with a deeply embedded sense of an angry, vindictive, violent God. And it has left many of them profoundly damaged.

But, Paul couldn't be clearer. No small print, no 'conditions apply' limitation clause.

Love never fails!

15

The crux

Most of us don't see things the way they are, we see things the way we are.[1]

'We preach Christ crucified,' announced Paul.[2]

The cross of Jesus is clearly a central theme in Paul's letters. In the light of this, it's not difficult to understand why it has grown to be the most distinctive of all Christian icons around the world, regarded as the very *crux* of Paul's writing and thinking.

So, for many, the cross has become not just central to the gospel; it has become the whole gospel. Because of the cross, God's anger is satisfied, we are forgiven, and our relationship is restored. Job done!

It's fascinating to see how many of the available booklets on 'becoming a Christian' simply stop at the cross. According to one popular online tract, the gospel is as simple as ABC:

---

[1] 'We do not see things as they are. We see things as we are.' A Talmudic saying attributed to Rabbi Shemuel ben Nachmani (*c.* 270–*c.* 330).

[2] 1 Corinthians 1.23.

Accept God loves you.
Believe that, even though you have sinned and fallen short, Jesus died in your place.
Confess your sins and receive forgiveness.

Jesus' death on the cross – often still portrayed in songs and sermons as his sacrifice in order to appease and pacify God's wrath by taking the punishment for our sin on his own shoulders – is the beginning and end of the story. Even if the resurrection is mentioned, it reads more like a 'happy ever after' than anything else. But when Paul announced that he was interested in nothing but 'Jesus Christ and him crucified', did he mean what we mean?[3] Once again, rather than jumping to conclusions, our challenge is to listen as hard as we can to Paul on his terms, rather than on ours. To see the world through Paul's eyes – not our twenty-first-century contact lenses! To see things as *they* are, not as *we* are.

We've propagated heartless courtroom scenes; the punishment must always fit the crime as cold unfeeling justice is delivered.

We've dressed up pre-Christian violent pagan ideas; the gods are angry and their wrath must be appeased by an innocent victim.

These, and many more contemporary theories about the way in which the cross works, detached from the socio-cultural setting in which Paul lived, have been

---

[3] 1 Corinthians 2.2.

cloaked in random decontextualized Bible verses to give them the false appearance of authenticity.

It is often claimed that Paul, along with all the other New Testament writers, was so taken up with what Jesus achieved on the cross – somehow solving the problem of sin – that he never got around to thinking very hard about precisely 'why' and 'how' this wonderful outcome was achieved. Thus, we are told, it was only centuries later that theologians began to get to grips with how exactly God was made 'at one with' humanity.

But, the way I see it, not only is this popular view extraordinarily arrogant, it's also one which, once you stop to think about it, makes no sense.

Paul is the genius who has the *mind* to recalibrate the teaching of Jesus as 'the Way' of living, not just for the Jewish people but for the whole world, and at the same time the *energy* to constantly 'road test' it all, however challenging and costly that task. To believe that he did all this – or that he could do all this – without ever reflecting on what his encounter with the crucified and risen Jesus of Nazareth on the Damascus road meant in terms of his worldview is simply ridiculous.

Saul had once spent his days hunting down the followers of Jesus. He regarded them as dangerously deluded vermin; their leader as nothing more than a cheap and fake messiah. But, now he was preaching 'Christ crucified' and staking his whole life on the message that sits behind it. In the light of this, the idea that he would be unable to tell you how – or wasn't bothered to put pen to paper to set down why – all this works is ludicrous.

In fact, Paul is very clear about how he sees all this. The problem is that he is just not saying what we have decided we want to hear.

Paul's back story, the cultural construct in which he lived, was, as we know, Second Temple Judaism. This is how he understood and negotiated the whole world. And, as we also know, as far as Paul – indeed all Jews – were concerned, a dead messiah was no messiah at all. A crucified messianic candidate, stripped naked, gasping for breath, for water and dignity, did not speak of liberation – it was an unmitigated disaster.[4] As Paul himself put it, a crucified Christ was bluntly 'a stumbling block to Jews' and plain stupidity to Gentiles.[5]

The cross was the ultimate means of exclusion in the Roman Empire. A symbol of imperial terror, it was the Romans' preferred instrument of execution for criminals and all those they regarded as threats to their national security. Designed to shame, humiliate and torture its victims publicly over an extended period of time before life finally ebbed away, it kept the Empire's reputation for violent, brutal social engineering in place. As Paul puts it, quoting from the Old Testament, 'Cursed is everyone who is hung on a pole.'[6]

It was Jesus' resurrection – and Jesus' resurrection alone – that changed the game. 'Paul never sanctifies or hallows death, pain, and suffering. He takes no masochistic delight in suffering,' wrote J. Christiaan Beker. For Paul, the death

---

[4] John 12.34: 'The Scriptures teach that the Messiah will live forever. How can you say that the Son of Man must be lifted up?'

[5] 1 Corinthians 1.23.

[6] Galatians 3.13, quoting Deuteronomy 21.23.

of Jesus is effective only because it stands within the radius of the victory of the resurrection.[7] Paul is nothing if not blunt with his friends in Corinth: 'If Christ has not been raised, our preaching is useless and so is your faith . . . If Christ has not been raised, your faith is futile.'[8] The cross without the resurrection is a disaster.

Only the resurrection explains why it is that Paul comes to believe that Jesus of Nazareth *is* the Messiah (or Christ) at all, rather than simply one more publicity-seeking fake.[9] It is only his blinding encounter with the risen Jesus, on the dusty Damascus road, that opens his eyes to the fact that God has finally done what Isaiah's prophecy spoke of.

Through Jesus, God has 'swallowed up death'[10] and now is delivering on the rest of his responsibilities; but this time not just for the Jews, but for all peoples of the earth – as well as for the entire cosmos.[11] Jesus has become the Christ; his resurrection authenticates him not only as the Jewish Messiah, but the Lord of the whole earth. The resurrection transformed the cross – an ignominious instrument of death and exclusion – into what would become a symbol of deliverance for the whole world.

[7] J. C. Beker, *The Triumph of God: The essence of Paul's thought* (Minneapolis: Fortress, 1990), p. 88.

[8] 1 Corinthians 15.14, 17. See also e.g. Romans 6.8, 10; 2 Corinthians 13.4; 1 Thessalonians 4.14.

[9] The Hebrew Messiah, המשיח, *Ha mashiach*, meaning 'the anointed one' or 'the liberator', is the equivalent of the Greek Christ, Χριστός, *Christós*. Paul uses the term 'Jesus Christ' (Jesus the Messiah) as well as the reciprocal 'Christ Jesus', meaning 'the Messiah Jesus'.

[10] Isaiah 25.6–8.

[11] 2 Corinthians 5.18–20; Ephesians 2.16; Colossians 1.20–21.

Our problem is that our individualistic, introspective Western worldview, and its overriding concern with personal salvation, has divorced Paul's writing from its socio-historical moorings. Its stranglehold has completely blinded us to the breadth of his theological orientation and perspective.

For Paul, Jesus' death and resurrection mark the new exodus, the ultimate exodus, through which the whole of creation is rescued and renewed. The Pharaohs of this world have been defeated once and for all. Because of the cross and the resurrection – which Paul sees as two scenes in one event – a new world order has been launched.

God, Paul declares in his letter to the Colossians, reconciles the entire cosmos through Jesus – the unconventional Messiah – who teaches, lives and dies by the upside-down, counter-cultural principles of love rather than the sword, forgiveness rather than revenge and meekness rather than arrogance. As he hangs on the cross Jesus takes his own medicine. He 'turns the other cheek', he refuses to return evil for evil. He exposes the false ideology that violence is the ultimate solution, as he willingly absorbs its impact within his own body. Finally, as Jesus emerges from the grave, he demonstrates that no political power, no unjust regime can defeat love.

The thought that on the cross Jesus is somehow placating God's anger is completely foreign to Paul. Instead, armed only with the non-violent power of truth and love, Jesus opposes and defeats the anger, sin and violence of humanity and the forces of evil that sit behind them. He soaks them up, but he will not submit to them. He absorbs their consequences, but they cannot absorb him. And his resurrection, three days later, turns the tables. Sin, evil and the threat of death could not defeat him; now he has defeated them!

This is the ultimate act of the faithfulness of Jesus to God as well as to humanity. The theology of the cross is the theology of service and sacrifice. And it's this story that, in turn, Jesus' followers are asked to live faithfully to. 'In your relationships with one another,' writes Paul, 'have the same mindset as Christ Jesus':

> Who, being in very nature God,
>> did not consider equality with God something to be used
>>> to his own advantage;
> rather, he made himself nothing
>> by taking the very nature of a servant,
>> being made in human likeness.
> And being found in appearance as a man,
>> he humbled himself
>> by becoming obedient to death –
>>> even death on a cross!
> Therefore God exalted him to the highest place
>> and gave him the name that is above every name,
> that at the name of Jesus every knee should bow,
>> in heaven and on earth and under the earth,
> and every tongue acknowledge that Jesus Christ is Lord,
>> to the glory of God the Father.[12]

Paul couldn't be clearer. It is what precedes and follows Jesus' death on the cross that makes his death redemptive. Christ's life, death *and* resurrection together are his victory over all the forces of evil 'in heaven and on earth

---

[12] Philippians 2.5–11.

and under the earth'. For Paul, Jesus' death on the cross, transformed by his resurrection, unmasked, disrupted and subverted the prevailing perceptions and structures of power. As N. T. Wright puts it, 'It took [Paul's] genius to see that the symbol which had spoken of Caesar's naked might now spoke of God's naked love.'[13]

The meaning of the cross is not that God the Father punished the Son in order to avoid punishing humanity, but rather that through Christ's faithfulness to walking the way of peace and forgiveness rather than power, control and retaliation, God absorbed the world's evil and its consequences into himself. The cross is the greatest symbol of divine love. It is the demonstration of just how far God the Father and Jesus the Son are prepared to go to prove that love and to bring redemption to their creation.

Jesus' death is redemptive, not because it satisfies some necessary condition in the way that many of our later Western doctrines of the cross have suggested, but because Jesus lived a life faithful to God's pathway of love and in response God raised him from death.

God didn't punish Jesus. God exalted him.

The cross of Jesus is about humanity's anger, cruelty, violence and longing for retribution. And it is about God's dogged love. On the cross, Jesus does not placate God's anger as he takes the punishment for sin, but rather he absorbs the consequences of all the injustice and sin in the society around him. History actually records that Jesus died

---

[13] N. T. Wright, *Paul: In fresh perspective* (Minneapolis: Fortress, 2005), p. 73.

because of the self-interest of the Jewish leaders, the pride of the Roman Empire, the detachment and weakness of Pontius Pilate (the Roman official in charge of Judea at the time), the manipulation of Judas and the fickleness of the ordinary people. According to Tom Wright:

> Jesus shouldered the burden, not so much of 'sin' in the abstract, in a kind of transaction which took place away from the actual events that led to his death, but rather of the actual weight – the power and results – of human sin and rebellion, the accumulation of the actual human pride, sin, folly and shame which, at that moment in history, concentrated themselves in the arrogance of Rome, the self-seeking of the Jewish leaders, and the distorted dreams of the Jewish revolutionaries, and the failures of Jesus' own followers.[14]

The cross speaks not of anger, but of love – summed up for all time in Jesus' own words: 'Father forgive them, for they know not what they do.'

God's power is revealed in weakness, not in strength. And Paul believes that this should be the guiding principle of the Church's identity – one that stands in total opposition and contrast to the popular values of status, power and wealth which dominate our society. Whatever our theories of the cross, unless they articulate this, they are wrong-headed. 'The crucifixion of Jesus is not only a past, datable, verifiable fact in the Church's memory, but also an everpresent reality to guide and determine the Church's life,' wrote Charles B. Cousar in his book, *A Theology of the Cross: The death of Jesus in the Pauline letters*.[15]

---

[14] Tom Wright, *Virtue Reborn* (London: SPCK, 2010), Ch. 4.

[15] C. B. Cousar, *A Theology of the Cross: The death of Jesus in the Pauline letters* (Minneapolis: Fortress, 1990) p. 4.

Why does this matter? Because what we believe is indissolubly linked to the way we behave. What we believe about the cross – and what God was doing there – will fundamentally shape our attitude towards, and involvement with, wider society. Inadequate and erroneous theology leads to distorted understandings of God and humanity, and inevitably results in immature engagement in community and wider society.

Has Christ's death on the cross any relevance or significance beyond the eternal destiny of his individual followers? Does the meaning of the cross speak to our government's foreign policy, the future of the Middle East, the war on terrorism, the challenge to the market economy of ethical trading, people trafficking and climate change? Does it address the hopes, ambitions and fears of our generation?

The centrality of the cross in Paul's letters, once freed from the sentimentality of Western theological introspection, is seen for what it is. It's a story of outstanding grace, of scandalous love and unending mercy; it's a story that is political, global and cosmic.

But, if all this is true, it leads us to another big question: What about life beyond death? What about heaven and hell?

16

Shades

Hell has a history, and it is an interesting one.

Through the millennia it's been written up as everything from a fiery vault somewhere beneath the earth, filled with worms and torture chambers, to a frozen tomb, all the way, in the words of Jean-Paul Sartre, to the bleak observation 'Hell is other people'.[1]

But before we explore it all, a short explanation.

The next three chapters don't mention Paul's writing very much – which might, at first, seem rather strange for a book bearing the title *The Lost Message of Paul*.

Instead, this chapter explores what it was that informed Paul's worldview around life beyond this one; the lens through which he saw the afterlife, the ideas that shaped his pre-understanding, while the following two explore what informs our worldview around life beyond this one;

---

[1] The quote comes at the close of the play *Huis Clos* (*No Exit*), which Sartre wrote in 1943. The play begins with three characters who find themselves waiting in a mysterious room. It is a depiction of the afterlife in which three deceased characters are punished by being locked into a room together for eternity.

144

the lens through which we see the afterlife, the ideas that inform our pre-understanding.

They are different. Very different indeed.

And that has caused a problem. Because, as we've already seen, reading Paul – or any text – outside of its original context, and then, though unconsciously, overlaying it with a completely different one, is always a prelude to countless errors. When we see things the way we are, rather than the way they are, we delude ourselves; we rob ourselves.

That's why, in order to get to grips with Paul's understanding of what we call hell, once again we need to begin with the ideas that informed his worldview and culture. Our goal is simple – as far as possible to see things the way he saw them, rather than trying to force him to reflect our own thoughts back to us. That's what this chapter is about.

The archaeologists tell us that the fertile crescent of Mesopotamia[2] and Ancient Egypt formed one of the 'cradles of civilization'; the region which, for this reason, was to become home to some of the world's most ancient, socially developed and influential states and empires including Sumer, Babylon and Assyria.

Stretching back at least six thousand years, these civilizations have left us with records of their early ideas around the concept of an afterlife. They also show us the slow

---

[2] Mesopotamia, 'land between rivers', was a historical region situated within the Tigris–Euphrates river system. In modern terms it roughly corresponds to most of Iraq, plus Kuwait, the eastern parts of Syria and south-eastern Turkey.

beginnings of what we've come to know today as the ideas of heaven and hell; ideas which, as they developed, passed into Greek culture, then on to the Romans, and finally to us. To really get to grips with all this, it helps to know something about the history of the area they came from.

The Sumerians and Akkadians, followed by the Assyrians and Babylonians, dominated Mesopotamia from the beginning of written history until the fall of Babylon in 539 BC, when it was conquered by the Persian Empire. Two hundred years later it was to fall again, this time becoming part of the huge empire of the Greeks under Alexander the Great in 332 BC. Then, following his death in 323 BC, as his empire was divided up between his four generals, it was Seleucus – the founder of the Greek Seleucid Empire – who claimed Mesopotamia, the Levant, Persia and part of India.

But by around 150 BC, things had changed again and Mesopotamia found itself under the control of the Parthian (Iranian) Empire, before some of its western parts eventually fell to Roman control in AD 116.

Likewise for Egypt. First it was conquered by the Persians and then by Alexander the Great, before, on his death, being claimed by another of his generals, Ptolemy. However, in 30 BC, the whole country was annexed by Octavian, the future Roman Caesar Augustus.

Just like us, the ancient peoples of earth were fascinated by the movement of the stars, and especially by the sun and its nightly journey under the earth through the hours of darkness. As they watched and studied, they began to apply what they saw to the journey of the human soul after death. It seemed clear to them that, just like the sun, they would be plunged into the darkness of the under-world. But, as we will see, slowly they also began to hold out the vaguest half hope that their souls might somehow at last reach the world of the stars (which they regarded as the home of the gods).

So, back to the people of Sumer, the most ancient people of Mesopotamia.

For Sumerians the afterlife of the soul was in a dark, dreary, bleak domain located deep below the ground and known as *Kur*. An individual's actions during his lifetime had no effect on how he would be treated in the world to come – everyone got exactly the same afterlife, where they continued a shadowy version of what they had known as life on earth.

The Ancient Egyptians, however, developed an element of moral fitness as a factor in determining the quality of your life after death. For them, the soul was required on death to give an account of its life on earth to the gods, in the presence of the Spirit of Truth. The soul resided in the heart, and the idea appears around 1400 BC, in the *Book of the Dead*, that on death your heart would be weighed in the Scales of Justice against an ostrich feather; the Feather of Truth.

If it turned out that your heart was lighter than the Feather of Truth, you were welcomed by Osiris, the god of the underworld, into the world of the gods – the Fields of Aaru (Fields of Reeds), where you would enjoy pleasure for ever. But, if your heart was heavier than the feather, because of the clinging effect of your misdeeds, your soul would be thrown into the jaws of Ammit, a crocodile/ hippopotamus monster demon – the Devourer of the Dead. Alternatively, at best, you might get to wander for ever among the punishments of the underworld.

But the good news was that, although this was the threat, in reality there was very little to worry about. It was possible both to anticipate and completely avoid a negative judgement by reciting a declaration before your death that you had not killed, or stolen, or been deceitful, in life. And, as an extra guarantee, you could also take offerings, which acted like bribes, with you into the tomb.

In short, although the details were hazy and vague, life beyond this one – in whatever form – was not worth worrying too much about.

It is fascinating that, as other ancient civilizations, such as India and China, arose in Asia – all among cultures situated along extensive and fertile river valleys – similar themes around the afterlife emerged.

In the fourth century BC, in China, the famous Taoist philosopher Chuang Tzu told the parable of the skull.[3] One day, on a long journey, he saw a skull by the roadside – clean and bare, but with every bone in its place. He bent down and began a conversation with it. 'Surely, if you could, you would clothe your bones once more with flesh and

---

[3] Translated by Arthur Waley in *Three Ways of Thought in Ancient China* (New York: Doubleday, 1956). Chuang-Tzu, 369–298 BC, also known as Zhuangzi, was probably the greatest prose writer of the Chou Dynasty.

skin, and return to your father and mother, wife and child, friends and home, I do not think you would refuse.'

'Among the dead,' answered the skull, 'none is king, none is subject, there is no division of the seasons; for us the whole world is spring, the whole world is autumn. No monarch on his throne has joy greater than ours.'

Chuang Tzu found this hard to believe, and told the skull so. A deep frown furrowed the skull's brow. 'How can you imagine', it asked, 'that I would cast away joy greater than that of a king on his throne, only to go back again to the toils of the living world?'

On, then, to the Ancient Greeks.

In Greek tradition the underworld was ruled over by the god Hades, who also gave his name to it. In the *Odyssey*, one of Homer's two great epic poems, Hades is painted as a tedious, joyless, grim, dreary, shadowy underworld – a miserable and boring place where the sun's rays did not penetrate; a giant holding bay where all people went when they died, regardless of status or how well or badly they had lived their lives on earth. Although a few famous sinners could be found there, who were being punished for ever, most of the souls or 'shades' (the spirits or ghosts of the dead) were simply waiting for some unknown and vague onward journey. So, though once more there was a faint threat, it was really not that much to get yourself worried about.[4]

---

[4] For more on what the Ancient Greeks thought about the afterlife, see the Appendix on page 290.

In Roman thought too, similar themes were developed. In the *Aeneid*, Virgil – who ranks as one of Ancient Rome's greatest poets – models his work on that of Homer, but also takes the ideas on a little and deepens them. Those who have done well in life enjoy beautiful afterlives; they are surrounded by joy and happiness. However, those who have been evil are physically punished and seem to be stuck. Aeneas, the hero of the *Aeneid*, sets out on a journey into Hades to gather knowledge and, in his pilgrimage, guided by Sibyl, travels to the gates of the city of Dis, where he can hear the groans and the rattle of chains of those who are trapped there.

Just as Virgil built on Homer, so his poetry in turn would, in time, have a deep influence on Western Christian thought and literature. This is especially true of Dante's *Divine Comedy*, in which he appears as Dante's guide in his journey through Hell and Purgatory. And all this, as we shall discover, has had a huge impact on Western theology.

So what about the Bible?

In the Old Testament, in a similar way to the literature of the Egyptians, the Greeks, the Romans and other ancient cultures, the whole issue of the afterlife lacks clarity. *Sheol* is a place of darkness to which *all* the dead go – the righteous and the unrighteous – regardless of the moral choices they have made in life. But there are few specifics, except that it is a shadowy, gloomy underworld, a place of neither pain nor pleasure, punishment nor reward, where you hope that God will protect you and lead you to something better.[5]

---

[5] The word *Sheol* occurs 65 times in the Hebrew manuscripts of the Old Testament, and means the grave (the place of the dead) or the pit, both for

Sheol's inhabitants are *shades* – just like those of Hades they lack personality and strength. Some texts also suggest that they can be contacted by the living; in one such story the Witch of Endor contacts the shade of Samuel for King Saul, even though such practices had been strictly forbidden by the book of Deuteronomy.[6]

It is also worth having two more bits of information.

First, when the texts of the Hebrew scriptures were translated into Greek in Alexandria, around 200 BC, the word *Hades* (the Greek underworld) was introduced to substitute for the Hebrew word *Sheol.*[7]

Second, aside from what we call the Old Testament, Paul, as a Second Temple thinker, would also have been well acquainted with other Second Temple texts, in which new ideas were developed. In some, *Sheol* was considered to be the home of both the righteous and the wicked, although they are separated into respective areas. In others *Sheol* was considered as a place of punishment for the wicked dead alone, and sometimes, within the Talmud,[8] it is

---

the righteous and the unrighteous, regardless of the moral choices made in life, where conscious souls face a shadowy existence.

6   Deuteronomy 18.10.

7   In most modern English-language Bibles the word *Sheol* is now helpfully retained rather than translated.

8   The Talmud has two components: the Mishnah (the original written version of Rabbinic Judaism's oral teaching around the Torah – the five books of the Law or Pentateuch – compiled around AD 200), and the Gemara (dating to around AD 500), the record of the rabbinic discussions following the writing down of the Mishnah. The entire Talmud runs to over 6,200 pages in standard print. It contains the teachings and opinions of thousands of rabbis, including their differences of view (dating from before

equated with *Gehenna* – the interesting idea that Jesus often talked about, but which itself has got mixed up with our modern concept of hell. More about this later too!

What is true, however, is that all agree we reach the end of the Old Testament – the Hebrew Bible – with no clear or firm ideas about the nature of the afterlife or what its purpose is, and no depictions of anything much to be dreaded. Indeed, according to King David, the composer of Psalm 16:

> My heart is glad and my tongue rejoices;
> my body also will rest secure,
> because you will not abandon me to the realm of the dead,
> nor will you let your faithful one see decay.

It may have been vague, but the Jewish people had the idea that there was hope rather than damnation beyond the underworld; they were after all the people that God loved and had chosen.

This is the worldview – the cultural and theological understanding of the afterlife – that Paul, the Hellenized (Greek-influenced) Second Temple Jew, inherited. But the worldview that we've inherited – the one that has developed since Paul's life and death – shaped by other empires and art, is, as we will discover, very different.

Christ through to the fifth century AD) on the Jewish law, ethics, philosophy, customs, history and much more.

17

Layers

It is a matter of fact.

We have no record of any extended depiction of the horror of the Church's version of hell until long after Paul's life. But even then, its fire and agony only became a dominant feature in the writings of the Western half of the Church; and even there, only as it found itself transformed by its uneasy relationship with the imperial Roman state.

Listen to Tertullian (*c.* AD 155–*c.* 240), a prolific early Christian author from Carthage in the Roman province of Africa. In his book *On the Spectacles*, written around the beginning of the third century, he warns his readers to avoid the Roman circus, theatre and amphitheatre – all of which were extremely popular at the time. Far from offering harmless pleasure, he teaches that the mass emotion they create can corrupt the conscience and seduce the followers of Jesus into abandoning their faith. More than that, he argues, how can they worship God in such settings? Some of these are the very arenas where Christians have been executed.

But Tertullian has good news for those Christians who love the theatre and games and will find it hard to give them up. Don't worry, he concludes, there's a spectacle to look forward to that will be far greater than even the most bloodthirsty entertainment available now. And, what is more, it will last for ever:

> The return of the Lord . . . that eternal Day of Judgement . . . How vast the spectacle that day, and how wide! What sight shall wake my wonder, what laughter, my joy and exultation? As I see those kings . . . groaning in the depths of darkness! And the magistrates who persecuted the name of Jesus, liquefying in fiercer flames than they kindled in their rage against Christians! . . . Such sights, such exaltation . . .[1]

It's a grotesque vision, but it soon becomes a popular one. In the first years of the fifth century AD Augustine explains, in his famous book *City of God*, that 'By a miracle of their most omnipotent Creator, they [the damned] will burn without being consumed, and suffer without dying.'[2] And, later in the same book, he is also able to assure his readers that those who enter 'into the joy [of God] shall know what is going on outside in the outer darkness . . . [their] knowledge, which shall be great, shall keep them acquainted . . . with the eternal sufferings of the lost'.[3]

But it's also really interesting that, about the same time, various other proselytizing religions, equally concerned about extending their 'offer' of conversion and salvation to the individual, were beginning to tread similar pathways of

---

1 Tertullian, *On the Spectacles* 30.
2 Augustine, *City of God* 21.9.
3 Augustine, *City of God* 20.22, 'What is Meant by the Good Going Out to See the Punishment of the Wicked'; 22.30, 'Of the Eternal Felicity of the City of God, and of the Perpetual Sabbath'.

persuasion. By the fourth century AD, in China, Buddhists and Daoists, who had begun to compete with one another for converts, were both vocal about the number of hells or layers of hell (Diyu, 地獄, the realm of the dead) they knew of that awaited the unfaithful.

The Buddhists suggested eight.

The Daoists countered with ten.

The Buddhists upped that to 18.

The Daoists recalculated and came back with 24.

All this paled into insignificance when the Buddhists weighed in with a new calculation which gave them 12,800 layers of hell under the earth and 84,000 other miscellaneous layers of various hells located at the edge of the universe. The Daoists, as far as we know, gave up.[4]

Equally in Hinduism, based on texts from the fourth and fifth centuries AD, we know that they developed a stream of teaching about 32 hells or layers of hell and 37 heavens. However, it is perhaps surprising that it was not until the bishops of the Western, Latin-speaking Church gathered in Rome's Lateran Palace for the fourth Lateran Council, convened by Pope Innocent III in 1215, that they formally committed to the doctrine of 'perpetual punishment with the devil' for those unworthy of Christ.

---

[4] Martin Palmer, Director of the International Consultancy on Religion, Education and Culture, speaking on 'Hell', an episode of *In Our Time*, BBC Radio 4.

The cynic might comment that this was a case of very good timing as economics and theology came together. Just as the Church's coffers were beginning to run dry and the Pope found himself searching for new ways to generate much-needed revenue, along comes a doctrine which scares the living daylights out of people by dangling them over an everlasting pit of living death, but then offers them a way out through penance and payment. The creation of fear through the threat of exclusion is a time-tested way of maintaining control.

So it was that Thomas Aquinas, the immensely influential thirteenth-century Italian philosopher, theologian and doctor of the Church, rubbed in the point that Augustine had made eight hundred years earlier:

> Nothing should be denied the blessed that belongs to the perfection of their beatitude . . . And in order that the happiness of the saints may be more delightful to them and that they may render more abundant thanks to God for it, they are allowed to see perfectly the sufferings of the damned.[5]

It seems that, far from ruining heaven, the sight of the tortures of hell enhance it. Who wouldn't want to pay for a ticket!

It was, perhaps, also extraordinarily helpful that just over two hundred years later Hieronymus Bosch (*c.* 1450–1516), a Dutch draughtsman and painter, began painting his terrifying and bizarre depictions of hell; a complex and hierarchical world of agonizing reality filled with the writhing bodies of tormented sinners, complete with monsters who

---

[5] Thomas Aquinas, *Summa Theologica*, III Suppl., q. 94.

were half human and half reptilian. It is often said, however, that all that Bosch did was to put into pictures the words of Durante degli Alighieri (1265–1321), commonly known as Dante.

Dante's most famous work, the *Divine Comedy*, which he began in 1308 but didn't complete until 1320, a year before his death, is divided into three parts: *Inferno*, *Purgatorio* and *Paradiso*. It describes the Italian poet's journey down into Hell, all to save the soul of his beloved Beatrice, before navigating his way back, with help, through Purgatory and on to Paradise. We will talk more about purgatory and paradise or heaven later, but for now let's stick with Dante's description of Hell in the *Inferno*.

Dante's work is an extraordinarily imaginative and terrifying vision of the afterlife which draws on both Western medieval Christian theology and philosophy, especially that of Thomas Aquinas (1225–74). What's more, as we have seen, it is in a conscious line of development of thought from Virgil, Homer and those who influenced them. And, in line with this, Dante's Hell has descending layers – this time nine.

Limbo is the first. Housed here are all those who although (in Dante's opinion at least) they have no guilt, equally in life they had no faith either. As a result, they are all just stuck there; virtuous pagans who were not sinful but were ignorant of Christ, and so will spend eternity in an inferior form of heaven. Here, Dante is introduced to many prominent people from classical antiquity such as Homer, Socrates, Aristotle, Cicero, Hippocrates and Julius Caesar. They live in a giant castle with seven gates which

symbolize the seven virtues,[6] but which is left cloaked in
fog – symbolizing the absence of God and of hope. This
means that they are left forever longing for the light.

In the second circle of Hell Dante and his guide, the
soul of Virgil, find people who were overcome by sins of
'incontinence' (passion), such as adultery and lust. These
people are punished by being blown violently backwards
and forwards by raging winds, which prevent them from
ever finding peace or rest. Once again, the punishment
is symbolic. The lustful couldn't control their emotions,
now they can't control themselves.

And so, as Dante continues to descend, guided by Virgil –
circle by circle, layer by layer, ever deeper, down into the
depths – the punishment always fits the crime.

In the fourth circle, for instance, Dante and Virgil see
the souls of people who are punished for greed. They are
doomed to drag enormous stones from place to place and
therefore have no alternative but to push them against
each other. These symbolize their self-centred lifestyles,
which mean they must now forever work in competition.
It is interesting that here Dante encounters hosts of cler-
gymen, including various cardinals and even popes.

Deeper down, the seventh circle is reserved for those who
have committed the sin of murder or violence. Dante
explains how those condemned to live there are sinking

---

[6] After Pope Gregory released his list of seven deadly sins in AD 590, the
seven virtues became identified as chastity, temperance, charity, diligence,
patience, kindness and humility. Practising them is said to protect one
against temptation from the seven deadly sins.

into a river of boiling blood and fire, while gnawing at each other's scalps. Meanwhile those who in life committed suicide have been turned into trees and bushes – robbed of freedom of movement for ever.

In the eighth circle reside the fraudulent. Here Dante discovers that those who committed various types of fraud are now punished in various fitting ways. The flatterers, for instance, are now buried in excrement – just like the excrement that came from their mouths in life. Meanwhile fortune tellers, their heads twisted backwards on their bodies, are compelled to walk backwards for ever, their eyes, as Dante tells us, blinded with tears. It is here that Muhammad is entombed.

The deepest circle of them all is the ninth. It is residence for all those who have committed what Dante and the Catholic Church regard as the ultimate sin; that of treachery. To be a traitor to your family, your feudal lord or the Church is as bad as it gets. Here, just as in some of the other circles, there are various categories. So, for instance, traitors to their families and friends are frozen in the circle's icy lake up to their heads, with their teeth chattering. Why? Because this cold lack of movement is, according to Dante, symbolic of the lack of soul which was required for their acts of betrayal in life.

Lastly, below it all sits a three-faced Satan – entombed in ice, chewing on people, covered in slime and weeping.

So profound was Dante's impact on European Renaissance culture that, two centuries later, Michelangelo (1475–1564) chose to paint bits of Dante's poetry into his latest commission. *The Last Judgement*, which covers the whole altar wall of the Sistine Chapel in Rome, took over four years to complete, and is a giant depiction of the second coming of Christ and the final, eternal judgement by God of all humanity.[7] Altogether Michelangelo's huge fresco depicts over three hundred figures, some ascending to heaven while others are being dragged down into hell. And, to add to its shock value, the artist originally painted almost all the males as nudes. One unfortunate man is being pulled into hell by his testicles, while another – generally agreed to depict Biagio da Cesena, one of Michelangelo's critics – is pictured with a snake devouring his genitals.

Not only are the scenes of damnation portrayed in *The Last Judgement* deeply disturbing; in the world of the sixteenth century its power as a piece of social media, positioned as it was on the wall of the Sistine Chapel in the centre of Renaissance Rome, was unparalleled. From the day it was unveiled, its reception was mixed; great praise but widespread criticism. So scandalous was this giant wall painting, and so shaken by its coarseness were many within the Church, that eventually, bowing to pressure, the Pope was forced to order a partial cover-up; various artists were commissioned to paint clothes onto many of the naked bodies.

The message of the medieval Catholic Church, though, was crystal clear: damnation will be everlasting – and it

---

[7] Michelangelo painted *The Last Judgement* near to the end of his life between 1536 and 1541. It is interesting to compare and contrast its style and attitude with his much earlier and equally famous painting *The Creation of Adam* on the ceiling of the Sistine Chapel, which is part of the fresco he painted *c.* 1508–12 as a much younger man.

will be a physical as well as spiritual hell. But the sobering reality is that the understanding of hell for the Western Roman Catholic Church was shaped at least as much by the poetry of Dante and the vivid images of artists such as Bosch and Michelangelo as by any theologian.

So, rather than being read on his own terms – as a first-century thinker, shaped by the story of Judaism, influenced by his Hellenized upbringing and revolution-ized by his encounter with Jesus – Paul, the great includer, was read through the thinking of all those who had lived since his life and work; viewed not only through the lens of Augustine and Anselm, but also through that of medi-eval poetry and paintings, as the champion of exclusion.

Whereas previously, although shadowy it was a place of hope, and in the works of Homer and Virgil it was even possible to visit and return from the underworld all the wiser for the experience, in Western Christian thought hell had become a one-way trip with no escape and a just eternal punishment for a sinful life.

But, as we will discover, this was never the only voice from the Church.

18

Different

Astonishing numbers of people have been taught that while only those who are Christians – and even the right kind of 'born again' Christians – will be 'saved' and 'go to heaven', the rest of humanity will spend eternity in torment and punishment in God's torture chamber of hell. More than that, they have also been told that this is simply 'what the Bible teaches'; a central truth of the Christian faith to reject which amounts to heresy.

I am convinced of two things:

First, this is not what the Bible teaches.

Second, this depressing, deadly and misguided notion has left our culture deaf to the real heart of Jesus' teaching; that of love, forgiveness and the path to well-being and hope. The very message that our society and world so desperately longs to hear.

I understand that there will be those who accuse me of arrogance. 'What right have you got to overturn two thousand years of Church teaching?' But, in truth, the popular Western view of hell is not based on two thousand years of Church history. It is well worth noting, for instance, that it forms no part of any of the ancient creeds of the

Church. Instead, as we have seen, it represents a toxic mix of medieval Catholic imagery plus five hundred years of post-Reformation Protestant teaching – although even here it is constantly disputed and always evolving.[1]

Far more importantly, however, it was never the teaching of the first Christians – and is still not that of the Eastern half of the Church, who rejected it on the basis of their understanding of the text of the Bible. This doom-laden vision of the afterlife belongs, to this day, almost exclusively in the Western half of the Church. For the Orthodox Church – the Greek-speaking Eastern Church – the focus was never on hell, complete with gruesome details of endless agony inflicted by a loving God, but on Christ and the genuine salvation he brings through what is known as the 'Harrowing of Hell'.

Based on Christ's journey into the underworld, alluded to in the New Testament in 1 Peter 3.19–20, which speaks of Jesus preaching to 'the imprisoned spirits', the harrowing of hell was the story of the triumphant descent of Christ into the realm of the dead between the time of his crucifixion and his resurrection. This, of course, is described in the Apostles' Creed, one of the earliest Christian creeds, and still recognized by the whole Church (both East and West):

> I believe in Jesus Christ, his only Son, our Lord,
> who was conceived by the Holy Spirit,
> born of the Virgin Mary,
> suffered under Pontius Pilate,
> was crucified, died, and was buried;

---

[1] See for instance Tom Wright, *Surprised by Hope* (London: SPCK, 2007), Chapter 9.

he descended to the dead [in some versions 'he descended into hell'].
On the third day he rose again . . .[2]

Orthodox icons and artwork of Christ's resurrection and judgement consistently tell this story. Look some up on Google. Christ stands over the broken gates of hell in triumph, trampling satan underfoot and offering an outstretched arm to Adam and Eve. Here you will find no scenes or depictions of terror and torture at all.

The Eastern Church teaches that, following his death, Christ has closed hell. He stands on its fallen gates and brings those trapped within it into salvation. Through his death he has defeated hades and emptied hell. As Paul explains in Colossians 2.15, Christ has 'disarmed the powers and authorities' and 'made a public spectacle of them, triumphing over them by the cross'.

Listen to the way that the early Eastern Church leaders speak of the impact of Jesus' death. Alexandria, in Egypt, was the intellectual centre of the Hellenistic world, and arguably the most important theological centre of gravity for the Christian faith prior to the rise of the imperial Roman Catholic Church. Speaking of the impact of Jesus' death, Athanasius, the Bishop of Alexandria (AD 296–373), wrote: 'While the devil thought to kill One [Christ], he is deprived of all those cast out of hades, and he [the devil] sitting by the gates, sees all fettered beings led forth by the courage of the Saviour.'

---

[2]   We will explore the lines that follow, 'he ascended into heaven, he is seated at the right hand of the Father', and specifically 'and he will come to judge the living and the dead', in the next chapters.

Didymus the Blind (*c.* 313–98), dean of the theological school of Alexandria, where he taught for about half a century, declared: 'In the liberation of all no one remains a captive! At the time of the Lord's passion the devil alone was injured by losing all of the captives he was keeping.'

Meanwhile John Chrysostom (d. 407), Archbishop of Constantinople, wrote:

> While the devil imagined that he got a hold of Christ, he really lost all of those he was keeping.

And Jerome (347–420), the translator of the Vulgate, was equally clear:

> Our Lord descends, and was shut up in the eternal bars, in order that He might set free all who had been shut up . . . The Lord descended to the place of punishment and torment, in which was the rich man, in order to liberate the prisoners.

This stunning Eastern picture of the emptying of hell by Christ as an expression of the extraordinary love of God for every single one of us stands in stark contrast to the condemnatory Western medieval Roman Catholic picture of God as a torturing tyrant.

Although the sixteenth-century Protestant reformers of the Western Church radically rethought the Roman Catholic view of the basis on which access to salvation took place, its stance on judgement, damnation and the nature of hell was in large measure simply taken as read. Calvin and Luther had very clear views on who would be 'saved' and how they would be saved, but Roman Catholic ideas of hell – its nature and the evolution of the doctrine from the pre-Christian roots – were never questioned.

So, for instance, listen to some more words of the eighteenth-century American Puritan and revivalist preacher Jonathan Edwards:

> When they [the inhabitants of Heaven] shall see the smoke of their torment [the damned in Hell], and the raging of the flames of their burning, and hear their dolorous shrieks and cries, and consider that they in the meantime are in the most blissful state, and shall surely be in it to all eternity; how will they rejoice![3]

> The saints in glory will know concerning the damned in hell, that God never loved them, but that he hates them, and [that they] will be for ever hated of God.[4]

Or his contemporary, Isaac Watts (1674–1748), the English clergyman and prolific hymn writer, best known for the lyrics of the popular Christmas carol 'Joy to the World'. Here's a verse from one of his less well-known hymns:

> What bliss will fill the ransomed souls,
> When they in glory dwell,
> To see the sinner as he rolls,
> In quenchless flames of hell.[5]

But this is not simply some discredited teaching of past centuries. In our own lifetimes, the words of Billy Graham

---

[3] Jonathan Edwards, 'The End of the Wicked Contemplated by the Righteous', *The Wrath of Almighty God* (Morgan, PA: Soli Deo Gloria, 1996), p. 373.

[4] *The End of the Wicked Contemplated by the Righteous. A sermon by Jonathan Edwards,* 1834, sec. III <http://www.biblebb.com/files/edwards/contemplated.htm>

[5] Isaac Watts, quoted by Edward T. Babinski, author of *Leaving the Fold* and contributor to various 'freethought' and 'atheist' publications, in a letter to *Christianity Today* magazine, May 2002.

in his last book, published in 2015, offer yet another vivid Western depiction of hell:

> Every person who rejects Christ and his atoning work will be cast into this horrible pit of despair . . . There will be 'no purposeful living' in Hell, just an existence beyond all misery.
>
> You may wonder what Hell is really like. Don't look to comedians for answers. The Bible tells you the truth. Hell is a place of sorrow and unrest, a place of wailing and a furnace of fire; a place of torment, a place of outer darkness, a place where people scream for mercy; a place of everlasting punishment.[6]

However, even within the Western evangelical Christian tradition, there have been other voices. For instance, John Stott, the world-renowned British theologian, prolific author and friend of Billy Graham, explained:

> The fact is that God, alongside the most solemn warnings about our responsibility to respond to the gospel, has not revealed how he will deal with those who have never heard it. We have to leave them in the hands of the God of infinite mercy and justice, who manifested these qualities most fully in the cross. Abraham's question, 'will not the Judge of all the earth do right?' (Genesis 18:25) is our confidence too.

But he goes on to explain that he has never been able to conjure up 'the appalling vision of the millions who are not only perishing but will inevitably perish'. Instead, he says he cherishes the hope 'that the majority of the human race

6 Billy Graham, *Where I Am: Heaven, eternity and our life beyond*. Quoted in Adelle M. Banks, 'Billy Graham warns of fire and brimstone in "final" book', 2 October 2015, <https://www.washingtonpost.com/national/religion/billy-graham-warns-of-fire-and-brimstone-in-final-book/2015/10/02/0c627a54-6940-11e5-bdb6-6861f4521205_story.html?noredirect=on&utm_term=.b96f573d43d0>. Graham is drawing here on metaphorical terminology used by Jesus in various parables. We will explore this in Chapter 23.

will be saved'.[7] Moreover, in the book *Evangelical Essentials*,[8] Stott defended what he called *annihilationism* – the view that 'unbelievers', as he called some people, are finally annihilated rather than experiencing the literal hell that Billy Graham wrote about with its everlasting torment.

Stott struggled with the idea of eternal punishment. 'Emotionally, I find the concept intolerable and do not understand how people can live with it without either cauterizing their feelings or cracking under the strain.' He argued that 'the ultimate annihilation of the wicked should at least be accepted as a legitimate, biblically founded alternative to their eternal conscious torment'.

The truth is that the theory of annihilationism was not new to Western theology, but had been around since at least the Middle Ages. But the fact that such a widely known and respected figure as Stott could present it as a possible alternative to the commonly accepted concept of a literal, everlasting hell for the 'damned', raised eyebrows among many traditionalists, some of whom went as far as to question whether he was ever a real Christian![9]

This, of course, raises another important question. The Church is filled with different voices. Our God-given responsibility is to discuss and debate – it is only in this way that we can possibly find light and truth: together, through discussion, including disagreement. So, why are

[7]   John Stott, 'The Logic of Hell: A Brief Rejoinder', *Evangelical Review of Theology* 18 (1994), pp. 33–4.

[8]   David L. Edwards and John Stott, *Evangelical Essentials: A liberal evangelical dialogue* (Leicester: IVP, 1988), pp. 312–20.

[9]   Stott came close to being expelled from the Evangelical Alliance.

some people so angry at, dismissive and judgemental of the theological views held by others?

At its heart, our behaviour is indissolubly linked to our beliefs. Although at times, of course, we fail to live up to our beliefs, this doesn't negate the core principle that our foundational beliefs will, in the end, always filter into our responses. Our values will have consequences for both our attitudes and actions. So, what we believe about God and divine behaviour will inescapably shape our attitudes and responses to others, including those with whom we disagree.

If I regard myself as the faithful servant of an angry God, then I will regard it as my duty to be angry.

If I regard myself as the faithful servant of a condemning God, then I will regard it as my duty to condemn. I will discount everyone with whom I disagree.

If our first understanding of God is more about divine anger and judgement than love, mercy and generosity, it is not only natural but inevitable that we come to reflect these values ourselves.

The god we serve shapes our responses. When we attack, slander and condemn others in aggressive and toxic tones from our pulpits – be they literal or digital – we reveal our understanding of the god we serve.

It is time to learn to listen to each other's voices and opinions without maligning, slandering, misrepresenting or demonizing those with views that differ from ours. All growth in understanding is built on the foundation of open debate. If we respect the Bible, we can't simply use it as an echo chamber to magnify our own thoughts and opinions. Of course we will have disagreements – but we have to learn to engage with differing opinions in a more gracious and graceful discussion together.

For the record, I strongly disagree with Billy Graham's view of life beyond death – as I'll explain later – but at the same time I have huge respect for him and the way he lived. He was a person of extraordinary integrity, and I do not doubt for a moment that I am a richer person for the opportunity I had to get to know and work with him in years past. That's the whole point! These issues are so important that our task must be to graciously debate them – and to do so globally – listening to voices from the Eastern Church as well as our own.

So I want to debate with Tom Wright, another much-respected friend of mine, and a world-class scholar from whom I have learned much. On the subject of hell Tom states:

> Jesus simply didn't say very much about the future life; he was, after all, primarily concerned to announce that God's kingdom was coming 'on earth as in heaven' ... We cannot therefore look to Jesus' teaching for any fresh detail on whether there really are some who finally reject God, and who as it were have that rejection ratified.[10]

He goes on to acknowledge:

---

[10] Wright, *Surprised by Hope*, p. 189.

The early Christian writers [including Paul] go along with this. Hell, and/or final judgement, is not a major topic in the letters . . . it is not mentioned at all in Acts; and the vivid pictures towards the end of the book of Revelation, while being extremely important, have always proved among the hardest parts of scripture to interpret with any certainty.[11]

But then, in the very moment he has explained that in the light of this we need to steer clear of making dogmatic statements about hell and judgement, he rushes on to make some. Tom identifies what he regards as the three normal views of hell:

1 Eternal conscious punishment – the idea of everlasting agony for 'the damned';
2 Annihilationism (which he prefers to call 'conditional mortality');
3 Universalism – the idea that all are finally saved (which we will explore in the next chapter).

He then explains that, in his view, none of these do justice to the New Testament:

I find it quite impossible, reading the New Testament, to suppose that there will be no ultimate condemnation, no final loss, no human beings to whom God will not say 'thy will be done'. I wish it were otherwise but 'the cheap and cheerful universalism of western liberalism has a lot to answer for.'[12]

So he proposes a new approach which he says combines 'the strong points of the first and third' of the above views:

---

[11] Wright, *Surprised by Hope*, p. 190.

[12] Wright, *Surprised by Hope*, p. 192.

My suggestion is that it is possible for human beings so to continue down this road, so to refuse all whisperings of good news, all glimmers of the true light, all promptings to turn and go the other way, all signposts to the love of God, that after death they become at last, by their own effective choice, beings that once were human but now are not, creatures that have ceased to bear the divine image at all.[13]

He goes on to explain:

With the death of that body in which they inhabited God's good world, in which the flickering flame of goodness had not been completely snuffed out, they pass simultaneously not only beyond hope but also beyond pity. There is no concentration camp in the beautiful countryside, no torture chamber in the palace of delight. Those creatures that still exist in an ex-human state, no longer reflecting their maker in any meaningful sense, can no longer excite, in themselves or others, the natural sympathy some feel even for the hardened criminal.[14]

This is horrific. It is grotesque. It is inhuman! Beyond natural sympathy? None of this is a matter of dry theological dispute or intellectual debate. On it hangs the mental health and well-being of countless millions of people. Why would a God who is defined as love choose to condemn anyone to everlasting punishment, still worse the punishment of being 'ex-human'? What makes any sense about that proposal? And, if it were the case, would that make this God morally superior to, or less than, us? We will explore this much more deeply.

But, for now, to quote Tom Wright just once more: 'It seems to me that the New Testament is very clear that

13 Wright, *Surprised by Hope,* p. 195.

14 Wright, *Surprised by Hope,* p. 195.

there are people who do reject God and reject what would have been His best will for them, and God honours that decision.'[15] This, of course, is a very common approach, but one which, the way I see it, not only avoids the real flow of Paul's thought, but also ignores the voice of the Eastern half of the Church, and, as we will discover later, our deepest understanding of human nature.

[15] N. T. Wright on Rob Bell and the Reality of Hell, <https://www.the gospelcoalition.org/blogs/trevin-wax/n-t-wright-on-rob-bell-and-the-reality-of-hell/>

19

The elephant

Does the God of love punish people with infinite, eternal torment based on decisions and actions taken in their few short years of life on earth?

I read a post on a blog which somewhat underplayed the horror of this prospect. It read: 'In a sense, it is shocking and horrifying. Think about people we know! . . . That should give us cause to stop, to be gripped by compassion for them, to pray for them and to weep over them.'

But here's my question. If you believe in a God who would do this, why bother praying for your friends in the first place? If you are gripped by *compassion for your friends*, why pray to the God who is either unable or unwilling to see or value the good that is in them and who, you believe, is therefore happy ultimately to condemn them, even though you are desperately concerned about their eternal well-being?

What kind of love is that? What kind of 'father' would, having sought to build a relationship with his children, suddenly call time, switch, and then inflict agony and torture on them? We all know that if we had evidence of a parent, any parent, we knew behaving in this way, we would have a civic duty to report them to the police or social services immediately.

Life in our globalized, multi-faith, multi-cultural world highlights freshly some big questions for the Church, ones which have always been there, but which have often been ignored. For instance:

Is salvation little more than a giant geographical lottery? What if the good residents of Kent had been raised in Kurdistan, or those born in Boston had found themselves starting life in Baghdad? Surely, many of us who are Western Christians are Christians only because we are Western? Or, put another way, if the most devout Christians had been raised in an Islamic context would they be, very likely, devout Muslims?

Would a God *of love* really create a world where only the Christian minority of the human race are treated *with love*? Would such a God really be content to consign the vast majority of the population of earth to judgement and then to some kind of hell?

Why is it that whenever any religious group claims that they understand a way of 'salvation', it always includes them and their friends, but excludes their enemies?

If God's grace is real grace – amazing, undeserved, non-discriminatory, uncontainable, extraordinary grace – then why isn't it available to everyone regardless of their geography, religious beliefs, social background or mental capacity?

In the end, is heaven mainly for those lucky enough to live near a church, and the kind of church that helps and welcomes them, rather than hinders and makes them feel unwelcome? What about the countless people who are turned away from Christ by the attitudes and behaviours of the Church?

At what age do you become morally accountable for your eternal destiny? 3, 5, 10, 14, 18, 21? Is there an age of innocence, and if so, when does it end? If you're going to die from cancer, is it better to die before you reach that threshold than after it?

It is often claimed that the New Testament is very clear that when people reject God, God, out of love – because love always grants you your own way – honours that decision. But, even in this statement, hell, whether as eternal conscious torment, annihilation, or through ceasing to be human, is subtly reinvented not so much with the emphasis on God's decision but rather on your own choice.

What has Paul got to say about such questions?

Hell has no place in Paul's message. He never uses the term once in any of his writings. Nor does the book of Acts refer to it as part of its account of his preaching (or, for that matter, in any other context).[1] If Paul did believe

---

[1] This is highly significant in and of itself. Acts contains what is often referred to as the *kerygma* (from the Greek word meaning 'to proclaim'), which among biblical scholars has come to mean the core of the early Church's oral tradition about Jesus. It should also be said that there is a mention of 'the realm of the dead' in Peter's sermon on the day of Pentecost in Acts 2. It occurs in both verse 27, where Peter quotes David from Psalm 16.8–11, 'Therefore my heart is glad and my tongue rejoices; my body also will rest in hope, because you will not abandon me to the realm of the dead, you will not let your holy one see decay', and in verse 31 where Peter applies David's words to the resurrection of Jesus: 'Seeing what was to come, he

in hell, he either forgets to mention it – or he has decided to keep his belief a big secret. Of course, many will want to remind me that, though the word might be missing, the concepts that sit behind it – of judgement and dealing with evil – are fully present. I agree. We will unpack my perspective on all this over the next few chapters.

Paul's seminal thinking on the subject of life beyond this one is set out in a number of passages within his writing. In one of the most important, contained in his letter to the infant church in Rome – the clearest articulation of his overall theology – he compares the effect of the sin of Adam with the effect of the sacrifice of Christ:

> Therefore, just as sin entered the world through one man, and death through sin, and in this way death came to all people, because all sinned . . . But the gift is not like the trespass. For if *the many* died by the trespass of the one man, how much more did God's grace and the gift that came by the grace of the one man, Jesus Christ, overflow to *the many* . . .
>
> Consequently, just as one *trespass resulted in condemnation for all people, so also one righteous act resulted in justification and life for all people.* For just as through the disobedience of the one man *the many were made sinners*, so also through the obedience of the one man *the many will be made righteous.* (emphasis added)[2]

It just couldn't be any clearer, either as a self-contained statement or as a conclusion reached thanks to Paul's wider understanding as a transformed Second Temple

---

spoke of the resurrection of the Messiah, that he was not abandoned to the realm of the dead, nor did his body see decay.' In a few translations confusion is caused because, rather unhelpfully, they have failed to translate the Greek Hades to 'realm of the dead'.

[2] Romans 5.12–19.

thinker. His logic is simple: what God has done for the Jewish people, he has now done for all.

The words and phrases that I have italicized cannot have one meaning in the first part of Paul's sentences but a different definition in the next. To teach this, as is sometimes done, is not only disingenuous but renders any understanding of any of Paul's writing impenetrable – for it is to conclude that he is so inconsistent that his words might mean anything he chooses in any particular moment, unrelated to anything he chose for them to mean a moment earlier.

Either Paul believes that eventually 'all' will enjoy God's presence because of Christ, or, if he doesn't, he uses such misleading language to tell us so that it becomes impossible to take seriously a word of what he says anywhere else.

However, various writers – including some New Perspective thinkers – have, in my opinion, sought to wriggle their way around the force of Paul's argument by interpreting 'all' in the clause '*one righteous act resulted in justification and life for all people*' to mean 'Jews and Gentiles alike without distinction' rather than 'everyone without exception'. In that way, they claim to be able to interpret 'all' to mean 'individuals from both groups' rather than 'everyone in both groups'. This allows them to talk 'New Perspective' while at the same time lacking the courage to finally let go of a sixteenth-century theological model which, as we've seen, was developed in reaction to the Catholicism of the day and which they have already, for the most part, chosen to reject.

That 'all' actually means 'some' is however an extremely weak argument, for the very reason that it attempts to do exactly what we've just talked about. It tries to give Paul's use of the term 'all' two completely different meanings in the two halves of the same sentence.

In addition, it asks us along the way to believe that, on one hand, the sin of Adam, which Paul says plunged 'all' humanity *universally* into sin, death and destruction, with no one escaping its devastation, has more impact than the effect of the sacrifice of Christ. And it does so even though it is obvious that Paul's literary intention is to craft a clear and careful balance between Adam and Christ in order to juxtapose the two equal but opposite and contrasting outcomes.[3]

The theologian John Piper uses the same kind of 'does-all-really-mean-all' argument to dismiss the power of Paul's magnificent declaration about Christ in Colossians 1.19–20:

> For God was pleased to have all his fullness dwell in him [Jesus], and through him to reconcile to himself all things, whether things on earth or things in heaven, by making peace through his blood, shed on the cross.

Piper claims that although some have used this statement from Paul to argue that 'all rebel creatures . . . will be reconciled to God in the end and there will be no eternal hell', this is not what it means:

> It's assumed that Paul means 'all things' in the universe *now* will someday be reconciled to God. I don't think he means that. I think he means that the blood of Christ has secured the victory

---

[3] For more on Paul's understanding of the story of Adam, see Chapter 13.

of God over the universe in such a way that *the day is coming* when 'all things' that are in the new heavens and the new earth will be entirely reconciled to God with no rebel remnants.

But, whatever the fancy exegetical footwork, in the end you have to do one of two things: either conclude that Paul was so loose with his choice of language as to be irresponsibly vague and misleading around the articulation of his central message, or accept that he meant very deliberately to say exactly what he did say. He really is talking about good news for all!

The big underlying issue is once again, of course, how you understand God in the first place. We are right back to the matter of our pre-understandings and prejudices. It is difficult for us – especially when reputations, friendships, jobs and income are at stake – but our task is to allow the authentic voice of Paul, the Second Temple Jew, who has had his thinking stretched by his encounter with Christ, to speak to and challenge us.

And there's no stopping him. Paul is convinced. He has discovered that this good news is not for his tribe alone; it is for the whole world, it is cosmic – and he is very keen to let people know.

Saul, the fundamentalist, nationalist Pharisee has become Paul the great includer and universalizer. He has come to believe that what God has already done for the Jewish people he has now, through Christ, done for the whole world. Jesus the Jewish 'Messiah' has become 'Lord' of whole world. The badge is no longer circumcision, but it is not faith either, it is simply this – being human.

Later in Romans – the letter that all regard as the theological centrepiece of his writing – Paul talks to his readers about those Jews who are opposing his message of grace for all. But he carefully explains that because of God's covenant with them, God will take away their sins anyway. He comments: 'As far as the gospel is concerned, they are enemies . . . . but as far as election is concerned, they are loved on account of the patriarchs, for God's gifts and his call are irrevocable.' He then goes on to address his non-Jewish audience and explains that likewise, in spite of their disobedience, they too have received mercy. For he concludes that what God wants is to have mercy on all.[4]

The theme of universal forgiveness is far from consistent in the Old Testament. Its different books are not always consistent with one another but, even more problematically for the casual reader, their authors are not always consistent with themselves. Yet, as Paul well knew, there are a significant number of Old Testament passages which grasp God's future redemption of all.

Although we have already explored Paul's understanding of some – such as Isaiah 25 – there are many more. For instance, in Genesis 19 the cities of Sodom and Gomorrah are destroyed, but later, Ezekiel, the prophet, declares that God will eventually restore the fortunes of Sodom and her daughters. Equally, the writer of Lamentations explains that 'no one is cast off by the Lord forever. Though he brings grief, he will show compassion, so great is his unfailing love'.[5]

---

[4]   Romans 11.28–29.
[5]   Lamentations 3.31–33.

Likewise, in Psalm 30 David writes of God:

> For his anger lasts only a moment,
>   but his favour lasts a lifetime;
> weeping may stay for the night,
>   but rejoicing comes in the morning.[6]

And in Psalm 103 he proclaims:

> The LORD is compassionate and gracious,
>   slow to anger, abounding in love.
> He will not always accuse,
>   nor will he harbour his anger forever;
> he does not treat us as our sins deserve
>   or repay us according to our iniquities.[7]

Meanwhile in Psalm 65 he announces:

> Praise awaits you, our God, in Zion ... to you all people will come.

And in Psalm 22, the very Psalm that Jesus quotes from the cross,[8] he writes:

> All the ends of the earth
>   will remember and turn to the LORD,
> and all the families of the nations
>   will bow down before him [God].

So Paul, with his understanding of all these words he has studied since childhood, re-energized by his relationship with and understanding of Jesus, writes to the young church in Philippi:

---

[6] Psalm 30.5.

[7] Psalm 103.9.

[8] See Matthew 27.46.

Have the same mindset as Christ Jesus:
Who, being in very nature God,
 did not consider equality with God something to be used to his
  own advantage;
rather, he made himself nothing
 by taking the very nature of a servant,
 being made in human likeness.
And being found in appearance as a man,
 he humbled himself
by becoming obedient to death –
 even death on a cross.
Therefore God exalted him to the highest place
 and gave him the name that is above every name,
that at the name of *Jesus every knee should bow,*
 in heaven and on earth and under the earth,
and every tongue acknowledge that Jesus Christ is Lord,
 to the glory of God the Father. (emphasis added) [9]

He just can't keep it to himself. He blurts it out to his multi-ethnic group of friends in the city of Rome: 'Since *all* have sinned and fall short of the glory of God; *they* are now justified by his grace as a gift, through the redemption that is in Christ Jesus.'[10]

Then, in the letter of 1 Timothy 4.10 – whether written by Paul or by one of his followers – comes this intriguing statement: '. . . we have put our hope in the living God, who is the Saviour of *all* people, and especially of those who believe.'

---

[9] Philippians 2.5–11. Most scholars agree that Philippians was written in or around AD 62, during the reign of Nero, Roman emperor 54–68. There is wide agreement among early Christian writers as well as non-Christian authors, such as Tacitus and Suetonius, that Nero persecuted the followers of Jesus. In fact, Eusebius tells us Nero's persecution led to the executions of both Peter and Paul. So Paul points out that Jesus is a new kind of emperor. He is no Caesar; he is not a bigger version of Nero. He is the Lord of love.

[10] Romans 3.23–24.

What an odd thing to say. First, yet again, the fact that Jesus is the universal saviour is emphasized. But then comes that strange addition: 'and especially of those who believe'. It's like saying 'absolutely everyone is invited to my party – and especially those that hold the same views as me'. On first reading the second clause seems some-what redundant. That is, of course, until you understand that biblically 'salvation' was never exclusively about life beyond death – but also, indeed primarily, about the quality of life, right here and now. It's just one more of those issues caused by a Western misunderstanding of an ancient Mediterranean mindset.

Paul's message is clear. To all whose question is 'Does God believe in me?' his answer is a definitive 'Yes!' He redefines all the social and religious assumptions of his day. Those who had formerly felt that the door of God's acceptance was slammed firmly in their faces now discover that it has been flung wide open. As he broadcasts to the church in Corinth: 'For as *all* die in Adam, so *all* will be made alive in Christ . . .'[11]

How can this be, his audience ask. Is the trigger our faith, our works, our effort, our ability to believe and avoid doubt? No, comes Paul's answer, it is a gift of God's grace to everyone, entirely as a result of the faithfulness of Christ.

That's the revolution!

---

[11] 1 Corinthians 15.22.

20

Credo

All men are Christ's, some by knowing Him, the rest not yet. He is the Saviour, not of some and the rest not. For how is he Saviour and Lord, if not the Saviour and Lord of all?[1]

Needful corrections, by the goodness of the great, overseeing judge . . . compel even those who have become more callous to repent.[2]

God does not take vengeance, which is the requital of evil for evil, but chastises for the benefit of the chastised.[3]

We can set no limits to the agency of the Redeemer to redeem, to rescue, to discipline in his work, and so will he continue to operate after this life.[4]

Some of the thoughts of Clement of Alexandria (AD 150–*c*. 215), who taught at the theological school in that famous city, and who tells us that as a young man he studied under a disciple of the original apostles.

---

[1] Clement of Alexandria, *Stromata* 7.2. Clement's theology survives in his substantial trilogy *Protrepticus* (The Exhortation), *Paedagogus* (The Tutor) and *Stromata* (The Miscellanies), a collection of theological treatises which he never completed.

[2] Clement of Alexandria, *Stromata* 7.2.

[3] Clement of Alexandria, *Stromata* 7.16.

[4] Clement of Alexandria quoted by Johann A. W. Neander (1789–1850), an influential German theologian and Church historian of the time. Cited in Philip Gulley and James Mulholland, *If Grace Is True: Why God will save every person* (San Francisco: HarperSanFrancisco, 2003), p. 212.

In turn, Clement's best-known pupil was Origen (185–254) who, born in Alexandria, spent the first half of his career there. Considered to be one of the great theologians and exegetes of the Eastern Church, Origen also became a famous early proponent of universal reconciliation to God through Christ:

> We assert that the Word, who is the wisdom of God, shall bring together all intelligent creatures, and convert them into his own perfection, through the instrumentality of their free will and of their own exertions. The Word is more powerful than all the diseases of the soul, and He applies His remedies to each one according to the pleasure of God, for the name of God is to be invoked by all, so that all shall serve Him with one consent.[5]

> The goodness of God, through Christ, will certainly restore all creatures . . .[6]

It is argued by some that Origen's work lacks credibility because he was eventually condemned as a heretic by the early Church. This is extremely misleading. Origen was actually condemned by the imperially backed Catholic Church in AD 553, almost three hundred years after his death, as it pushed doctrine in its own particular direction. But in his own day, he was universally respected by the whole Church.

---

[5] Origen, *De Principiis* (On the First Principles). *De Principiis* was the first-ever systematic exposition of Christian theology. Origen composed it as a young man between the years 220 and 230 while he was still living in Alexandria. Fragments of his Greek original are preserved in *Philokalia*, an anthology of Origen's texts, probably compiled by Basil the Great and Gregory Nazianzus. The vast majority of the text has only survived in an abridged Latin translation produced by Tyrannius Rufinus in 397.

[6] Origen, *De Principiis.*

One hundred and fifty years later, Gregory (*c.* 335–94), Bishop of Nyssa and another leading theologian of the Eastern Church, explained Christ's faithfulness would lead to:

> The annihilation of evil, the restitution of all things, and the final restoration of evil men and evil spirits to the blessedness of union with God, so that He may be 'all in all,' embracing all things endowed with sense and reason . . .[7]

Just like Origen, Clement and many others, Gregory even went so far as to maintain that satan, 'the originator of evil himself will be healed'.[8] And his contemporary Jerome wrote:

> The nations are gathered to the Judgement . . . that in Jesus' Name every knee may bow, and every tongue may confess that He is Lord. All God's enemies shall perish, not that they cease to exist, but cease to be enemies.[9]

The ancient creeds of the Church are attempts to summarize its belief. The word 'creed' is derived from the Latin *credo*, which means 'I believe'. In the first few hundred years after the death of Christ, the Church faced various disputes and differences of opinion. Out of these debates and disputes, statements of belief were formulated. These historic creeds – especially what is formally known as the Niceno-Constantinopolitan Creed (the amended form of the earlier Nicene Creed), written in 381 at a gathering

---

[7] Quoted from Gregory of Nyssa, *Sermo Catecheticus Magnus* (Large Catechetical Sermon).

[8] Gregory of Nyssa, *Catechetical Orations* 26. *The Catechetical Oration of Gregory of Nyssa*, ed. James H. Srawley (Cambridge, 1903), p. 101.

[9] Jerome, *Commentary on the New Testament.*

known as the First Council of Constantinople – are still today regarded as foundational by most Christian denominations. The Niceno-Constantinopolitan Creed is, for instance, recited week by week in Anglican, Catholic and Orthodox churches around the world.

Much of the task of these ecumenical councils, as they were called, was to define orthodox faith. As part of this they chose to denounce various beliefs with which they didn't agree, going on to label them heretical.[10] The centrality of the teaching of the universal redemption of all people through Christ, however, was never questioned by any of the great ecumenical councils of the early Church.

The second council, held in Constantinople in 381, which produced the updated version of the Nicene Creed, was presided over by a small group of senior leaders including Gregory Nazianzus.[11] We know from his writings that Gregory was a convinced advocate of universal reconciliation through the faithfulness of Christ.

More than that, one of the new clauses in this second version of the creed – 'I believe in the life of the world to come' – was added at the initiative of Gregory of Nyssa, who as we have already seen was firmly committed to the view that Christ's work would redeem all of humanity. Even Augustine, at the beginning of the fifth century, while making it clear that his was a different position, recognized that 'There are very many [in the Church] who

---

[10] They denounced various doctrines including Arianism and Pelagianism, Apollinarism and Sabellianism.

[11] Gregory's fellow leaders were Timothy of Alexandria, Meletius of Antioch and Nectarius of Constantinople.

though not denying the Holy Scriptures, do not believe in endless torments.'[12]

But in contemporary Western culture, there is a long list of theologians who queue up to explain that, although they believe that God is love, they side with Augustine rather than the leaders of the Eastern Church. In spite of his concern over the 'the appalling vision of the millions who are not only perishing but will inevitably perish' and the cherished hope 'that the majority of the human race will be saved', John Stott also wrote 'I am not and cannot be a universalist . . .'[13] Tom Wright thinks the same: 'I am not a universalist. I've never been universalist,' he says, before adding intriguingly, 'someone quoted a theologian saying, "I'm not a universalist, but maybe God is."'[14]

Miroslav Volf is Croatian by birth. His profound book *Exclusion and Embrace* takes as its starting point his attempt to make sense of the civil war and ethnic cleansing that took place within his lifetime in the former Yugoslavia. From there it explores reconciliation and the primacy of grace in the search for justice.[15]

---

[12] The original Latin, *imo quam plurimi*, could also be translated 'majority', but not as a 'small number'. From Augustine, Enchiria, *ad Laurent, c.* AD 29. Quoted in E. Christopher Reyes, *In His Name* (Trafford Publishing, 2014), p. 531.
[13] David Edwards and John Stott, *Essentials* (London: Hodder and Stoughton, 1988).
[14] N. T. Wright on Rob Bell and the Reality of Hell, <https://www.the gospelcoalition.org/blogs/trevin-wax/n-t-wright-on-rob-bell-and-the-reality-of-hell/>
[15] Miroslav Volf, *Exclusion and Embrace: A theological exploration of identity, otherness, and reconciliation* (Nashville: Abingdon, 1996).

Credo

Forgiveness, he explains, marks the sacred ground between exclusion and embrace. This is the logic of the New Testament mandate to love your enemies, he suggests. It shows that 'at the core of the Christian faith lies the persuasion that the "others" need not be perceived as innocent in order to be loved, but ought to be embraced even when they are perceived as wrongdoers'.[16]

> At the heart of the cross is Christ's stance of not letting the other remain an enemy and of creating space in himself for the offender to come in . . . The cross is the consequence of God's desire to break the power of human enmity without violence and receive human beings into divine communion . . . The arms of the crucified are open – a sign of a space in God's self and an invitation for the enemy to come in.[17]

However, in his last chapter Volf goes on to argue that a proper biblical understanding of our ethical obligation not to retaliate against evildoers must be set in the larger framework of God's justice. The chaotic powers that refuse to accept God's redemption in the cross of Christ will come to the end of God's patience with them.

'Every day of patience in the world of violence means more violence,' says Volf. So he concludes that 'final exclusion' by God is a 'deeply tragic possibility'. 'Without such judgement, that is, the violent judgement of God, there can be no world of peace, of truth and of justice.'[18]

---

[16] Volf, *Exclusion and Embrace*, p. 85.

[17] Volf, *Exclusion and Embrace*, p. 126.

[18] Volf, *Exclusion and Embrace*, p. 297

Asked about this, Volf explained that to write the end of the book differently he would 'have to have a much more optimistic view of human nature and . . . would have to affirm that the lure of divine love will in the end be successful'. And when asked if he was a universalist, he replied, 'Well, I say I am not, but God may be. I'm desperately hoping for hell to be empty . . . I'm very clear that I do hope for universal non-refusal of the divine offer of grace. Anything less than that kind of hope would not be adequate to the view of how God has revealed himself to be in the cross of Christ.'[19]

At least we now know the identity of Tom Wright's mystery theologian!

And, agreeing with Volf, Wright equally concludes:

> OK, there's stuff in Scripture which is a little puzzling about this, and we can't be absolutely sure all down the line. But it seems to me that the New Testament is very clear that there are people who do reject God and reject what would have been His best will for them, and God honours that decision.[20]

We are back to that one! But, as I've already said, why the pessimism? Why the fear that 'God can't be that good'? What an extraordinary view of the Creator of the universe. Why believe in a god who, in the final analysis, is morally less than even we can imagine a God of love might be?

---

[19] 'Conversations with Miroslav Volf on his book Exclusion and Embrace: A Theological Exploration of Identity, Otherness, and Reconciliation (1996)', *The Conrad Grebel Review* 18:3 (Fall 2000), <https://uwaterloo.ca/grebel/publications/conrad-grebel-review/issues/fall-2000/conversations-miroslav-volf-his-book-exclusion-and-embrace>

[20] 'Conversations with Miroslav Volf on his book Exclusion and Embrace'.

Part of the worry, of course, is the fear of boxing God in; of limiting God, because nothing can impinge on the free decision of God. But God is love and, whatever else, this much is certain and undeniable: none of us has any right to place any sort of limit on God's loving-kindness. Instead, perhaps it is our duty to try to comprehend just how much greater God's grace might be than we have ever begun to imagine.

Although some church leaders will be forever suspicious, gloomy and worried about this kind of thinking, and want immediately to balance it with statements about judgement, I find two things really quite disturbing.

First, that so many Christians seem determined to tell us that they are absolutely sure they know precisely who is going to be rejected by God and why. And second, that it seems to me that – on any more thoughtful reading of Jesus' words, although without ever condemning any one individual to eternal punishment – his constant warnings about judgement (as I've said, we'll come to the meaning of that word later) were always directed towards those who spoke and acted judgementally to others, so turning their lives into a living hell.

Jesus' whole emphasis was consistently to include the very people ostracized by the religious authorities of his day, as well as to challenge them about their own attitudes and behaviour. The last day, he kept warning them, will be a day of big surprises (we'll also talk more about what he meant by that a little later).

As the famous theologian Charles Moule wrestled with the issue of how to balance human free will with God's mercy, forgiveness and infinitely patient love, he talked about the tenacity of God as portrayed in the book of Hosea:

> The prophet finds he cannot give up his wicked wife, try as he will. Can we believe the love of God in Jesus to be less tenacious? I cannot believe that such love does not pursue us even in hell. If we cannot rest without knowing that our loved ones are right with God, is it conceivable that God can be content to let them go?[21]

The problem is that the ambiguity of the answers given by so many modern-day Western 'experts' create on one hand a huge level of theological confusion and, on the other, terrible pastoral distress. Imagine the pain of a young widow who has lost her husband to cancer, who sits in a church building each Sunday to hear time after time that the man she still loves and longs to be reunited with is condemned to hell, separated from her and their children for ever because he just could not believe in God. She is already living in hell.

No amount of clever marketing, trendy website design, great coffee, trained welcomers, comfortable seating or sophisticated outreach programmes can cover things up when, at the heart of it all, a church worships a God who – though the hymns and sermons speak of love – has a much darker side.

---

[21] Quoted in Mark Koonz, 'The Old Question of Barth's Universalism: An Examination with Reference to Tom Greggs and T. F. Torrance', p. 42, <https://research-repository.st-andrews.ac.uk/bitstream/handle/10023/5685/Koonz_2011_TiS_TheOldQuestion.pdf;jsessionid=89F67D8A0F7CFAF3B88638054E441010?sequence=1>

Let's be honest. The idea of untold masses of people suffering for ever brings no glory to God. The thought of everlasting acrimony and agony undermines any real discussion of a God of love. Only the promise of restoration and reconciliation can do the opposite.

It's the way that any and every good school works. As I write, I, or rather the team at Oasis, the charity I founded, are responsible for 52 schools across England, and around thirty thousand students. We are duty bound to work to include even the most difficult kids. Every exclusion is a failure of love. In this I'm always inspired by a story I first heard some years ago from the well-known educationalist Sir Ken Robinson.

By the time Gillian was eight years old, she was already viewed as a problem student. She had the habit of not working, fidgeting noisily, being constantly distracted, and disturbing the other children in her class as she sat with a blank expression on her face. Her teachers said she had a learning difficulty. Today she would have probably been diagnosed with attention-deficit/hyperactivity disorder and put on medication. But this was the 1930s and the ADHD label hadn't been invented at the time. So instead, Mrs Lynne, Gillian's mother, decided to take her to see a psychologist for specialist assessment.

During that meeting the specialist asked to speak to Mrs Lynne privately in the corridor, and left Gillian alone in his office with the radio on, telling her as firmly as he could not to move from the wooden chair she was seated on. But, in the music-filled room, Gillian soon began to tap her feet, then jiggle, before finally getting up and beginning to dance around the room. The psychologist, secretly watching from the corridor, turned to her mother and said, 'You know, Mrs Lynne, Gillian isn't ill or rebellious. She's a dancer. Take her to a dance school.'

She did. The outcome: Gillian Lynne went on to join the Royal Ballet Company, performing all over the world and starring in various Hollywood films. Then, as that phase of her career ended, she began to produce shows and eventually, meeting Andrew Lloyd Webber, went on to choreograph musical hits like *Cats* and *Phantom of the Opera*. In 2014 she was honoured by the Queen when she was made a dame for services to dance and musical theatre.

Although her school had all but written her off, mistaking her extraordinary talent for some form of bad and disrespectful behaviour, Gillian wasn't a problem child. Instead, what she needed was to be understood. If it had not been for the far-sightedness of the psychologist, Gillian would have been lost.[22]

Every exclusion is a failure of understanding and ultimately of love.

The question is, do we believe that the God who is love understands that?

---

[22] A story told in Robinson's extremely popular 2006 TED talk 'Do schools kill creativity?'

21

A twist in the tale

Back to that big question. Are we saved by grace – undeserved love – demonstrated in the faithfulness of Christ? Or are we saved by our ability to make a rational 'decision' which we call 'faith'? Whatever the answer is – it can't be both.

The theologian James Dunn makes a good point. He is clear that he wholeheartedly agrees with Ed Sanders' correction of the misguided Christian idea that Judaism was a 'works based' religion designed to seek acceptance from God. But, having done that, he goes on to make a further telling point. He explains that Sanders' understanding of Paul still suffers from what he calls a Western 'individualizing exegesis'.[1]

The way he sees it, we wrongly interpret the Bible – an ancient document produced in a very different culture – when we impose our Western assumptions on it. Chief among these misunderstandings is our modern Western view of the world as individualistic. The ancient Mediterranean world's understanding of society was far more collective and communal. It is the difference between a 'me' centred culture and an 'us' view of life.

---

[1] James Dunn, *The New Perspective on Paul* (Grand Rapids: W. B. Eerdmans, 2005).

Modern-day Westerners ask, 'How can I be saved?' 'What does this mean for me?' We read the whole Bible through that lens. But, as we've already observed, we don't see things the way they are, we see things the way we are. If we are to take the words of James Dunn seriously, the salvation of individuals through a rational personal 'decision' they take called 'faith' amounts to a huge shrinking of the good news of the New Testament and of Paul's teaching. 'Faith in Christ' rather than the 'faithfulness of Christ to all' became the banner under which the Western reformers dismantled the theology of grace extended to all and opened the door to modern individualism.[2]

Paul's theology is thoroughly collective. In the passage that we have already referred to from his letter to the Colossians he explains that, through Christ, God was pleased 'to reconcile to himself all things, whether things on earth or things in heaven'.[3]

Paul has a big vision. Resurrection in the Old Testament was a metaphor for the restoration of Israel,[4] but in his understanding it has now become about the renewal of the whole cosmos. Somehow, although he doesn't know all the answers, without in any way denying his focus on human beings, his theology is signalling God's eventual all-encompassing redemptive transformation through

---

[2] See Robert Morgan, 'Paul's Enduring Legacy', in *The Cambridge Companion to St Paul*, ed. J. D. G. Dunn (Cambridge: Cambridge University Press, 2003), p. 251.

[3] Colossians 1.20.

[4] As in Acts 1 and the question to Jesus: 'Lord, will you at this time restore the Kingdom to Israel?'

Christ not only of the individual, but of the community and the entire cosmos.

As he writes in Romans 8, although 'we know that the whole creation has been groaning as in the pains of child-birth right up to the present time', it 'will be liberated from its bondage to decay'.[5] And in that very context he goes on to reassert his confident hope that

> In all these things we are more than conquerors through him who loved us. For I am convinced that neither death nor life, neither angels nor demons, neither the present nor the future, nor any powers, neither height nor depth, nor anything else in all creation, will be able to separate us from the love of God that is in Christ Jesus our Lord.[6]

If it is clear that Paul believes that God is renewing the entire universe, why would that not include all people, and why would that not be his meaning here?

In line with this idea, the great Swiss theologian Karl Barth had a thoroughly brain-stretching response to the question of who gets included by God: 'I don't believe in universal-ism, but I do believe in Jesus Christ, the reconciler of all.'[7]

It's an answer that is brilliant – and brilliantly subtle.

It's an answer that deliberately picks up on Paul's powerful assertion to the Colossians that 'God was pleased to have

---

[5] Romans 8.20–22.

[6] Romans 8.37–39.

[7] Quoted in Eberhard Busch, *Karl Barth: His life from letters and autobi-ographical texts*, trans. J. Bowden (Philadelphia: Fortress, 1976), p. 394.

all his fullness dwell in Christ, and through him to reconcile to himself all things'.

It's an answer that comes from the man many regard as the
greatest Protestant theologian of the twentieth century.

And it's an answer that takes a huge amount of thinking
about.

As a result, countless books and articles have been written
about the puzzle of whether Barth was a universalist or not.
I have a feeling that Barth was much smarter than many
of his interpreters, who in my view have often missed the
nuance of his writing and got themselves hung up on
the wrong issue. Asking whether Barth was or wasn't a universalist is the wrong question. Barth is actually addressing something subtly different.[8]

We all think we know what we are talking about when we
talk about universalism. But there is a problem. In much
Western thinking, it has come to be understood as the
view that there are many pathways – each of equal value –
that lead to life beyond death, and that Christianity is just
one among many. Which is why, in my view, we miss the
real point that Barth was raising.

In one short but profound sentence, he opens up a completely different way of thinking. He is clear. He flatly

---

[8] In fact, a host of world-class theologians, including Bloesch, Balthasar,
Berkouwer and Brunner, suggested that Barth's doctrine of election necessarily implied universalism. Though they did not all believe that he explicitly articulated this, they all speak of the inner necessity of it in his account
of election. But the big question is 'What did Barth mean by universalism?'

rejects any idea of a Christ-less universalism. But he wholly embraces and celebrates his conviction that Jesus is the reconciler of all. He unpacks this theology in his book *The Coming of God*, and addresses the issue in more detail in his short book *The Humanity of God*. There he makes three short observations 'in which one is to detect no position for or against that which passes among us under this term [universalism]'.[9]

First, he declares: 'One should not surrender himself in any case to the panic which this word seems to spread abroad, before informing himself exactly concerning its possible sense or non-sense.'

Second: 'One should at least be stimulated by the passage, Colossians 1:19, which admittedly states that God has determined through His Son as His image and as the first-born of the whole Creation to "reconcile all things (τά πάντα) to himself," to consider whether the concept could not perhaps have a good meaning.'

Third: 'This much is certain, that we have no theological right to set any sort of limits to the loving-kindness of God which has appeared in Jesus Christ. Our theological duty is to see and understand it as being still greater than we had seen before.'

Rather than falling into the trap of hastily dismissing or accepting the idea with a cheap 'yes' or 'no' answer, Barth wants us to think about the issues.

---

[9] Karl Barth, *The Humanity of God* (Richmond, VA: John Knox Press, 1960), pp. 61–2.

His point becomes crystal clear. There is no automatic universalism in and of itself. For him everything was about Jesus – Christ sat at the very centre of all his writing and thinking. Ask anybody who has ever read, or attempted to read, his giant masterpiece *Church Dogmatics*.[10] 'Jesus Christ is the elected man,' he says. All others: us, them, everyone – we are also 'elect', but only 'in Him' – because of him. God chose Jesus – an election that is all-inclusive, universally meaningful and effective.[11]

The way I see it, this is exactly what Paul is talking about when he declares so emphatically in his letter to the Galatians: 'It is no longer I who live, but Christ lives in me.'[12] God elects everyone through Jesus!

Barth is reconstructing John Calvin's old doctrine of election. Calvin, of course, had argued a doctrine of 'limited atonement'. That's what the 'L' in TULIP stands for.[13] He had been clear – the way that he saw it, only the minority of humanity will be saved:

> For though all, without exception, to whom God's Word is preached, are taught, yet scarce one in ten so much as tastes it; yea, scarce one in a hundred profits to the extent of being enabled, thereby, to proceed in a right course to the end.[14]

---

[10] *Church Dogmatics* comes in 13 volumes and runs to over six million words.

[11] Karl Barth, Preface to *Church Dogmatics: The Doctrine of God* II.2. Vol. 10 (London: T & T Clark, 2010), p. 116.

[12] Galatians 2.20 (NLT).

[13] For more about TULIP, see Chapter 13.

[14] John Calvin, 'Psalm 119.101', in *Complete Commentary*, Volume 2: Psalms to Isaiah.

In Barth's view this destroyed assurance. Although the fact that people were predestined was meant to give them comfort, how could you be absolutely sure that you were actually one of the elect? This caused – and still causes – huge 'salvation anxiety'.

Barth grew up within a Calvinist framework and as a young leader he had loved Calvin's writing. However, as time went by, he radically shifted his view, as is shown by the many volumes of *Church Dogmatics* which he published throughout the rest of his academic career. His mature position is best expressed in his preface to Volume II, written in 1942:

> I would have preferred to follow Calvin's doctrine of predestin-ation much more closely, instead of departing from it so radically. I would have preferred, too, to keep to the beaten tracks when considering the basis of ethics. But I could not and cannot do so. As I let the Bible itself speak to me on these matters, as I meditated upon what I seemed to hear, I was driven irresistibly to reconstruction.[15]

To use a long word, Barth's whole theology is centrally and essentially Christological. And it is from this standpoint that his fundamental criticism of John Calvin comes. 'All the dubious features of Calvin's doctrine result from the basic failing that in the last analysis he separates God and Jesus Christ,' he writes.[16] Barth was never talking about universalism, but the inclusion of all through Jesus. In fact, Hans Urs von Balthasar, who according to Barth himself was his most astute interpreter, concedes that, although Barth never said it explicitly, the principle of universal

---

[15] Barth, *Church Dogmatics*, Preface.

[16] Barth, *Church Dogmatics*, p. 111.

redemption for all through Christ is clearly built into the very groundwork of his theology.

Some will argue, of course, that this is a wishy-washy, soft and soppy, easy-going tolerance of everything, born out of Western liberalism. I know, I have read their books. But there is a very simple response to their claim.

Karl Barth's understanding of the Bible was worked out in and through the harsh context of Nazi Germany. The question of evil for him was not some lazy old chestnut of a conversation over a cup of tea, a glass of wine or a round of golf; the monstrous atrocities of Nazi Germany and his costly public opposition to Adolf Hitler were part of his everyday reality. Barth was largely responsible for the writing of what we know as the Barmen Declaration, which rejected the influence of Nazism on German Christianity by arguing that the Church's allegiance was to the God of Jesus Christ, not to other lords. He mailed this declaration to Hitler personally. It became one of the founding documents of the Confessing Church.[17]

John Calvin's work was all about grace, but a deficient grace because it was not grace for all. In Barth, grace is for all – even those who defy grace remain objects of grace. Despite their folly all are claimed by grace.[18] The old categories are done away with. Through Christ, God has elected everyone![19]

---

[17] The very words of Barth I have just quoted were written in 1942.

[18] See Donald G. Bloesch, *Jesus Is Victor!: Karl Barth's doctrine of salvation* (Nashville: Abingdon, 1976), p. 70.

[19] Hans Urs von Balthasar, *The Theology of Karl Barth*, trans. John Drury (New York, Chicago, San Francisco: Holt, Rinehart and Winston, 1971), p. 170.

So, for the record, I am not a universalist – but I do agree with the Apostle Paul. I believe that when Paul explained that Christ is the reconciler of all, he meant it.

Old-style exclusivity rightly insisted that Jesus is the only way. But it then made a mistake. It wrongly concluded that without an explicit knowledge of and relationship with Christ, salvation was impossible. It said that only those with 'saving faith' were 'in'. It claimed that everyone who was not actively committed to the Christian faith (sometimes a particular version of the Christian faith) was excluded from salvation.

Old-style universalism insisted that faith in Christ was merely one of many paths to salvation. In our multi-cultural, multi-ethnic, multi-linguistic, multi-ideological, multi-faith society it is up to you to choose your route. I believe that what Paul speaks of is a 'Christ-centred' exclusivity beyond these old categories – both of which failed to understand the worldview he inhabited. Paul believes that Jesus the Jewish Messiah has become the Messiah for the whole world. Jesus is the way; Jesus is the only way.

Paul's exclusivism is revolutionary because it is totally inclusive. Through Christ all things were made; and through him all things and all people will be reconciled to God.

None of this is to ignore the problem of sin, or to excuse the problem of sin. Nor is it simply a case of wishing for the best and hoping hell will be empty. Rather, it is an outcome of his encounter on that Damascus road. What God had done for Israel, God has through Jesus Christ achieved for all humanity.

22

Judgement

'Faced with a world in rebellion, a world full of exploitation and wickedness, a good God *must* be a God of judgment,' writes Tom Wright.[1]

Absolutely. I agree. And Paul is clear; we will all face judgement. 'We must all appear before the judgement seat of Christ,' he tells the church in Corinth, 'so that each of us may receive what is due us for the things done while in the body, whether good or bad.'[2]

Making the same points to the young church in Rome, he reminds them that 'God will judge people's secrets through Jesus Christ, as my gospel declares', before going on to ask: 'You, then, why do you judge your brother or sister? Or why do you treat them with contempt? For we will all stand before God's judgement seat . . . Therefore let us stop passing judgement on one another.'[3]

There will be a judgement through which God, the creator of the world, will set the world right, once and for all. We must all appear before the judgement seat of Christ.

---

[1]   Tom Wright, *Surprised by Hope* (London: SPCK, 2007), p. 150.

[2]   2 Corinthians 5.10.

[3]   In Romans 2.16; 14.10–13.

But . . .

If God is a good God – a just God – perhaps that is only half the story. Perhaps the outcome of any divine judgement will be a huge surprise. Tom Wright has this to say on the matter:

> I find it quite impossible, reading the New Testament on the one hand and the newspaper on the other, to suppose that there will be no ultimate condemnation, no final loss, no human beings to whom . . . God will eventually say 'Thy will be done'. I wish it were otherwise . . .[4]

I have the greatest respect for Tom. I owe so much to him. But it strikes me that Paul understands how all this works at a deeper level than some of Tom's writing appears to recognize. Preachers and theologians queue up to tell us that in order to restore justice – to right what is wrong – in the end the wicked must be judged. But the real questions are, who are the wicked and what does this judgement consist of?

In a world of systematic injustice and inequality, why do so few see the link between the abandoned 8-year-old boy whose story a charity uses to tug at donors' heart strings, and the young man of 18 who has joined a gang, been dragged into the world of drugs, stabbed a rival, and is now doing 'time', having fathered a child he is not there for?

Why do so few see the connection between the innocent child who is habitually sexually abused and the 30-year-old who has become a habitual sexual predator?

---

[4] Wright, *Surprised by Hope*, pp. 192–3.

Why do so few see the connection between the vulner-able teenage girl who was trafficked and the cold-hearted woman who now runs the brothel?

It hardly needs stating that the world looks very differ-ent from our pulpits and theological lecture halls than it does from a dole queue, a refugee camp, a brothel, a shop doorway, a prison cell or a damp and overcrowded council house. Power and privilege easily blind us – me included – to what we most need to be able to see.

It is fascinating to observe the stance that the world-famous German Protestant theologian Jürgen Moltmann takes in all this. Moltmann was acquainted, first hand, with the brutality of war. As a young man, forced to serve as a German soldier, he was taken prisoner by the Allied forces. Constantly tormented by stories and images of Auschwitz, Buchenwald and Bergen-Belsen, he says that he often felt he would rather die, along with many of his comrades, than live to face the evil of what his nation had done.

As a prisoner in Belgium, he met a group of Christians who were also in the camp, and was given by an American chaplain a copy of the New Testament and Psalms. He says that he gradually felt more and more identification with the Christian faith, later claiming that 'I didn't find Christ, he found me.' Returning to Germany after the war at the age of 22, he worked as a pastor and began to study theology, eventually becoming Professor of Systematic Theology at the University of Tübingen. In his book *The Coming of God*, in a chapter entitled 'The Restoration of All Things', he discusses the idea of eternal life for some and eternal death for others (what is sometimes referred to as 'double-destination' theology), but reaches a very different conclusion from Wright and others, suggesting that final judgement was originally the idea of hope for the losers of history, and that only under Augustine was it transformed from this liberating expectation into a threatening and fear-filled idea.[5]

The first sustainable community project that I set up, back in the 1980s, as part of Oasis was a safe house which to this day provides accommodation for disadvantaged young women who have been abused, exploited and betrayed. It exists to equip and empower them on their journey towards living independently.

Before opening, we kitted out the whole building with a great deal of care. We bought artwork for the bedrooms and hallways and, in the shared lounge, we placed a huge TV. But within weeks of our first residents' arrival, every-thing had gone. Stolen and sold. The walls were bare. The unit on which the TV had once been placed stood empty.

More than that, there was rarely a 'please' or a 'thank you' from any of our young women. With some it proved impos-sible even to make eye contact. For me, this was the steepest learning curve. But slowly I came to see that the problem was really mine. I am ashamed to admit it, but because the disability of these young people was psychological it was too easy to misread their responses and, as a result, to react rather than respond to them, and so to judge them negatively. If theirs had been a physical rather than an

---

[5] For an understanding of Moltmann's position, see Jürgen Moltmann, *The Coming of God* (Minneapolis: Fortress Press), 1995.

emotional disability, I would have been ready to compensate for them far more easily.

It is too easy to judge others based on nothing more than our own limited understanding and prejudices. Our perception becomes our reality. Having never stood in the ill-fitting shoes of the 'other', it is too easy to jump to misconceived conclusions and hasty misjudgements.

Caricatures and stereotypes abound. Misinformation and over-simplification leave us blinded by our ingrained ideologies. We edit complex stories into simple tales of right and wrong which leave us blameless and others in the dock. But, in the words of Martin Luther King, Jr. I have already quoted, 'There is some good in the worst of us and some evil in the best of us. When we discover this, we are less prone to hate our enemies.' The evils of consumerism, racism, sexism, class, power, inequality, wealth distribution, empire, privilege and entitlement implicate us all. None are free from complicity and a measure of responsibility – despite our best self-justifying stories. Sin and its effects are corporate, communal and complex, not merely personal.

But, the argument goes, if you are going to take Paul seriously, even if the term 'hell' was not part of his rhetoric, there is no denying that the concept of judgement and his haunting language with respect to 'the righteousness of God' can't be dismissed.

In 1 Corinthians 5 Paul confronts his audience: 'It is actually reported that there is sexual immorality among you, and of a kind that even pagans do not tolerate: A man is sleeping with his father's wife.' His simple solution: 'hand this man over to Satan for the destruction of the flesh, so that his spirit may be saved on the day of the Lord.'[6]

It's a frightening line. But what does handing over some-one to satan actually mean?

Sarx – the New Testament's term for 'flesh' – is easily mis-understood. Our challenge is that Paul uses it as a meta-phor rather than literally – just as we often do in our twenty-first-century culture.

In our culture, 'flesh' has besides its literal meaning a variety of metaphorical uses, which we understand only because of the phrase or sentence it appears in. For instance, 'he's here in the flesh' gives 'flesh' the meaning of physical presence; 'I want my pound of flesh' gives it the meaning of entitlement; 'let's try to flesh this out' gives it one of a search for a more comprehensive explanation; and 'the flesh trade' one of prostitution or sex.

The problem is that Paul's metaphoric framework is very different from ours. Although his usage very slightly over-laps with ours, it is in the main significantly different. When Paul uses *sarx* metaphorically he uses it to 'desig-nate our human condition in its fallenness or our human opposition to the Spirit of God'.[7]

---

[6] It is not the only time that Paul uses this phrase. He uses exactly the same term in his letter to Timothy, urging him to hold 'on to faith . . . which some have rejected and so have suffered shipwreck'. Among the latter, he says, are Hymenaeus and Alexander, 'whom I have handed over to satan to be taught not to blaspheme'.

[7] Douglas J. Moo, '"Flesh" in Romans: A Challenge for the Translator', in *The Challenge of Bible Translation: Communicating God's word to the world. In*

Here's the challenge. In order to understand what Paul means by his use of the term 'the destruction of the flesh' – and read his work well – we have to ignore our cultural pre-conceptions and step into Paul's worldview. It's another case of working at seeing things the way they are, rather than the way we are.

When we do this, it becomes clear that Paul's instruction to hand this man 'over to Satan' for the 'destruction of the flesh' in order that 'his spirit can be saved on the day of the Lord', is actually a way of talking redemptively. The sense of Paul's words is 'Let him go his own way. Leave him to live with the consequences of his behaviour – because that is the only thing that is going to bring him to his senses and turn him around as a human being.'[8]

None of this should surprise us; it's exactly in line with Paul's language, as we've already seen in Romans 1, where he talks about God 'giving people over' to their sinful ways to reap what they have sown.[9] It is interesting that our misunderstanding of Paul's motive here is reflected in our modern use of the popular expression 'to teach someone a lesson', which no longer means what it says. Instead we have come to understand it, rather illogically, as 'to punish'.

Throughout the Old Testament, God's coming judgement is thought of as a good thing: something to be celebrated,

---

honour of Ronald F. Youngblood, ed. Glen S. Scorgie, Mark L. Strauss and Steven M. Voth (Grand Rapids: Zondervan, 2003), pp. 365–79.

[8] Likewise Hymenaeus and Alexander, whom Paul says he has 'handed over to Satan to be taught . . .' There's the clue again – it's not for destruction, but for correction, it's for refinement and change.

[9] See Chapter 13.

longed, yearned and hoped for. Why? Because injustice will be corrected. Things will be put right. The poor, the oppressed, the unheard, the forgotten, the misunderstood, will all be able to breathe a huge sigh of relief. In the words of Isaiah:

> The wolf will live with the lamb,
> the leopard will lie down with the goat,
> the calf and the lion and the yearling together;
> and a little child will lead them.[10]

It's a metaphor, of course, but the question is, a metaphor for what?

In their most far-sighted moments, its authors understood that this hope extends to the whole world, not just Israel:

> Sing to the LORD a new song,
> for he has done marvellous things . . .
> The LORD has made his salvation known
> and revealed his righteousness to the nations . . .
> all the ends of the earth have seen
> the salvation of our God . . .
> Let the rivers clap their hands,
> let the mountains sing together for joy;
> let them sing before the LORD,
> for he comes to judge the earth.
> He will judge the world in righteousness
> and the peoples with equity.[11]

Paul's cultural heritage was steeped in this universal redemptive vision. The Hebrew scriptures are filled with a

---

[10] Isaiah 11.6.

[11] Psalm 98.1–9.

sense of longing for God to bring judgement and justice, to set the whole world right.

Over the centuries immediately before his lifetime, however, that inclusive story was eroded. It slowly became not only nationalist – focused on Israel's longing to see God overturn the oppressive regimes of the Gentile world around them – but also, even for the Jewish people, increasingly exclusive. Take, as just one example, the role of shepherds in Jewish society. Not only was their most famous king, David, originally a shepherd boy, but in later life he pictured God in Psalm 23 as the great shepherd of his people. Yet, by the time of Jesus, shepherds had sunk to the bottom of the social pile. It was the job that no one wanted to do. Only the despised ended up 'keeping sheep'. Their profession was their badge of shame, and there was no disguising it, because they stank of sheep. People avoided them. They were categorized as 'sinners'. Their testimony was not even recognized in courts of law.

As a young man the cultural air that Paul breathed filled him with this poisonous, legalistic, nationalistic and elitist worldview. As a hard-line, rules-driven Pharisee, he was not only sure that he was right, he was equally certain that the followers of 'the Way', who besides anything else were beginning to share their tables and food with Gentiles, were both wrong and dangerous. He was also convinced that the punishment for their heresy must fit their crime.

Then, on that Damascus road, Paul discovered grace for himself. He encountered the risen Christ. He recognized that he had been wrong. He understood the consequences. But, to his surprise, he was not dealt with as he believed he deserved. And he never got over it. In fact, if you read his letters, in every single one, within the first few sentences he just can't help himself. He has to talk about grace. In the light of his encounter with Jesus, Paul had come to re-focus his cultural story: God's justice is always grace-filled, always restorative, but never retributive.

The problem is that, in the West, the word judgement has come to carry some very negative overtones, becoming almost synonymous with 'punishment'. So, over time, we've come to understand the core of Paul's theology around God's redemptive action through Christ largely in terms of what has become known as the doctrine of justification.

'Justification' is an important word for Paul. But it has suffered hugely in the West from being recruited by Luther and the other reformers as a technical term, and as a result has lost its original meaning. The doctrine of justification was central to the Reformation. In the Western Church, the word 'justification' has slowly changed its meaning, explains Alister McGrath in his study of the history of the doctrine. Since the Reformation, it has become a way of talking about conversion – or the initiation of the Christian life. For Luther and the other reformers, what mattered above all was a legal sense of 'justification'.[12]

So, when the sixteenth-century Protestants read the first chapters of Romans, they read it in terms of a cold law-court

---

[12] Alister E. McGrath, *Iustitia Dei: A history of the Christian doctrine of justification*, 3rd edn (Cambridge: Cambridge University Press, 2005). His book became the leading reference work on the whole subject after its initial publication in 1986.

setting. All humans are in the dock, God is the judge, and we are guilty. But, as we've already seen, the belief that a person was justified by his or her faith became their central theme. Only when an individual, through a deliberate act of her choice, places her faith in what Jesus has achieved on her behalf – and in her place – through taking what would have been her punishment in his death on the cross, is that person judged by God as not guilty.[13]

As a result, a strong tradition also grew up around another of Paul's often-used phrases, *dikaiosyne theou* (δικαιοσύνη θεοῦ). Normally translated into English as 'the righteousness of God', it can sound terrifying.

Since the Reformation, many in the West have chosen to understand it as an impossibly high standard that no human being can reach by his own energy and therefore as a gift, or status, that is bestowed by God on those individual humans who have faith and, in John Calvin's thinking, have been chosen for salvation.

But, as we have seen in earlier chapters, in Paul's thinking and writing things are very different. We are justified not by our faith but by *pistis Christou* – the faithfulness of Christ. So rather than justification being about how a particular individual becomes a Christian, it is instead Paul's way of stating that we all – Gentiles as well as Jews – now share the same status because of what Christ has done for us all.

---

[13] In fact, it is only in Romans 1—3 (See Romans 1.17; 3.21, 22) that it's possible to 'read into' Paul's words any kind of legal feel at all. You just can't do this even in Romans 4, let alone in his long passage about justification in chapters 9 and 10. Equally, the reformers' imposed 'law court' setting doesn't fit with Paul's thought in Galatians 2 and 3 or Philippians 3.

So, other theologians have suggested that *dikaiosyne theou* is much better understood as 'the deliverance of God,'[14] 'the justice of God', God's 'covenant faithfulness' or 'unswerving commitment to do what is right'. However you choose to translate it, *dikaiosyne theou* refers to the right-ness of God's restorative character: covenant love, faithfulness, trustworthiness, goodness and wise judgement.[15]

Once you understand that undeserved grace is Paul's theme, the rest is pretty straightforward. Whatever other terms Paul chooses to use – judgement, justification, the righteousness of God – they are all subsumed in that of love, his overarching theological category. Although our society often writes Paul off as authoritarian and judgemental, the truth is that it's we who cling to a medieval 'them and us' view of the world which too readily demonizes others without understanding their inner story.

Paul's view is different:

> I am convinced that neither death nor life, neither angels nor demons, neither the present nor the future, nor any powers, neither height nor depth, nor anything else in all creation, will be able to separate us from the love of God that is in Christ Jesus our Lord.[16]

Or, as he explains later in the same letter, 'love is the fulfilment of the law.'[17]

---

[14] Douglas A. Campbell, *The Deliverance of God: An apocalyptic rereading of justification in Paul* (Grand Rapids: W. B. Eerdmans, 2009).

[15] Tom Wright argues for God's 'covenant faithfulness'.

[16] Romans 8.38–39.

[17] Romans 13.10.

23

The pruning

So, Paul never mentions hell, and for him judgement was about justice rather than punishment.

But before we go any further, I know that some will want to remind me again that in the end, because Paul was a follower of Jesus and not the other way around, we have to take seriously what Jesus said, and Jesus said a lot about hell, the gnashing of teeth and eternal punishment. So let's take a deeper look at the understanding of judgement that Paul inherited from Jesus.

The word most often translated as 'hell' or 'hell fire' in the New Testament is *Gehenna*. It occurs on 12 occasions, and it's Jesus who uses it on 11 of these.[1] Most English translations replace the word *Gehenna* with 'hell'. Here's just one example:

> And if your eye causes you to stumble, gouge it out and throw it away. It is better for you to enter life with one eye than to have two eyes and be thrown into the fire of hell (Gehenna).[2]

---

[1] Matthew 5.22, 29, 30; 10.28; 18.9; 23.15, 33; Mark 9.43, 45, 47; Luke 12.5; James 3.6.

[2] Matthew 18.9.

This is confusing. It would be far better to leave it untranslated, since Gehenna is the name of a specific geographical location. The outcome of the confusion caused by its clumsy, unnecessary and misleading translation is that huge numbers of people assume that Jesus' references to *Gehenna* are his way of talking about the medieval images of hell that we have grown used to.

It is now very well known that in Jesus' day, the valley of *Gehenna* (its Greek name) – or *Ge Hinnom* (in Hebrew) – was a smouldering municipal garbage dump just outside the old city of Jerusalem. In fact, to this day, the Valley of Hinnom remains the name of the valley surrounding Jerusalem's old city, on its south-west side.

In Jesus' day, Gehenna was notorious for the child sacrifices offered there to the god Molech during the reigns of Ahaz and Manasseh, kings of Judah.[3] Ever since then it had been regarded as cursed. This is why the Old Testament tells us Manasseh's grandson, Josiah, eventually had it turned it into a rubbish heap.[4] And, it's also why, as the dogs and wild animals fought over scraps of rotting food there, you would have often been able to hear snarling and gnashing teeth.

What is not so well known is that Jesus wasn't the first to use Gehenna as a metaphor for God's fiery judgement. The Old Testament's eighth-century prophets, Isaiah and Jeremiah, both speak of it in this same way. Of course,

---

[3] 2 Kings 16.3; 2 Chronicles 28.3; 33.6; Jeremiah 7.31–34; 19.6.
[4] 2 Kings 23.10: 'So no one could ever again use it to sacrifice a son or daughter in the fire as an offering to Molech.'

Jesus – as well as his Jewish audience – knew this, which is why he can use it so freely without explanation.[5] Because Gehenna lies outside the walls of Jerusalem and represents judgement, it is the worst place to end up. It is a stinking, disease-infested pile of putrid waste beyond the protection of the city.

Some theologians suggest that Jesus' use of the term 'Gehenna' was almost entirely to do with his prediction of the fall of Jerusalem which finally took place, some years later, in AD 70. Jesus was warning that unless they turned back from the aggressive and violent stance that so many in Jewish society were taking towards the Roman machine, the Empire would smash their holy city to pieces. They claim that this is the primary meaning of Jesus' reference to Gehenna: as a metaphor to warn his contemporaries that, without the change in spirit and attitude that he was calling for, the rubbish dump was where they would all end up.

The way I see it, however, although Jesus' symbolic use of Gehenna definitely includes this focus, it also had a far wider application. He is famous for his non-violent approach to all conflict. So his use of the threat of Gehenna was also connected to his teaching about the implications of failing to respond, in a way that echoes God, to the whole spectrum of human relationships, as well as the array of other strains and tensions that life brings us:

> You have heard that it was said to the people long ago, 'You shall not murder, and anyone who murders will be subject to

---

[5] Isaiah 30.33; 66.24; Jeremiah 7.31–32; 19.2–6.

judgement.' But I tell you that anyone who is angry with a brother or sister will be subject to judgement . . . And anyone who says, 'You fool!' will be in danger of the fire of hell (Gehenna).[6]

If Jesus was trying to simply focus the use of the term 'Gehenna' on the context of the political problem in Jerusalem, then clearly James – the only other person to use the word in the New Testament – who was writing to Jews 'scattered among the nations' about taming the tongue, didn't get the memo:

The tongue also is a fire, a world of evil among the parts of the body. It corrupts the whole body, sets the whole course of one's life on fire, and is itself set on fire by hell (Gehenna).[7]

In the light of all this, let's take a look at two key prophecies about the Valley of Hinnom in the Old Testament; prophecies either forgotten – or perhaps sometimes deliberately ignored – by modern Western preachers, but well known to Jesus as well as his contemporaries.

Jeremiah says:

'Behold, days are coming,' declares the LORD, 'when the city will be rebuilt for the LORD from the Tower of Hananel to the Corner Gate. The measuring line will go out farther straight ahead to the hill Gareb; then it will turn to Goah. And the whole valley of the dead bodies and of the ashes, and all the fields as far as the brook Kidron, to the corner of the Horse Gate toward the east, shall be holy to the LORD; it will not be plucked up or overthrown anymore forever.'[8]

---

6 Matthew 5.21–22.

7 James 3.6.

8 Jeremiah 31.38–40 (NASB).

This explosive prophecy describes an extension of the boundaries of Jerusalem to encompass the whole region including Ge Hinnom, here referred to as the 'valley of the dead bodies and of the ashes'. Jeremiah declares that all this will become 'holy to the Lord'; the fortunes of Gehenna will be turned around. It turns out, after all, that it is not an *everlasting* pit of fire.

And it's not just one isolated thought. Joel says,

> In that day [the coming day of final judgement] the mountains
>   will drip new wine,
>   and the hills will flow with milk;
>   all the ravines of Judah will run with water.[9]

All the ravines of Judah flowing with water will of course include the valley of Gehenna. Nothing – even Gehenna – is beyond the redemptive reach of the God of love.

Although in the sayings of Jesus, the stench of Gehenna was a powerful metaphor for the inevitable consequences of a broken way of being human, it had had nothing to do with everlasting punishment in hell. When Jesus warned his contemporaries about Gehenna, he wasn't telling them that unless they repented in this life they would burn for ever in the next one. Instead he was warning them that to live out of sync with the values that he was teaching (the values of the kingdom of God) was stupid and self-destructive. Don't settle for living on life's rubbish dump – it stinks!

Jesus and Paul – both scholars of the Old Testament – would have taken all this for granted, even if we can't.

---

[9] Joel 3.18.

Which is why Paul made no provision for belief in the idea of the unending infernal torment of 'the wicked', but rather taught, as we've already seen, that all things in heaven and earth and under the earth will be reconciled to God, and every tongue 'confess that Jesus Christ is Lord, to the glory of God the Father'.[10] Our problem is simply that, as time has passed, the relevant history and geography has been forgotten and the images now conjured up, instead of being generated by Jesus, are more likely to come from Dante, Bosch and Michelangelo.[11]

In this context it is important to take a look at Jesus' famous parable, where, having separated the peoples of the earth into two groups – sheep and goats – on the basis of their responses to the hungry and thirsty, the lonely and sick, the prisoners and destitute, he sent the goats away to what various English Bible translations tell us was 'eternal punishment'.[12]

But is that what Jesus meant?

'Eternal punishment' is a well-known cultural term which comes from the Greek *kolasis aiónios* (κόλασις αἰώνιος), but one which, in my view, would be much more accurately

---

[10] Philippians 2.11.

[11] And, more recently, William Blake (1757–1827). Blake's poetry ('I will not cease from Mental Fight, Nor shall my Sword sleep in my hand: Till we have built Jerusalem [here])' speaks of what recent theologians would call 'inaugurated eschatology', but does so long before their ideas developed. The pioneer of this theological approach was Oscar Cullmann (1902–99), whose work was popularized by George Eldon Ladd (1911–82). See Chapter 29.

[12] Matthew 25.31–46. The phrase 'eternal punishment' (in the form κολασιν αιωνιον) occurs in verse 46.

rendered as a 'time of pruning'. I know that it sounds ridiculous at first, but hear me out.

The first word in the phrase, *kolasis*, originally meant to prune or to lop in order to nurture, to cut back, curb, check or correct. But even when used in an ethical context as a metaphor, it was used to describe suffering which produces improvement. As William Barclay, the influential Greek scholar who was Professor of Divinity and Biblical Criticism at Glasgow University, points out, 'it is true to say that in all Greek secular literature "kolasis" is never used of anything but "remedial punishment".'[13]

More than that, *kolasis* is the only word used in the Gospels for 'punishment' in regard to God's dealings with wrongdoers. But, as Aristotle – who has much to say in his writings about the nature of justice – explains, this is the kind of punishment which 'is inflicted in the interest of the sufferer', that is to say, it is always for the betterment or improvement of the person being punished. He contrasts this with *timória* (τῑμωρῐ́ᾱ), which he says is the kind of punishment that is 'inflicted in the interest of him who inflicts it, that he may obtain satisfaction'.[14]

The root of *aiónios*, the second word in the phrase *kolasis aiónios*, is *aion*. This originally meant 'generation' or 'a limited period of time'. So, in Homer as well as in the work of other classical Greek scholars, including those contemporary with the writing of the New Testament, it typically

---

[13] William Barclay *A Spiritual Autobiography* (Grand Rapids: W. B. Eerdmans, 1977), p. 65.

[14] Aristotle, *Rhetoric*, 1369b13. Also see Niels Aslak Christensen, 'Aristotle on Anger, Justice, and Punishment' (University College London, 2016).

refers to a space of time which is clearly defined and marked out.[15] That's why in Matthew 28.20, Jesus' promise to his disciples is translated as 'I am with you always, to the end of the age (*aion*)', rather than what would be the completely nonsensical statement, 'I am with you always, to the end of eternity.'[16]

All this becomes even more marked when you realize that there are a number of other words, frequently used in classical Greek, which do mean 'endless'. Of these, the word that is most commonly employed to signify things that have no beginning or end was *aidios* (ἀΐδιος). It is this word that Aristotle chooses to use to define eternity.[17]

The Pharisees and Sadducees were both influential Jewish sects at the time of Jesus; sects which held conflicting views on a wide range of issues to do with faith and politics. One of their areas of disagreement related to the afterlife. A number of divergent scenarios concerning the afterlife had developed within various Jewish traditions during the intertestamental period. The Sadducees denied the resurrection of individuals because, they said, it wasn't written in the Torah, but this was fiercely countered by the Pharisees who had come to believe both in the resurrection of the body and in the immortality of the soul. They taught that

---

[15] Check out the revered Liddell-Scott-Jones Greek Lexicon, <http://www.perseus.tufts.edu/hopper/text?doc=Perseus:text:1999.04.0057:entry=ai)w/n>

[16] According to Jude 1.7, Sodom and Gomorrah were destroyed with 'πυρὸς αἰωνίου', translated as 'eternal fire'. But, of course, the fire wasn't eternal. It had been out for a very long time even when Jude wrote. Once again it is clear that αἰωνίου here refers to a defined period of time, which has a beginning and an end.

[17] Aristotle, *On the Heavens* 2.1.

after death the soul will wait until the messianic era begins, when it will be rejoined to the body in the land of Israel at the time of resurrection. But, being tough on those they regarded as unsuitable to play a part in this resurrected Israel, they developed the novel idea that the penalty for 'sinners', as they called them, would be torment without end. They stated their doctrine in unambiguous terms, as Josephus records in his book *Wars of the Jews*:

> [The Pharisees] believe that wicked spirits are to be kept in an eternal imprisonment (*eirgmon aidion*). The Pharisees say all souls are incorruptible, but while those of good men are removed into other bodies those of bad men are subject to eternal punishment (*aidios timória*).[18]

Wanting to make it clear to his Greek audience that the Pharisees believed in eternal punishment, Josephus knew that *aiónios* (a period of time) would not convey his meaning, and so purposely used instead the word *aidios* (ἀΐδιος) meaning eternal or endless.

All of which means that, if Jesus had intended to endorse this innovative doctrine of the Pharisees, then he had a perfectly good term with which to do so. But the word that he chooses to use both here in the parable of the sheep and the goats, and also in his encounter with the rich young ruler, is *aiónios*.

Never once does Jesus ever endorse the Pharisees' doctrine of endless punishment. Rather, he takes a strategic stand against their teaching by deliberately using *aiónios* instead

---

[18] Josephus, *Wars of the Jews* 2.8.14, quoted in F. W. Farrar, *Mercy and Judgement* (1881), pp. 379–80.

of *aidios*. Moreover, he warns his followers not to fall prey to the teachings of the Pharisees (Matthew 16.12).[19]

Jesus was never talking about 'eternal punishment'; his whole understanding of the term *Gehenna* would have precluded that anyway. For him, as for his original audience, *kolasis aiónios* had one obvious meaning, 'a time of pruning'.[20]

The Greek text of the New Testament contains two other words that have sometimes – but not always – equally

---

[19] In fact, in the whole New Testament the word *aidios* (eternal/endless) is only used twice. In Romans 1.20, Paul uses it in the context of a discussion of God's attributes: 'since the creation of the world his [God's] invisible attributes, his eternal (*aidios*) power and divine nature, have been clearly seen.' The other usage is in Jude 6, which refers to 'eternal bonds' that hold fallen angels captive until the Day of Judgement. Even there these bonds, although they are said to be endless, only endure until the Day of Judgement.

[20] In passing, it is worth pointing out that, although it is often suggested that, in the Parable of the Rich Man and Lazarus, Jesus implies eternal judgement for some, Joseph Ratzinger (later Pope Benedict XVI) explains that this is clearly meant as nothing more than an earnest warning to the living to have mercy on the beggar at their door. Tom Wright agrees. He quotes Ratzinger and then explains that it is 'only by extension, and with difficulty, that we can extrapolate from the many gospel sayings . . . what may happen after death itself. The two parables which appear to address this question directly are, we should remember, parables, not actual descriptions of the afterlife. They use stock ancient Jewish imagery, such as "Abraham's bosom", not to teach about what happens after death but to insist on justice and mercy within the present life.' He adds: 'Jesus simply didn't say very much about the future life; he was, after all, primarily concerned to announce that God's kingdom was coming "on earth as in heaven". He gave . . . no fresh teaching on the question of the resurrection . . . he was content to reinforce the normal Jewish picture. In the same way, he was not concerned to give any fresh instruction on post-mortem judgement . . .'

unfortunately been translated as hell: *Hades* (which occurs 11 times) and *Tartarus* (which occurs just once).

When the Old Testament was translated into Greek, in ancient Alexandria, around 200 BC, the old Hebrew word *Sheol* that we've looked at was substituted by the word *Hades*.[21] As we saw earlier, it is now generally agreed that neither word refers to a place of everlasting punishment, but rather to the temporary abode of the dead. So, helpfully, most modern New Testament translations now use the term 'the grave', 'the pit' or 'death' instead of hell.[22]

Jesus uses the word *Hades* four times and his usage, of course, always fits with this.[23] For instance, 'And I tell you, you are Peter, and on this rock I will build my church, and the gates of Hades shall not prevail against it.'

---

[21] According to Steve Holmes, a theology professor at St Andrews University in Scotland, by Jesus' day Hades was seen as a synonym for Gehenna – 'a place of fiery purgation where evil souls resided until the final judgement'. See https://shoredfragments.wordpress.com/2011/03/28/rob-bell-love-wins-7-hell/

[22] In Greek mythology, Hades was the ancient god of the underworld, the only god not to reside on Mount Olympus, dwelling instead in a dark palace beneath the earth, which eventually took his name. This was the place where souls went after death. At the moment of death the soul was separated from the corpse, taking on the shape of the former person, and was transported to the entrance of Hades.

[23] Matthew 11.23: 'And you, Capernaum, will you be exalted to heaven? You will be brought down to Hades. For if the mighty works done in you had been done in Sodom, it would have remained until this day'; Matthew 16.18: 'And I tell you, you are Peter, and on this rock I will build my church, and the gates of Hades shall not prevail against it'; Luke 10.15: 'And you, Capernaum, will you be exalted to heaven? You shall be brought down to Hades'; Luke 16.23: 'In Hades, being in torment, he lifted up his eyes and saw Abraham far off and Lazarus at his side.'

Lastly, *Tartarus*, another Greek term, occurs just once in the New Testament, in 2 Peter 2.4: 'For if God did not spare the angels who sinned, but cast them down to hell (*Tartarus*) and delivered them into chains of darkness to be reserved for judgement.'

Its subject is fallen angels rather than human beings, but once again, both unhelpfully and inaccurately, especially for a Western audience steeped in Dante, most, but not all, English Bibles still translate it as 'hell'. Actually, just like *Hades*, it was originally the name of a Greek deity, which also came to be used as a designation for another subterranean place of divine punishment in Greek thinking, and seems to be used here as an alternative to *Hades*.[24]

So, is it 'eternal punishment' or 'a time of pruning'? It makes a huge difference not only to the way we read the Bible, but just as importantly to the way we see the world.

---

[24] Tartarus in Greek thinking became the name for a subterranean place of divine punishment even lower than Hades; it was where Zeus cast the Titans along with his father Cronus after defeating them.

24

Wired

'Twelve-year-old thug arrested for drug running.' Why does the headline read that way? Why doesn't it read 'Twelve-year-old boy rescued from drug gang'?

Why does our language promote fear and condemnation rather than compassion and empathy? Perhaps it's because we are far more medieval in our thinking about human behavioural development than we sometimes like to think.

That's why Paul's teaching is so revolutionary. Both for his time, and for ours. 'Do not conform to the pattern of this world, but be transformed by the renewing of your mind,' he writes.[1]

Paul is intuitive. He understands that a human mind can be renewed. And he understands that love is the only way to achieve it. In fact, remarkably, he chooses to argue that it is possible to sum up the whole of the Hebrew Bible's law in just one phrase: 'Love your neighbour as yourself.'[2] What's more, he does it again. He tells the church in Rome that 'whoever loves others has fulfilled the law . . . whatever other command there may be, [they] are summed up

---

[1]   Romans 12.2.

[2]   Galatians 5.14.

in this one command: "Love your neighbour as yourself."'
Put differently, he articulates the principles of what we
today would call a therapeutically informed approach to
human development.[3]

A good friend of mine, a child psychologist, confessed to
me that 20 years ago, when she began her work, she assumed
that violence was a selfish, immoral, outrageous exercise of
personal power and that punishment was the only way to
redress the balance. She smiled as she explained to me how it
was only as she spent time with children from chaotic backgrounds who have experienced trauma and neglect that she
was enabled to see things as they really are.

We all have a tendency, while excusing the reasons for some
of our own moral weaknesses, to attribute 100 per cent of
the challenging behaviours of others to a state of failed personal morality; what they do reflects who they are.

Much has been written about this fascinating human
trait (known by psychologists as Fundamental Attribution
Error), which means that in contrast to our interpretation
of our own behaviour, where we tend to attribute our
mistakes to environmental factors, we are prone to ignore
such things in the behaviour of others and cling to the
belief that, unlike us, they do bad things because they are
bad people.[4]

---

[3] I recommend reading a good psychology book, for example one of
Dr Tina Payne Bryson and Dan Siegel's bestsellers, *The Whole-Brain Child*,
No-Drama Discipline or *The Yes Brain*.
[4] For more on Fundamental Attribution Error, see <https://ethicsunwrapped.
utexas.edu/glossary/fundamental-attribution-error>

Throughout the seventeenth and eighteenth centuries, the Bethlem Hospital – nicknamed Bedlam – was England's most notorious public asylum or 'madhouse'. In *The Treatment of the Insane without Mechanical Restraints,* published in 1856, Victorian doctor John Conolly wrote in stark terms about life there in the 1700s. The treatment of its patients, about which Conolly repeatedly expresses his personal disapproval, was barbaric. Bleeding, forced vomiting, cold baths, debilitating drugs, the use of cages, whips and chains were all administered in the attempt to weaken the animal spirit which was believed to be producing madness.

The 'lunatics', as they were called, had lost their power of reason, which at the time was considered by many to be the very essence of what it was to be human. Only these brutal treatments might put things right for them.

In fact, so famous did Bedlam become that until 1770 the general public were allowed in to 'spectate' the patients from the institution's galleries. For this purpose, the 'lunatic keepers', Conolly tells us, adopted the role of showmen, getting their 'star' patients to 'perform' by provoking them for the amusement of the crowd, much like circus animals.

But, besides providing the entertainment of this 'freakshow'[5] and creating a fund-raising opportunity (a small entrance fee was charged), Bedlam's 'open to the public' policy was designed to provide visitors with moral instruction.[6] The

[5] Roy Porter, *Madmen: A social history of madhouses, mad-doctors and lunatics* (London: Tempus, 2006), p. 157.

[6] Jonathan Andrews, 'Bedlam Revisited: A History of Bethlem Hospital *c.*1634–*c.*1770' [Ph.D. thesis] (London: Queen Mary and Westfield College, London University, 1991), pp. 23–4.

received wisdom of the day was that 'madness' and the life that followed within the living hell of the asylum was the consequence of allowing your 'passions and appetites' to dethrone reason. It was hoped that the experience of a visit to Bedlam would provide all the warning you would ever need to keep well away from the dangers of immorality and vice.

Two hundred and fifty years later, although the worst excesses of this kind of self-serving – not to mention hypocritical – 'moralizing' have, perhaps, long been swept away, its remnants are all too evident in our society. 'Good' people are thought to be 'good' because they control their behaviour and act in a socially appropriate and morally responsible manner. On the other hand, 'bad' people are 'bad' because they display antisocial behaviours and make morally bankrupt choices. And, sadly, this is where much theology – even that of some leading scholars – is still stuck.

Over the last 50 years, however, we have learned more about neuroscience – the science of how the human brain works – than through the rest of human history.

In evolutionary terms, the brain stem, part of the hindbrain, is the brain's most primitive part. It is responsible for some of the most basic functions of life, such as breathing and movement – the involuntary bodily processes necessary for survival.

The limbic system, part of what is known as the forebrain, serves as the brain's emotional motor system. Its task is to process and collate input from all our sensory systems – vision, touch, hearing, taste and smell.

The highest-level brain processes such as sensation, voluntary muscle movement, thought, reasoning and memory are housed in what is known as the prefrontal cortex, which covers the front of the frontal lobe. This is considered to be the moral centre of the brain, because it is responsible for our ability to differentiate between conflicting thoughts and to recognize future consequences of current actions, to determine good and bad, wise and unwise, better and best, same and different, to plan and work towards defined goals, and provide us with social 'control' (our ability to override urges that, if not suppressed, could lead to socially unacceptable outcomes). Psychologists refer to the prefrontal cortex as being responsible for our executive function or *cognitive control*: our ability to select and successfully monitor behaviours that facilitate the attainment of chosen goals.[7] In other words, its job is to manage our responses to external stimuli and events and to keep us calm.

But its capacity to do all this is dependent on healthy development, and that's down to the love and security we enjoy, ideally from our primary caregivers, as we bond with them, as well as close relationships with extended family members and other significant carers.

The human brain works a little like a nuclear power plant, used to produce and then control the enormous energy needed to drive turbines and generate electricity. Whenever the question is asked about whether nuclear power is 100 per cent safe, operators are keen to explain

---

[7] Y. Yang and A. Raine, 'Prefrontal Structural and Functional Brain Imaging Findings in Antisocial, Violent, and Psychopathic Individuals: A meta-analysis', *Psychiatry Research* 174 (November 2009), pp. 81–8.

that every reactor has inbuilt systems which are specifically designed to cool, manage, moderate and even shut down their output if monitoring detects any unusual or dangerous readings. In the same way, the brain's prefrontal cortex is designed to manage and moderate the limbic system.

A child who has experienced strong attachments has far greater potential to become an adult whose prefrontal cortex is well developed and is therefore able to control his or her own emotions and impulses. Through childhood – and indeed for the rest of our lives – our 'executive function' gradually develops, learning to regulate our energy and emotions, generate responses which are protective, life-affirming and 'pro-social', and inhibit impulses which are not. This is known as self-regulation.[8] However, just as it can be improved, it can also be adversely affected.[9]

So, if you've been annoyed and wound up by someone taking a long time to get on or off the bus when you are in a hurry, but have been able to refrain from exploding by thinking through the reasons why this has happened, you owe it to your prefrontal cortex. It has managed to cool your limbic system down and so successfully self-regulate your response. But if, on occasion, your prefrontal cortex is unable to control your heated-up limbic system, that's when you have a tantrum – you shout or throw something, or behave aggressively or are intolerant.

---

[8] See S. W. Porges, 'The Polyvagal Theory: New insights into adaptive reactions of the autonomic nervous system', *Cleveland Clinic Journal of Medicine* (2009), <https://www.ncbi.nlm.nih.gov/pmc/articles/PMC3108032/>

[9] Adele Diamond, 'Executive Functions', *Annual Review of Psychology* 64 (2003), pp. 135–68.

But what about children and young people who have been exposed to chronic insecurities: family dysfunction and breakdown, violent neighbourhoods, food poverty; those who have been raped, abused or forced to witness violence and maltreatment? What about the child who can't self-regulate his or her emotions and energy?

This leads us to the problem of a 'dysregulated' limbic system. Traumatized children and young people can have severe emotional or physical reactions to triggers from past traumatic events, flashbacks to terrible memories, or a fear of particular places, activities or people that create reminders of those events, as well as being prone to sudden negative emotional swings of mood or even physical responses. It is also fairly common for children who've been maltreated to confuse new people they meet with the adults who first abused them.

A child or young person with a dysfunctional limbic system can experience an overload of her prefrontal cortex. It is simply unable to cope, to cool her down; to regulate her. And once this happens, lower-brain activity takes over; she is at the mercy of her dysregulated limbic system. If the child cannot find a legitimate way to regulate her tension or stress, then she may have no choice but to discharge it, usually through explosive aggression or violence, either to others or to herself.

Some young people refer to losing control in this kind of uninhibited way as 'switching'. But, although the resulting aggression and violence is distressing (for them and for those around them), anything that enables them to escape from the nightmare that has taken over their brain is cathartic.[10] The violence has the same impact as the release of steam from a pressure cooker. It restores equilibrium, and the exhaustion that follows brings temporary peace. Even suicide can be a way of managing emotions.

When the brain's social system of survival is overwhelmed, either in a child or an adult, that person may engage in more primitive and impulsive strategies in response to triggers. Stress hormones, including adrenalin and cortisol, can be secreted at high volume. Adrenalin increases the heart rate and makes breathing rapid, which causes the brain to become hyper-vigilant and narrow down its field of perception, in order to focus all its energy on the distressing experience.

---

[10] We now also know that childhood trauma alters gene activity and can be passed on to future generations; that our genes shape the way we cope with our environment. A study examining the offspring of children evacuated during the Second World War revealed they were up to four times more likely to suffer from serious mental health conditions than those whose parents were able to stay at home. But, although the authors acknowledge that this effect may be partially explained by the impact of these experiences on the evacuees' subsequent parenting, they believe it also shows a wide-scale link between childhood trauma, especially in women, and the mental health of the next generation. This is due to what are known as 'epigenetic' alterations in that second generation: changes caused to the evacuees' gene activity which are then inherited by their children.

Previous smaller studies with the children of survivors of the Holocaust, the Vietnam and Iraq wars have also reached the same conclusions; that genes have a 'memory'. The experiences of your parents and even your grandparents can directly affect you, even though you never witnessed their experiences yourself.

For more on this, see Rachel Yehuda and Amy Lehrner, 'Intergenerational Transmission of Trauma Effects: Putative role of epigenetic mechanisms', *World Psychiatry* 17:3 (2008), pp. 243–57. <https://www.ncbi.nlm.nih.gov/pmc/articles/PMC6127768/>

At this point, the person may have very poor access to any social method of problem solving or to high-level cognitive processes such as the ability to rationalize. Her preoccupation is survival. Energy preservation demands that engagement is focused only on those activities that guarantee safety and dominance. The person often also becomes individualistic, with a diminished capacity to empathize. She has little room to think about somebody else's needs; she is ready to fight in order to survive.

None of this is 'them' and 'us'. All this has the potential to happen to any of us when put in a challenging situation, but especially so for those whose prefrontal cortex and executive functioning have not developed in the first place. They are less likely to have the adaptive responses or mechanisms to fall back on.

The old world of black and white thinking around morality would describe these children, young people and adults as selfish and morally flawed. The reality is that they are victims of circumstance who have often appropriately adapted to the dysfunctional world they are being forced to endure. They don't decide to explode; their sense of identity is often fragile and their capacity to manage emotions limited. Something triggers them and they 'lose it'; they 'switch'. It feels to them as though they are being spun out of control in a tornado. Only after the whirlwind has passed can they regain a sense of conscious awareness and realize the terrible thing they did or desired.

And all this can be intergenerational. It leaves its legacy. A parent whose prefrontal cortex has not developed well may be incapable of being socially responsive to his or her child. But, because the parent's responses are not helpful, the child may engage with him or her less, or develop an internal working model which causes challenges later on. And the cycle begins again.[11]

This all happens because deep in the brain, clusters of neurons play a vital part in our development. Neurons – brain cells – of which a fully grown adult has over 100 billion, come in three main types: motor neurons (which control our muscles), sensory neurons (which are stimulated by our senses), and the all-important inter-neurons which connect the other neurons together, so creating neural pathways. A neural pathway is a string of connected neurons that sends signals from one part of the brain to another – for instance, from our limbic system to our prefrontal cortex. They are the brain's autobahns.

Our brains develop new neural pathways throughout our lives – but they do so much faster in childhood and our early teen years. A neural pathway develops in the same way as a physical track across a field. If you keep using the same route, a pathway forms; a behaviour in response to a stimulus becomes a habit.

If a baby smiles and is rewarded with a kiss and a cuddle, a neural pathway begins to form. If a young child touches something sharp and it hurts, a neural pathway begins to be laid down. But not all experiences are beneficial. A young child who has witnessed domestic violence may develop neural pathways which lead him to feel fear and withdraw from situations involving confrontation. A girl who is

---

[11] See <https://www.tutor2u.net/psychology/topics/internal-working-model>

sexually abused by a man may shut down emotionally and not let any man near her. She may begin to find ways of deliberately hurting anyone who gets too close to her.

If, since childhood, you've come to associate chocolate with comfort, reward and feeling good and you need an emotional lift, you will automatically take the path – physically as well as psychologically – to that box of chocolates. And every time you do it, that pathway is reinforced. (By the way, this is why, although a diet will help you lose weight in the short term, unless you change those pathways your weight loss will never be sustainable.) Or take another example. Why is it that whenever you walk to the shop, you automatically follow the same route?

The good news is that just like a real road system, however well-worn that pathway has become, there is the potential for it to be changed or adapted. Hope is always real. The brain is ever-changing. You can always forge new pathways and create new habits. This flexibility is known as neuro-plasticity. This is how some people who've had strokes are able to retrain themselves to speak or walk again. And it's this that enables you, with support, training and effort, to overcome bad habits that you thought were unbreakable and master new ones.

From the 1950s onwards, research began to highlight the need for young children to enjoy a secure emotional bond with a primary caregiver.[12] This creates a safe base

---

[12] Known as attachment theory. John Bowlby (1907–90) was a British psychologist, psychiatrist and psychoanalyst. Bowlby is notable for his interest in child development and for his pioneering work in attachment theory.

from which to explore the world and begin to form other relationships, and it can affect a child's psychological, behavioural and emotional development.[13] In the words of Howard Thurman, 'Everyone must be at home somewhere before they can feel at home everywhere.'

Ground-breaking research in the USA in the 1990s found strong links between traumatic or abusive events, known as 'adverse childhood experiences' (ACEs) – sexual abuse; physical abuse or neglect; emotional abuse or neglect; domestic violence; imprisonment of a household member; substance misuse; mental illness; parental separation, divorce, etc. – and the likelihood of physical and mental health issues occurring later in life.

Subsequent extensive study confirms these initial findings time after time, but also highlights the breadth of the physical implications of poor psychological development. Neurodevelopmental factors interact with environmental factors. For instance, the higher the number of adverse childhood experiences, the lower an individual's overall life expectancy and the higher the occurrence of conditions such as cancer, heart disease, stroke, emphysema and diabetes.

But, as well as physical effects, traumatic experiences in childhood are also known to increase the risk of poor psychological health throughout life. For instance, people with a history of child trauma are more likely to experience

---

[13] 'Trauma-informed Care in Response to Adverse Childhood Experiences' (2018), <https://www.nursingtimes.net/roles/nurse-educators/trauma-informed-care-in-response-to-adverse-childhood-experiences/7024813.article#.W3PIqjWYSJc.twitter>

depression, anxiety, anger, failed marriages and relation-ships, as well as addiction to gambling or shopping. They are also more likely to develop risky health behaviours such as being violent, smoking, alcohol and drug misuse, mul-tiple sexual partners, morbid obesity and suicide attempts.[14]

Behaviours that stem from reactions to violence and abuse can have very lengthy incubation periods. They can be like time bombs. A small child is often not big or strong enough to intervene in the violence he witnesses. Instead he may become detached or 'disassociate', but the inter-nalized impact of the violence takes its toll and can have repercussions throughout life. What happens to a per-son at the age of two is relevant when he is 42. Thus the behaviour that we see in an angry, aggressive 42-year-old man is likely to be inextricably linked to the violence that he witnessed as a 2-year-old boy. Study after study over the last half century tells us the same thing. The care and protection extended to or withheld from a child has reper-cussions throughout life. When circumstances provoke an association, violence can become a way of responding to memories (whether conscious or unconscious) dating back decades.

Of course, no two people in conditions of adversity are the same. Not all traumatized individuals will react in the same way. There are a number of factors which can mod-erate behaviour. But those who end up in a stabbing frenzy may well have poor brain development, brain damage or a brain injury, which results in their aggressive behaviour.

---

[14] <www.independent.co.uk/life-style/health-and-families/childhood-trauma-effects-life-expectancy-mental-health-relationships-a7470106.html>

And childhood trauma is much more common than you might think. In 2015 the Welsh government carried out cross-sectional research. Almost half (47 per cent) of those interviewed reported at least one adverse childhood experience. Fourteen per cent reported four or more.

The shock for me was that, compared with participants who reported no ACEs, those with four and over were four times more likely to be high-risk drinkers; six times more likely to have had sex before the age of 16; 15 times more likely to have committed violence in the previous 12 months; 16 times more likely to have used crack cocaine or heroin; and 20 times more likely to have been in prison at some point in their lives.[15]

Research from the Prison Reform Trust suggests that children aged 10 to 17 who are 'in care' (for example in multiple foster placements) are more than five times as likely as their peers to be in trouble with the law. And, although fewer than 1 per cent of children and young people in England and Wales are 'in care', they make up a third of boys and 61 per cent of girls in custodial settings.[16]

To use a metaphor that does not appear in Paul's letters, the cards we are dealt in life are not evenly stacked for all. If being judged 'good' in life is based on our behavioural choices, then the brain making those choices must surely be developed and adapted enough to select socially beneficial responses.

---

[15] For this research 2,028 people aged 18–65 were interviewed.

[16] June 2015, <https://www.bbc.co.uk/news/uk-33221247>

This is why the 'pull-your-socks-up' method of behaviour management is impotent. The threat of punishment doesn't work. It never did. It simply perpetuates the internal working model that sees others as threatening and dangerous. Only love, empathy and support create the possibility for recovery and secure attachment. Paul knew this, and yet only now are we beginning to understand the extent to which our modern understandings of attachment theory and neuroscience support it. A better starting point for human behavioural and moral development is always affirmation rather than condemnation.

Jesus was never a member of that notorious terrorist gang of his day, the Zealots. He did not believe the popular doctrine that violence commands respect or that the punishment should fit the crime. His pathway was different, born of love rather than anger. 'Father, forgive them, for they do not know what they are doing.'[17] 'I tell you, love your enemies and pray for those who persecute you.'[18] Love means that no one is completely stuck where they are. There's always hope. There's always redemption. There is always the potential to feel safe again.

And Paul got the memo:

> May you have the power to understand, as all God's people should, how wide, how long, how high, and how deep his love is. May you experience the love of Christ, though it is too great to understand fully.[19]

---

[17] Luke 23.34.

[18] Matthew 5.44.

[19] Ephesians 3.18–19 (NLT).

He had it sussed. It's grace that makes people moral because it heals them enough to begin to make appropriate choices. Not only can we be changed by love – in reality love is the only power in the world that can change us. After all, it's exactly what Paul had experienced himself.

The big question, then, is how all this affects the Church's theology and understanding of sin, both personal and institutional.[20] How should it influence our social policy? What would be the benefits of using a trauma-informed model of care as a framework for understanding and supporting the people we are here to serve? How could we help rather than hinder those who have suffered trauma?

It's a lot to wrap our heads around, but that's why I believe that a deeper multi-disciplinary conversation between theologians, psychologists and psychotherapists would help the Church into a less 'black and white' understanding of 'sin', and of what are more complex issues than our current thinking sometimes admits.

---

[20] We will look at institutional sin – the systems which carry their own responsibility for creating and perpetuating some of the circumstances which lead to the issues raised here – in Chapter 28.

25

Refined

So let's go back, just once more, to that old chestnut; the one about how because God is love, when people choose to reject a relationship with God in this life, God honours their freedom and their free will and leaves them to their own hell for eternity.

I have two problems with this.

One. In the light of what we've just talked about, if God has any understanding of the human struggle – and I believe God has the deepest possible understanding of it – the statement makes no sense.

Two. It is clear that Paul believes something very different:

> No one can lay any foundation other than the one already laid, which is Jesus Christ. If anyone builds on this foundation using gold, silver, costly stones, wood, hay or straw, their work will be shown for what it is, because the Day [of Judgement] will bring it to light. It will be revealed with fire, and the fire will test the quality of each person's work. If what has been built survives, the builder will receive a reward. If it is burned up, the builder will suffer loss but yet will be saved – even though only as one escaping through the flames.[21]

---

[21] 1 Corinthians 3.10–15.

Scholars agree that Paul is deliberately drawing on the imagery of the words of the Old Testament's prophet Malachi, who described the Day of Judgement and the refining fire of God: 'But who can endure the day of his coming? Who can stand when he appears? For he will be like a refiner's fire or a launderer's soap.'[22]

Read that again. The purpose of the fire is to cleanse not to destroy – as is made clear by the second metaphor, the launderer's soap.

Some preachers try to make the argument that because Paul is writing to the church in Corinth his words are only applicable to those who have already 'put their faith in Christ'. But, as we've seen, this fails to do justice to Paul's core theme – that we are all in the same boat, all saved, not because of our effort, but because each and every last one of us is dependent on the faithfulness of Christ.

And, having explained that some build with gold, silver and precious stones, but others with a great deal of wood, hay and straw, Paul is pretty honest about his own track record:

> I do not understand what I do. For what I want to do I do not do, but what I hate I do . . . For I have the desire to do what is good, but I cannot carry it out. For I do not do the good I want to do, but the evil I do not want to do – this I keep on doing.[23]

---

22 Malachi 3.2.
23 Romans 7.15–19.

Perhaps that is why he explains to the Corinthian church: 'We have this treasure in jars of clay to show that this all-surpassing power is from God and not from us.'[24]

However, is Paul suggesting that some people are going to end up with a better deal – a bigger reward – than others? Paul is not talking about competition. He's not handing out medals. He's talking about the value of what we do in and of itself; much more like when someone really gives themselves to the discipline of painting, or singing, or writing, or design, or swimming, or running, or serving – or, as he puts it, building!

In all these pursuits it is the thing itself that becomes the reward. It is the joy that is gained through the doing of it. It is the privilege of being able to invest, to pursue a goal and leave a legacy. So, as Paul also explains to the Corinthians: 'Always give yourselves fully to the work of the Lord, because you know that your labour in the Lord is not in vain.'[25] Nothing good is wasted – it is an investment in what God is doing.

Once again we realize that Paul has absolutely nothing negative to say about the idea of our human effort and our 'good works'. In fact, the very opposite is true. It is clear that – although it has been dropped from much of Western Christianity – the idea of a final judgement according to the way we have lived our whole lives is as much part of Paul's thinking, in company with mainstream Second Temple Judaism, as it was of Jesus' teaching.

---

[24] 2 Corinthians 4.7.
[25] 1 Corinthians 15.58.

Similarly, until the sixteenth-century reformers ditched it, the Western Church believed in some kind of purging or redemptive process after death where people were cleaned up and made ready for heaven.[26] It was a little like Ebenezer Scrooge's agonizingly painful but ultimately redemptive journey in Charles Dickens' nineteenth-century classic novel *A Christmas Carol.*

The problem was that, over the centuries, 'purgatory' slowly evolved in Roman Catholic theology from being thought of as a process to become a place, where the souls of most of those ultimately destined for heaven were purified, through suffering and torment, from the consequences of their sins, waiting for their release.[27]

It was this ugly idea that the second part of Dante's *Divine Comedy* is devoted to. He chooses to depict Purgatory as a mountain on the far side of the world in the southern hemisphere. Having survived the depths of Hell, the author, accompanied by Virgil, ascends the mountain of Purgatory with its seven terraces, each corresponding to one of the seven deadly sins, and, once again, each with its own ironic punishments and tortures. Only when they reach the top do they find themselves in the garden of Eden itself, and thus, cleansed of all sin, they wait in this earthly paradise before ascending to Heaven.

---

[26] Various branches of Judaism also believe in the possibility of after-death purification. They even use the term 'purgatory'.

[27] Medieval Catholic theologians slowly developed their thinking around the idea of purgatory. The word first appears as a noun in the twelfth century, but did not become a formal doctrine until the First Council of Lyon (1245), after which it was augmented by the Second Council of Lyon (1274), the Council of Florence (1438–45) and the Council of Trent (1545–63).

To put in a kind word for Dante, he was a poet; a poet who simply used his extraordinary gift of words to create a vivid picture from what he had learned from the priests and theologians he trusted. But, rather than being wrong-footed by all this, if we go back to Paul and read again his words in 1 Corinthians 3 at the start of this chapter, we will see he does not define the purging he speaks of as a place, as a torture, or even as a period of time.

Once again, the vast majority of early Church writers appear to have believed that God's 'fire' was always cleansing; that it would cure those who went through it of the false identities and fallenness they had accumulated during their lifetimes. Clement of Alexandria is the earliest writer that we know of to speak of God's fire as a 'wise fire' which burns away sins, leaving behind only pure gold. Origen says that we will all be saved through 'divine fire',[28] while Gregory of Nyssa in his *De anima et resurrectione* (On the Soul and the Resurrection) propounds the notion of fire as a furnace of cleansing which purifies the soul of all that tainted it throughout life:[29]

> When such, then, have been purged from it and utterly removed by the healing processes worked out by the fire, then every one of the things which make up our conception of the good will come to take their place.[30]

---

[28] Edward Moore, *Origen of Alexandria and St. Maximus the Confessor: An analysis and critical evaluation of their eschatological doctrines* (Boca Raton, FL: Dissertation.com, 2005), p. 96.

[29] Gregory of Nyssa, 'On the Soul and the Resurrection', in *Nicene and Post-Nicene Fathers – Gregory of Nyssa: Dogmatic Treatises, etc.*, ed. Philip Schaff and Henry Wace, vol. V, Second Series (Peabody, MA: Hendrickson, 1995), pp. 430–648.

[30] Gregory of Nyssa, 'On the Soul and the Resurrection', p. 468.

Here is the biggest twist. What if the fire is simply a meta-phor for Christ?

The Catholic theologian Joseph Ratzinger, who eventually became better known as Pope Benedict XVI, enlarges on his understanding of Paul's words about the 'wood, hay and stubble' of our lives being 'burned off' and the mean-ing of this purging. He argues that it is a giant mistake to understand purgatory as a place where humans are sent in order to have their sins cleansed. He suggests that it is neither a place nor a length of time. Instead it is a person. Jesus himself is the purging fire, burning away our dross through the heat of his transforming love. He expresses it this way:

> The encounter with [Christ] is the decisive act of judgement. Before his gaze all falsehood melts away. This encounter with him, as it burns us, transforms and frees us, allowing us to become truly ourselves. All that we build during our lives can prove to be mere straw, pure bluster, and it collapses. Yet in the pain of this encounter, when the impurity and sickness of our lives become evident to us, there lies salvation. His gaze, the touch of his heart heals us through an undeniably painful trans-formation 'as through fire'. But it is a blessed pain, in which the holy power of his love sears through us like a flame, enabling us to become totally ourselves and thus totally of God.[31]

As Ratzinger had pointed out in his earlier book *Eschatology*: 'Simply to look at people with any degree of realism at all is to grasp the necessity of such a process.'[32]

---

[31] Pope Benedict XVI, Encyclical *Spe Salvi* (30 November 2007), paragraph 47.

[32] Joseph Ratzinger, *Eschatology: Death and eternal life* (Catholic University of America, 1988), pp. 230–1.

The searing heat of the love of Christ melts even the iciest of human hearts. To be embraced by – to be enfolded in – pure love, even for a moment, is enough for anyone and everyone:

> Enough for the broken;
> and for those whose sense of inner well-being and worth has been stubbed out.
> Enough for those whose anger always burns because they have known no justice;
> and for those who have never been heard or listened to.
> Enough for those who have been betrayed,
> and for those who have never been loved.
> Enough for those who cannot love themselves and therefore cannot love others.
> Enough for us all.
> Perfect love cleanses all.

That was Paul's point: 'Love never fails'!

26

In heaven's name

'If everyone gets to go to heaven, what's the point of being a Christian?'

It's a question I hear often. But the unspoken motive that betrays itself every time it's voiced is, of course, 'Are you trying to say that I've been wasting my time with all this church stuff for absolutely nothing?' It's just another symptom of the popular Protestant myth which assumed that the goal of the Christian life was to avoid God's anger by making sure you were 'saved' and guaranteeing your seat in 'heaven'.

Our problem, once again, is that, along with generations of Westerners before us, we've slipped into the myth of thinking of 'heaven' as being somewhere else. But it's fake news, manufactured through the very same process – the mix of medieval ideas with ancient pagan stories and a smattering of Bible verses and metaphors yanked out of context, and then over-literalized – that brought us the opposite story; the one about the fiery lake and torture in an everlasting hell. And besides being profoundly unbiblical, it has left us very confused.

It is said that St Thomas Aquinas once suggested, 'In the end language can only be related to what is here, and

given that the hereafter is not here, we can only infer.'
Unfortunately, it's never stopped us trying!

We've already explored Dante's fourteenth-century view
of hell and purgatory. His depiction of heaven was just
as fascinating and influential. Heaven, as he presents it in
Paradiso, the third part of the *Divine Comedy*, is the abode
of God, the angels and 'the blessed'. And, just like his version of hell and purgatory, it's ranked and hierarchical.
With Earth sitting at its base, it consists of ten ascending levels or spheres,[1] topped off by the Empyrean, the
dwelling place of God.[2]

Although Dante admitted that his version of heaven was
simply a personal vision, his words, together with various
other medieval cultural images, are the ones that the West
has not only absorbed, but is somehow still half tied to.
We are all familiar, one way or the other, with pictures of

---

[1] These are related to his understanding of the four cardinal virtues
(Prudence, Justice, Temperance and Fortitude) and the three theological
virtues (Faith, Hope and Charity). First are the heavens of the seven plan-
ets (as Dante understood them): the Moon, Mercury, Venus, the Sun, Mars,
Jupiter and Saturn. Then on to the outer firmament of the fixed stars (the
eighth heaven), then the Primum Mobile (the ninth heaven and the place
of the physical origin of life, motion and time) and lastly the tenth, the
Empyrean – the dwelling place of God. The model adopted by Dante of
a cosmos with the Earth at its centre, surrounded by the heavens, is generally known as the Ptolemaic concept of the universe (after Ptolemy, an
Alexandrian polymath of the second century AD). This was broadly shared
by all medieval thinkers, although there are various differing opinions
regarding the exact relationship between God, the different heavens and
Earth.

[2] The *Divine Comedy* actually finishes when Dante glimpses the Trinitarian
God, and, in a flash of understanding that he cannot express, finally grasps
the mystery of Christ's divinity and humanity, as his soul becomes aligned
with God's love.

heaven as a place with pearly gates manned by St Peter, complete with puffy clouds, standard-issue harps and bejewelled streets, and God – a bearded old gentleman – sitting on a golden throne, surrounded by a celestial choir of angels and 'the happy saints' who have made it, all dressed up in white.

There's an ancient story, often credited to the Buddha but with variations also found in Jewish, Christian and Muslim sources, which tells us that once there was a fish, which, because it was a fish, had lived all its life in water and knew nothing whatever of anything else. One day, as it swam in the lake where all its days had been spent, it happened to meet a turtle friend, who had just come back from an excursion on the land.

The fish greeted the turtle, 'I've not seen you for a long time. Where have you been?'

'Oh,' said the turtle, 'I've just been for a trip on dry land.'

'Dry land!' exclaimed the fish. 'What's that? Is it wet? Is it cool? Is it clear? Can you swim in it?'

'No,' said the turtle. 'I just can't describe it to you.'

'Why not?' asked the fish.

'Because there is nothing in your experience that you can compare it to,' replied the turtle.

Paul acknowledges to the church in Corinth that, frankly, his language about the future is at best like gazing through a glass, darkly; an exercise which is unlikely to reveal anything but a dim and distorted image:

> For we know in part and we prophesy in part, but when completeness comes, what is in part disappears . . . For now we see only a reflection as in a mirror; then we shall see face to face. Now I know in part; then I shall know fully, even as I am fully known.[3]

However, although he is aware of his limited grasp, he still believes he has signposts; not maps or photographs, but at least reliable signposts which give him *part* of the answer and point him in the right direction. He sets out his most systematic thinking around this great mystery, which he sees as the renewal of the whole cosmos, in chapter 8 of his letter to the Romans: 'I consider that our present sufferings are not worth comparing with the glory that will be revealed in us. For the creation waits in eager expectation . . .' Though at present it is subject 'to frustration' and 'has been groaning as in the pains of childbirth', it 'will be liberated from its bondage to decay . . .'[4]

For Paul, the future isn't about how he – or anyone else – is going to escape Earth. Instead, it's about what God is doing with the whole earth, the whole of creation. His message isn't about how individuals 'get saved' and fly off somewhere else, it's about what God's doing here and now with us all.

The word 'heaven' (and the associated term 'heavens') appears over four hundred times throughout the whole

---

[3]   1 Corinthians 13.9–10, 12.
[4]   Romans 8.18–22.

Bible, from the very first verse of Genesis to Revelation's penultimate chapter.[5] But, although in the Old Testament it is consistently used with reference to the sky – the home of the moon, the stars, the sun and of God[6] – its use in the New Testament is different. Although sometimes deployed exactly as it is in the Old Testament,[7] it is also used in a very distinctive and innovative way.

Intriguingly, Matthew's Gospel often uses the term 'the kingdom of heaven' to articulate exactly the same meaning the other Gospels do when they speak of 'the kingdom of God'.[8] So, whereas Matthew tells us that 'Jesus said to

---

[5] Genesis 1.1: 'In the beginning God created the heavens and the earth'; Revelation 21.1: 'Then I saw a new heaven and a new earth, for the first heaven and the first earth had passed away.' However, the grammar, structure and style of Ancient Hebrew and Greek are very different from English, which means that it is impossible to make a literal word-for-word translation into English – there is no single correct way to do so. Therefore, the number of times any particular word appears in our English Bibles differs from version to version.

[6] The Bible's ancient cosmology regards the earth as a flat disc which floats on a vast cosmic ocean, somehow all resting on giant pillars thrust up from beneath. The sky is a solid dome with windows and gates, and the sun, moon and stars all hang in the heavenly vault at no huge distance from the earth. Heaven, according to ancient Jews, is where God sits in the highest section. It is also clear, from a huge amount of ancient evidence, both textual and archaeological, that this belief simply reflects the common worldview of the time.

[7] Revelation 21: 'Then I saw a new heaven and a new earth . . .'

[8] Whereas Mark and Luke often use the term 'kingdom of God', John uses it only twice, both times in the same story. Speaking to the Pharisee Nicodemus, Jesus said, 'Very truly I tell you, no one can see the kingdom of God unless they are born again.' 'How can someone be born when they are old?' Nicodemus asked. 'Surely they cannot enter a second time into their mother's womb to be born!' Jesus answered, 'Very truly I tell you, no one can enter the kingdom of God unless they are born of water and the Spirit' (John 3.3–5).

his disciples, "Truly I say to you, it is hard for a rich man to enter the kingdom of heaven," Mark explains that 'Jesus, looking around, said to his disciples, "How hard it will be for those who are wealthy to enter the kingdom of God!"'[9]

Why?

Yahweh was the personal name of the God of Israel, the name that was revealed to Moses through the burning bush.[10] But the Jewish people so revered this special name that they refused to write it down. Instead they chose to abbreviate it to YHWH by leaving out the vowels.[11] In fact, if you look at some Jewish websites, you'll discover that the term G-D is still often used instead of GOD for exactly the same reason. That's why Matthew – whose target audience was Jewish – chooses, mostly, to replace the term 'kingdom of God' with 'kingdom of heaven'.

But when he does this, he is not talking about a physical space called 'heaven'. His intended meaning is altogether different. That's one of the things that confuses modern audiences. When Jesus – and therefore Paul – talk about 'heaven', they do not mean a place, separated from earth, where you might go when you die. Instead it's their way of referring to God's kingship or reign, coming to birth here on earth. This is why, in Matthew 6, Jesus explains to his disciples that they should pray this way:

---

9 Matthew 19.23; Mark 10.23.
10 Exodus 3.
11 YHWH occurs about seven thousand times in the Old Testament and is known as the Tetragrammaton. Most English translations use LORD in small capital letters to replace it.

'Our Father in heaven,
hallowed be your name,
your kingdom come,
your will be done,
on earth as it is in heaven . . .'

Whereas Jesus' famous prayer describes God as being 'in heaven', at the same time he was very well known for making it clear that this same kingdom – the kingdom of God – is right here on earth! So Luke records Jesus' words: 'The coming of the kingdom of God is not something that can be observed, nor will people say, "Here it is," or "There it is," because the kingdom of God is in your midst.'[12]

The kingdom of heaven, or the kingdom of God, is intermingled with our kingdoms. God's dimension (heaven) and ours (earth) are so closely related to each other that they overlap. So when Jesus talks of entering the kingdom, or suggests that someone's reward in heaven is great[13] or challenges his listeners to store up treasures in heaven[14] – he is speaking of giving attention to God's dimension of life, here and now.

We are told that we live in a 3D world, with three spatial dimensions: length, width and depth. But, at the same time, we are also aware of a fourth; the one we call time, which, although we can't see it, is just as real. Now,

---

[12] Luke 17.21.

[13] Luke 6.22–23: 'Be glad in that day and leap for joy, for behold, your reward is great in heaven.'

[14] Matthew 6.19–20: 'Do not store up for yourselves treasures on earth, where moths and vermin destroy, and where thieves break in and steal. But store up for yourselves treasures in heaven . . .'

however, according to string theory physicists, there are at least six other dimensions, each one just as real as the four we can see or perceive.

What Paul and the other New Testament writers, all following Jesus, are saying is that this has always been true of the dimension called heaven – though always present, it is often unseen or ignored. The closest Paul ever gets to talking about what we would regard as heaven as a place is in 2 Corinthians 12, when he uses the language of being carried up into the 'third heaven'. As he tells the story, he explains that he is uncertain about whether this experience was or wasn't 'in the body', as he puts it. In fact, although Paul tells this story in the third person ('I know a man who . . .'), most scholars believe that he was talking about himself and that it is highly probable he was referring to his visionary and life-transforming experience on that road to Damascus. However, his dominant thought about heaven – the framework of his writing – lies in a different direction.[15]

All Jews believed that history – the history of the entire universe – was heading somewhere. God had not abandoned his creation. A new era was coming. The golden age of God. What was promised by the Hebrew prophets in key passages such as Isaiah 25 or Isaiah 2.4 became the shared longing of all the Second Temple Jewish people:

> He will judge between the nations and will settle disputes for many peoples. They will beat their swords into ploughshares

---

[15] 2 Corinthians 12.2–4.

and their spears into pruning hooks. Nation will not take up
sword against nation, nor will they train for war any more.

So important to, and deep within, the national psyche was
this idea, that another prophet, Micah, repeated the cry
almost word for word:

> He will judge between many peoples
> and will settle disputes for strong nations far and wide.
> They will beat their swords into ploughshares
> and their spears into pruning hooks.
> Nation will not take up sword against nation,
> nor will they train for war any more.[16]

In the Old Testament the 'Day of the Lord' becomes the
term that describes this ultimate act of God's (Yahweh's)
judgement, justice and blessing.[17] It will occur when
human history has reached its divinely determined goal

---

[16] Micah 4.3.

[17] The Day of the Lord is not a one-off event. There are past references to historical events of judgement on various nations, including Israel (Amos 5.18, 20) and Judah (Lamentations 1.12; 2.1, 21–22; Ezekiel 7.19; 13.5; Zechariah 1.7–13; 2.2–3) as well as future references (Isaiah 2.10–22; 34.1–8; Obadiah 15; Joel 3.1–16; Zechariah 14.1–3, 12–15). For instance, the phrase 'Day of the Lord' is used to describe the plague of locusts that destroyed crops and resulted in famine (Joel 1.15–20) as well as the imminent invasion of powerful armies (Joel 2.1–11).

Sometimes God's blessing is prominent (Isaiah 4.2–6; 30.26; Hosea 2.18–23; Joel 3.9–21; Amos 9.11–15; Micah 4.6–8; Zephaniah 2.7; Zechariah 14.6–9) and sometimes God's judgement (Joel 2.1–2; Amos 5.18–20; Zechariah 1.14–15) is characterized by an outpouring of anger. (For a definition of God's anger, see Chapter 9.)

Sometimes the past and the future are telescoped together. But, despite this variety of opinion about the Day of the Lord in various OT writers and passages, ultimately the Day of the Lord becomes a picture of God's permanent undoing of evil and the triumph of his justice – the day when the losers win. See the reference to the work of Jürgen Moltmann in Chapter 22.

and will usher in a life in which all humanity is completely under the rule of God.[18] John Stafford Wright suggests that its hearers would take it to mean 'the day when Yahweh would intervene to put Israel at the head of the nations, irrespective of Israel's faithfulness to Him'.[19]

But, transformed by his encounter on the Damascus road, Paul came to understand that, through Jesus, what belonged to the age to come was already breaking into the here and now – bringing hope not only for his own people (the Jewish nation) but for all people, all nations, all languages, all tribes, all colours and all classes; for everyone. So he reframed this well-known Hebrew phrase in terms of his new understanding of Christ as the judge of humankind.[20] As he explains to a meeting of the Areopagus (the aristocratic ruling council of ancient Athens): '[God] has set a day when he will judge the world with justice by the man he has appointed. He has given proof of this to everyone by raising him from the dead.'[21]

For Paul, the Day of the Lord will see the dimensions of earth and heaven completely integrated. Our earthly realm and God's kingdom will finally become one and the same. But for now, as we long for that day's dawn, our challenge,

---

[18] Remember that the Hebrew term for day (יוֹם) and its derivatives are not always used literally. It can also mean a period of time, a number of years, a lifetime or an age, etc. See G. M. Burge, 'Day of Christ, God, the Lord', in *Evangelical Dictionary of Theology*, ed. Walter A. Elwell (Grand Rapids: Baker, 1984), p. 295.

[19] J. S. Wright, 'Day of the Lord', in J. D. Douglas, *The New Bible Dictionary* (Inter-Varsity Fellowship, 1962), p. 296.

[20] Some examples are 1 Corinthians 1.8; 1 Corinthians 5.5; 2 Corinthians 1.14; Philippians 1.6, 10; 2.16; 1 Thessalonians 5.2; 2 Thessalonians 2.2.

[21] Acts 17.31.

whatever the cost, is to choose to live in sync with the way the universe is heading: 'I consider that our present sufferings are not worth comparing with the glory that will be revealed in us. For the creation waits in eager expectation for the children of God to be revealed,' Paul writes to the Romans, adding that 'creation itself will be liberated from its bondage to decay'.[22]

The term 'thin place' is a fascinating metaphor with origins in the ancient Celtic Christian tradition. It speaks of an ordinary physical place – a beach, a bench, a building, a garden – where human beings experience God more readily and the boundary between heaven and earth collapses.

But, if you were to ask Paul . . .

A *thin place* could and should just as easily be a community of people following Christ. Just as he reminds the young church in Philippi, their 'citizenship is in heaven'; they belong to that incoming kingdom, not to the empire of Rome.[23]

---

22 Romans 8.18–21.
23 Philippians 3.20.

27

Metaphor

'All the world's a stage,' said William Shakespeare.

'Books are mirrors of the soul,' explained Virginia Woolf.

'Conscience is a man's compass,' wrote Vincent Van Gogh.

The dictionary tells us that a metaphor is 'a figure of speech in which a word or phrase is applied to an object or action to which it is not literally applicable'.[1] Put differently, a metaphor makes sense only until the point when it is taken literally; then it becomes a lie. Our problem is, of course, that although we intuitively understand metaphors from our own culture ('glass ceilings', 'sticky wickets', 'night owls', 'easy pickings', 'melting pots', 'cold feet', 'slippery slopes') it is often harder to recognize, let alone read, those from ancient times and languages.

And, to make it all even more puzzling, just as a single word within our culture is capable of one meaning when used literally but a completely different one if used metaphorically ('star', 'diamond', 'day', 'heart', 'fox', 'pig'), exactly the same is true, as we will discover, within Paul's writing.

---

[1]   Google Online Dictionary.

Growing up, I was taught by my local church that I lived in a barren and blasphemous world, where our task was to hang on until the day we would be rescued by the second coming – or parousia – of Christ. This was the moment when we would be suddenly 'caught up in the air' (or 'raptured' as it was called) with all the other 'believers'. Leaving this wicked old world behind us, we would escape the horrors that would then be afflicted on all those who suffered the fate of being 'left behind'.[2]

This always worried me a little. Knowing that the world is a sphere, and assuming, of course, that the UK was positioned centrally (as I did), I realized that when Christians living in other parts of it floated up into the atmosphere – Mary Poppins style – they would be headed in the wrong direction!

Much of this highly dramatic 'end-time' imagery is based on Paul's first letter to the Thessalonians,[3] even though everything Paul tells them he explains in much plainer 'down-to-earth' language (both literally and metaphorically) to others.[4] It is just that, when Paul writes to the Thessalonians, he is in a highly metaphorical mood and

---

[2] *Left Behind* is a hugely popular and influential series of religious novels (published between 1995 and 2007 by Tyndale House) by Tim LaHaye and Jerry B. Jenkins. Several of the books have also been adapted into films. There is even a PC game. LaHaye and Jenkins cite the influence on their thinking of Russell Doughten and his 1970s and 80s series of 'Thief in the Night' feature-length films about the Rapture and Second Coming; these in turn echoed the refrain of the 'Christian rock' song by Larry Norman, 'I Wish We'd All Been Ready', in which he sings, 'There's no time to change your mind, the son has come and you've been left behind.' They're the ones that scared me!

[3] 1 Thessalonians 4.13–18.

[4] 1 Corinthians 15.51–54; Philippians 3.20–21.

so borrows several wonderful, well-known images from various Hebrew and Roman sources to add flavour to his core message. But the problem is that, because we don't understand them, we all get a little 'left behind':

> We who are still alive, who are left until the coming of the Lord, will certainly not precede those who have fallen asleep. For the Lord himself will come down from heaven, with a loud command, with the voice of the archangel and with the trumpet call of God, and the dead in Christ will rise first. After that, we who are still alive and are left will be caught up together with them in the clouds to meet the Lord in the air. And so we will be with the Lord forever. Therefore encourage one another with these words.[5]

By the way, the Greek verb that Paul uses for 'will be caught up' in verse 17 is ἁρπαγησόμεθα. And that's where the whole idea of the rapture as we know it got started.

In the Vulgate, Jerome translated ἁρπαγησόμεθα into the Latin verb *rapiemur*, and from there we arrived at the English word 'rapture'. All that stuff about Christians suddenly flying up into the atmosphere, planes being left without pilots, empty cars crashing on motorways, children discovering that their parents have 'been taken to be with the Lord', and the multi-billion dollar sales of the Left Behind series of books and films, have flowed from this.

It's scary. But it's science fiction, not reliable theology.

At the very heart of it all sits the phrase 'we who are left until the coming (*parousia*) of the Lord Jesus'. This has given us the misleading phrase 'the second coming', which

---

5   1 Thessalonians 4.15–18.

creates a sense of leaving and returning. But when Paul used the term *parousia*, his original audience would have instantly understood exactly what he was, and wasn't, talking about, and that was something very different from what many of us have made of it.[6]

In fact, at one level, *parousia* (a transliteration of the Greek word παρουσία) was an ordinary Greek word. In classical Greek it simply referred to 'presence' or 'arrival'; the arrival of any person, anytime and anywhere. Paul uses it of his planned visit to Philippi, as well as that of Titus to Corinth.[7] He also uses it as a way of remembering his visit to – his presence with – the church in Corinth,[8] as well as a visit that a group of his friends had made to them: 'I was glad when Stephanas, Fortunatus and Achaicus arrived (*parousia*), because they have supplied what was lacking from you.'[9]

However, over time, *parousia* also began to be used in two more nuanced ways.[10] The first was to denote the ceremonial arrival of an official in a Roman town. Occasionally

6 Both the Ascension of Jesus and the Parousia are central to the early Church's belief. As the Nicene Creed says, '[Christ] will come again in glory to judge the living and the dead, and his kingdom will have no end.' But this 'returning' is in the sense of parousia, which as we will discover has a subtly different meaning.
7 Philippians 1.26; 2 Corinthians 7.6–7. It is also used in 2 Thessalonians 2.9 to refer to the presence of 'the lawless one', the Pauline opponent of Christ at the end of history.
8 2 Corinthians 10.10 (see also Philippians 2.12).
9 1 Corinthians 16.17.
10 The evidence for both is well summarized in Adolf Deissmann, *Light from the Ancient East: The New Testament illustrated by recently discovered texts of the Graeco-Roman world* (London: Hodder & Stoughton, 1910), pp. 372–8.

even Caesar might make a royal visit to one of the Empire's main cities. When this happened, the people who lived there would head out of the city gates in order to meet him, then turn round and escort him back into it, exactly where they had just come from. But, of course, in reality Caesar was always present. Every city was part of his kingdom. Roman law applied everywhere, it was always active across the whole Empire. So a royal *parousia* was not about a sudden return to re-establish a role that had been forgotten, but rather about celebrating the undeniable presence and rule of one whose kingship and influence was already very real.

But the word *parousia* had acquired a second, equally fascinating use. It came to describe the perceived presence or appearance of a Greek deity during worship. So, for instance, an inscription from the ancient city of Epidaurus in the third century BC talks about a manifestation of Asklepios (Latin: Aesculapius), the Greco-Roman god of medicine, to his devotees as a *parousia.*

That's why the adoption by Paul of a word that already contained full regal and even divine meaning was perfectly natural, and why, of the 13 times he uses it, around half of them refer to Christ's parousia. For Paul, and his original audience, it spoke of the moment when the presence of Christ, whose kingship and influence was already very real, would become an undeniable reality; the moment when the kingdom of heaven and the kingdom of earth would at last be fully integrated.[11]

---

[11] Of Paul's 13 uses of the word *parousia*, 7 refer to Christ: 1 Corinthians 15.23; 1 Thessalonians 2.19; 3.13; 4.15; 5.23; 2 Thessalonians 2.1, 8. It is

But Paul's use of this one-word metaphor is also a piece of multi-cultural genius. Because he used it to tie together two cultural narratives; to create a bridge between the world of Greco-Roman thought and that of Second Temple Judaism. This was in line with Paul's central mission.

In his classic book *The First Urban Christians*,[12] Wayne Meeks analyses the letters of Paul, which are the earliest extant documents of Christianity. He does so in order to build a picture of the life – including the tensions and pressures – of the young churches that Paul was working with. Meeks makes the point that each one of them was, by intention, ethnically and socially mixed. It was Paul's strategy.

Each of Paul's revolutionary cell groups was deliberately developed to be a microcosm of the global reality that Paul believed was coming; a foretaste of the promised future. He had no interest in starting, let alone supporting and encouraging, any community that was not ethnically diverse and socially inclusive. As he said to the Galatians, 'There is neither Jew nor Gentile, neither slave nor free, nor is there male and female, for you are all one in Christ Jesus.'[13]

So, through his use of the term *parousia* and much of the other imagery that he surrounds it with, Paul is making the intentional link between the political rhetoric of the Roman Empire and the Jewish idea of the Day of the Lord

---

also used in the same technical way in James 5.7, 8; 2 Peter 1.16; 3.4, 12; 1 John 2.28.

[12] Wayne A. Meeks, *The First Urban Christians: The social world of the apostle Paul*, 2nd edn (New Haven and London: Yale University Press, 2003).

[13] Galatians 3.28.

(the coming kingdom of God), by using language that alludes to both.

The Old Testament's book of Daniel is written in a style known as Apocalyptic: a literary genre heavily character-ized by symbolism and developed in post-Exilic Jewish culture following the return of the people from Babylon.[14] Daniel chapters 7—12 concern the end of the present age, when God will intervene in history to usher in the Day of the Lord.[15]

In Daniel 7 the author tells us that:

> In my vision at night I looked, and there before me was one like a son of man, *coming with the clouds of heaven*. He approached the Ancient of Days and was led into his presence. He was given authority, glory and sovereign power; all nations and peoples of every language worshipped him. His dominion is an everlasting dominion that will not pass away, and his kingdom is one that will never be destroyed.[16]

It is brilliant. In one word – *parousia* – Paul speaks directly into both cultures, because, of course, there is also the tie-up with the fact that Jesus himself had adopted the title 'son of man' as a metaphor to describe his self-understanding. 'At that time people will see the Son of Man coming in clouds with great power and glory,' he had explained as a way of speaking about himself.[17]

---

[14] See 1 Thessalonians 4.16–17; 2 Thessalonians 2.3–10.
[15] Richard B. Hays, *Echoes of Scripture in the Letters of Paul* (New Haven: Yale University Press, 1989), pp. 14–21, 29, 173–8. It is fair to say that almost all the subsequent studies in this area are in some way indebted to Hays' work.
[16] Daniel 7.13–14.
[17] Mark 13.26. Also see Mark 14.62.

Metaphor

What's more, although Paul's passage in 1 Thessalonians is filled with other pieces of what to us is strange imagery, its interpretation was equally plain for his Jewish audience. Clouds, alongside trumpets, are also a feature of the other famous Jewish story that his language echoes: the story of Moses coming down the mountain having just received the Hebrew law (the Torah) from God.[18] Moses tells the people that in three days' time 'the Lord will come down on Mount Sinai in the sight of all the people'. The text then tells us: 'On the morning of the third day there was thunder and lightning, with a thick cloud over the mountain, and a very loud trumpet blast . . . Then Moses led the people out of the camp to meet with God.'[19]

While heavily cloaked in metaphor, then, Paul's message to the Thessalonians turns out to be completely consistent with his message to other churches. When the Day of the Lord comes, all those who are alive will be transformed and those who have died will be resurrected.

But the specific reason for Paul's writing to the new Christians in Thessalonica was that, as he says, he is aware that they are wondering and worrying about what will happen, on the Day of the Lord, to their friends and family members who have already died. He reassures them. All those who have died will be raised from the dead and will experience Christ's parousia (the great transformation of the present world to which all Scripture points, otherwise known as the Day of the Lord) along with the living.[20]

18 Exodus 19 and 20.
19 Exodus 19.11, 16, 17.
20 In fact, for all those readers who recognize that our verse and chapter divisions were not part of Paul's original writing, this is what he says, explicitly,

Although Paul does not explain, nor does he know, exactly how the presence of the risen Christ will be recognized around the world by all humanity, his use of the term *parousia* is simply another way of referring to that moment when the dimension of heaven that is already here will become so real and so solid that a new world is born; when the kingdom of God will appear in its fullness, when swords will be beaten into ploughshares, when nation will not take up sword against nation nor train for war any more.[21]

Heaven is not somewhere 'up there'. We are not flying away. Paul's message is not about some mass migration from a doomed world to a blessed heaven. It is about the divine transformation of our earth, not its devastation. It is about the end of this era of war and violence, injustice and oppression. It is about a new world of justice and peace.[22]

---

a few lines further on when he talks directly about the 'day of the Lord'. 1 Thessalonians 5.2.

[21] Although Paul equated the parousia with the time of God's final judgement upon all people, the timing of all this, inferred from his teaching, has become hotly debated. Most scholars argue that Paul expected to live to see it, but at the opposite end of the spectrum are the opinions of those who have worked to save Paul's blushes by attempting to prove that as far as he was concerned it was an event that would take place sometime in the remote future. In truth, any serious analysis of Paul's words in 1 Thessalonians 4.12–18 makes it impossible to avoid the conclusion that he writes as if the parousia was, at very least, a real possibility within his own lifetime.

[22] As the Nicene Creed says, '[Christ] will come again in glory to judge the living and the dead, and his kingdom will have no end.' But, as you will also see, it makes no mention of us going anywhere.

28

Rescued

I can guess what you might be thinking.

If all this is true, if everyone's in, then why did Paul spend so much of his life travelling, preaching and writing, while enduring constant threats, frequent rejection, and various imprisonments and several shipwrecks (not to mention eventual execution)?[1]

It's a good question. A very good question. However, at risk of sounding a little like a politician in a radio interview, I'd like to explore another question first.

---

[1] To quote Paul himself from 2 Corinthians 11.23–30: 'I have worked much harder, been in prison more frequently, been flogged more severely, and been exposed to death again and again. Five times I received from the Jews the forty lashes minus one. Three times I was beaten with rods, once I was pelted with stones, three times I was shipwrecked, I spent a night and a day in the open sea, I have been constantly on the move. I have been in danger from rivers, in danger from bandits, in danger from my fellow Jews, in danger from Gentiles; in danger in the city, in danger in the country, in danger at sea; and in danger from false believers. I have laboured and toiled and have often gone without sleep; I have known hunger and thirst and have often gone without food; I have been cold and naked. Besides everything else, I face daily the pressure of my concern for all the churches. Who is weak, and I do not feel weak? Who is led into sin, and I do not inwardly burn?' Paul was also later shipwrecked again towards the end of his life on his way to Rome to face trial; see Acts 27.

The Ancient Jews, as we've discovered, were not the legalistic community that Church history sometimes portrays
them as. Far from the arrogance of believing that they
could achieve their own 'salvation' through good works,
they felt that they were 'saved' simply because they had
been chosen by God.

Their story was about amazing grace; nothing to do with
them and everything to do with God; a story based not
only on the historical reality of their exodus from slavery
but on God's unbreakable promises about the future. So
they kept the Hebrew law not as a way of trying to gain
divine acceptance, but as a way of honouring the fact
that they were already accepted. Although their flawed
attempts at faithfulness could only ever amount, at very
best, to a faint echo of God's faithfulness to them, they
were expressions of gratitude for what they knew was
already true. The motto of their prophets would have been
something like: 'In spite of ourselves we are all in, so now
let's live like it!'

So, perhaps the biggest question about Paul's theology
that we've not yet tackled is, what did this first-century
Second Temple Jew think he was talking about when he
spoke of 'salvation' and 'being saved'? I have a hunch that
if we can answer this one, perhaps the other question – the
one about why Paul was willing to endure so much opposition and hardship – will solve itself.

Broadly speaking, it's true to say that salvation is the overriding theme of the entire Bible. Our problem however is
that, as a leftover of the historic Lutheran and Calvinist
way of seeing things as much as of medieval Catholicism,

being 'saved' has been shrunk, for many, down to little more than the hope of life beyond death.

This was never how Paul – or any other biblical writer – understood things. In both Greek and Hebrew thought, salvation was always a much broader and more holistic term than it has become in its English religious use. But, not only is it all-encompassing, it's never purely orientated towards the future. It is always about down-to-earth liberation – shalom – the whole of you being made whole in the here and now, as well as about hope for the future.[2]

The New Testament's word for salvation, the one Paul used, is *soteria* (σωτηρία). It is a noun whose commonest use in classical Greek was 'physical health'.[3] Even more frequently, Paul uses *sozo* (σῴζω), the verb form of the same word, which means to rescue from danger and deliver into safety; once more the emphasis is on health, well-being and wholeness.

An assumption, they say, is a conclusion reached without its owner even knowing she's reached it. Because *soteria* and *sozo* are often (though not always) translated in our English Bibles simply as 'salvation' or 'save', we get confused into thinking it's somehow all to do with life beyond this one. This is even though, beyond our thoughts about religion, we still use the term 'saved' far more widely. For instance, to speak of a goalkeeper who 'saved' a shot on

---

[2] In fact, its verb form (*sozo*) occurs over 90 times in the New Testament and as a noun (*soterio*) 46 times.

[3] In Greek mythology Soteria was the goddess of safety and salvation, deliverance and preservation from harm.

goal, of money 'saved' in the bank and of a person 'saved' from bad relationship.

Once we stop to think about it, however, we see that this is true even in our English Bibles. So, for instance, in Acts, Luke tells the story of Paul in Lystra meeting a man who was lame: 'Paul looked directly at him, saw that he had faith to be healed (*sozo*) and called out, "Stand up on your feet!"'[4] The word Luke uses is *sozo*. But our translators know that the story is about the man's physical healing and so present it that way.

On another occasion, Luke tells the story of how he and Paul were shipwrecked in a hurricane-force storm while Paul was on his way to Rome as a prisoner to face charges. As Luke explains: 'We took such a violent battering from the storm that . . . when neither sun nor stars appeared for many days and the storm continued raging, we finally gave up all hope of being saved (*sozo*).'[5] Here, although the word *sozo* is translated into English as 'saved', common sense tells us that it is being used in the sense of 'rescued'.

The next example is even more pertinent. When Paul wrote to the Roman church he explained: 'I am not ashamed of the gospel, because it is the power of God that brings salvation (*soteria*) to everyone who believes: first to the Jew, then to the Gentile.'[6]

---

[4] Acts 14.8–10. The actual word used in the text is σωθῆναι, the aorist passive infinitive of the verb σώζω (*sozo*).

[5] Acts 27.13–20. The actual word used is σῴζεσθαι, the present middle-passive infinitive of the verb σώζω (*sozo*).

[6] Romans 1.16. The actual word used is σωτηρίαν – noun, the feminine accusative singular of σωτηρία (*soteria*).

This usage highlights our challenge. If you scan the internet for comments on this and various other verses where Paul uses *soteria* or *sozo* in this way, you will discover that, as one preacher's blog states, 'More often than not these words refer to salvation in a spiritual sense.' But this is one of those huge assumptions, made in denial of all the facts. It's the result of the mistake of importing dualistic Western concepts, which it would have been impossible for Paul to think about in ancient Eastern language, into our modern worldview.

For Paul – as for every Jewish thinker – the 'spiritual', as we call it, was never detached from the 'material' here and now. Paul's point is completely different. He is saying that salvation for those 'who believe' – those who choose to live faithfully to the message of Jesus – starts right here. The purging love – the refiner's fire – has already begun to do its therapeutic work. Which is exactly the point he makes in 1 Corinthians 1.18, where he explains that the message of the cross 'is the power of God' to those of 'us who are being saved (*sozo*)'.[7] The multi-dimensional offer of well-being is about life after birth, not just life beyond death.

Paul does, however, sometimes talk about salvation in a specifically future sense. So, in Romans 13.11–12, he writes: 'The hour has already come for you to wake up from your slumber, because our salvation (*soteria*) is nearer now than when we first believed. The night is nearly over; the day is almost here.' He's not thinking here, however, of some future disembodied state of the soul beyond death,

---

[7] The actual term used is σῳζομένοις, the dative plural masculine participle present passive of the verb σῴζω (*sozo*).

but instead about the 'Day of the Lord', the very down-to-earth and material renewal of the whole cosmos.

In fact, this should be obvious because, as we discovered earlier, the Greek words Paul uses are only ever vehicles – the best that he can find – to translate his Hebrew world-view into the language of a wider audience; to bring the story of Jesus the Jewish Messiah to the whole world.

The Old Testament uses an array of terms that explore the various aspects of salvation. These cover themes as diverse as deliverance, liberation, welfare, escape, release, relief, relaxation and rescue. However, not only did the Old Testament's authors see salvation as very physical and material, they also viewed it as far more communal than individual. So, although sometimes individuals are singled out – for instance, Abraham, Moses, Joseph or Esther – even this is usually presented as being for the good of the whole community.

Of all the words used in the Old Testament for salvation, *yasha* (ישע), meaning to rescue, save, deliver or set free, is probably the most frequently found. But in this case, not only does it have a rich history, it has an even richer future.

The Hebrew name Yeshua (which we translate as Jesus) is a shortened form of the name Yehoshua (Joshua), made up of two parts.[8] The first part, *Yeho* (an abbreviation of Yahweh),[9] was often used as a prefix for longer names,

---

[8] In English the Y sound slowly became a J.
[9] The Tetragrammaton (Yod-He-Vav-He), YHVH, was later modified by scholars who replaced the third letter V with a W, as it is believed this is more authentically how the original letter was pronounced.

such as Jehoshaphat and Jehoiachin, while the second half *shua* is a form of *yasha*. So, for Paul, as for his Jewish audience, even the very name Yeshua conveyed the idea that 'God saves and rescues, individually and communally, practically and materially, globally and cosmically, universally and eternally.'

Paul's life was turned around by his encounter with Christ. In that moment he was saved – rescued – revolutionized. What was more, he realized that what God had done historically for the Jews, he had now done for the whole world. But, for Paul, this salvation – this rescue – was never simply a future tense thing. This salvation was about life after birth – not just the promise for all of life beyond death. And that's why he travelled. He had to tell the world what he had discovered. He didn't want anyone to miss out.

Although Paul has so often been written off as the champion of misogyny and exclusion, he was the very opposite. Paul was the great includer, the great universalizer. This, and only this, provides the answer to that question about why he spent so much of his time travelling despite the personal cost. An excluder would have simply stayed at home!

29

The revolution

They say that a wise person listens to her best friends and her fiercest critics, simply because they are both speaking the truth from slightly different perspectives!

The German philosopher Friedrich Nietzsche (who was a scholar of both Latin and Greek) was, as most people know, a profound critic of the Church, as well as of other religions. In his book *Twilight of the Idols*, he makes a telling point:

> The most general formula on which every religion and morality is founded is: 'Do this and that, refrain from this and that – and then you will be happy! And if you don't . . .'
>   In my mouth, this formula is changed into its opposite . . . An admirable human being, a 'happy one,' instinctively must perform certain actions and avoid other actions; he carries these impulses in his body, and they determine his relations with the world and other human beings. In a formula: his virtue is the effect of his happiness.[1]

Nietzsche's point is profound. And, in this, he perhaps understands something of Paul's wisdom better than most of us. Too often, religion breaks people. It promises freedom but delivers control.

---

[1] Friedrich Nietzsche, *Die Götzen-Dämmerung* (Twilight of the Idols) (1895), trans. Walter Kaufmann and R. J. Hollingdale, <http://www.handprint.com/SC/NIE/GotDamer.html>

Luther looked at medieval Catholicism and didn't like what he saw. It had become a system of control. It created and then abused power. It excluded. It induced shame, fear and guilt. In reaction, he proposed a 'reformation'. But, this too soon produced another system of control. It creates and then abuses power. It excludes. It induces shame, fear and guilt. 'Do this and that, refrain from this and that – then you will be happy! But if you don't . . .'

None of this fits with the words of Paul the great includer. 'It is for freedom that Christ has set us free. Stand firm, then, and do not let yourselves be burdened again by a yoke of slavery,' he tells his Galatian friends.[2]

It is time for a new reformation. It is time to find a way of following Christ which offers liberation and welcome rather than control. Virtue is the outcome of hope, as Nietzsche in his brokenness realized, rather than the other way around.

Paul writes, near the conclusion of his letter to the Romans: 'The hour has already come for you to wake up from your slumber, because our salvation is nearer now than when we first believed. The night is nearly over; the day is almost here.' Then he adds: 'So let us put aside the deeds of darkness and put on the armour of light . . .'[3]

To the Colossians he says similar things and then exclaims:

> Therefore, as God's chosen people, holy and dearly loved, clothe yourselves with compassion, kindness, humility, gentleness and patience. Bear with each other and forgive one another if any of

---

[2] Galatians 5.1.
[3] Romans 13.11–12.

you has a grievance against someone. Forgive as the Lord for-
gave you. And over all these virtues put on love, which binds
them all together in perfect unity.[4]

The way we live matters. The decisions we make here and
now matter. This is how we begin to experience salvation;
right here, right now. But Paul's approach is all about car-
rots rather than sticks.

Since you are already counted in, Paul is saying, live like it!
There are habits and behaviours that have no place in the
coming age: greed, violence, injustice, exploitation, pride,
anger, abuse, torture, jealousy, hatred, bigotry, arrogance.
None of these fit.

According to Paul, however, we are never left to achieve
any of this on our own. We are not doomed to live off our
own supply of self-perpetuating energy. 'The fruit of the
Spirit', Paul explains, 'is love, joy, peace, forbearance, kindness, goodness, faithfulness, gentleness and self-control.'[5]

We live in a culture where some sections of the Church
operate with an almost magical 'let go and let God' theology of the Holy Spirit. But Paul's theology is integrated
with the rest of his thought. He did not suffer from the
dualism that has dogged Western Christianity, in which
what we call the 'sacred' is juxtaposed with the 'secular'.
As James Dunn sets out in his exhaustive study of the theology of Paul, the Holy Spirit plays a key role in Paul's
thinking, as well as one which is inseparable from the rest
of his message. Rather than a dualistic 'either/or' approach,

---

4   Colossians 3.12–14.
5   Galatians 5.19–23.

it is thoroughly 'both/and'; an intrinsic part of his thinking rather than a separate subject.[6]

What does it take to ride a bicycle, keeping it upright and balanced, without crashing? Surprisingly, perhaps, scientists have been puzzling over this question since bikes were first invented in the early nineteenth century. It turns out, however, that there's no single answer to the question. Instead, a bicycle's balance and stability is dependent on a complex mix of gravity, inertia, mass, aerodynamics, gyroscopics and weight distribution, as well as various skills of the individual rider, such as her flexibility, strength and balance.

You can't unpick it. You can't pull it apart. Riding a bike is to do with you and not to do with you. It's to do with your effort, and at exactly the same time it's not your effort at all.

Why does a church grow? Is it the power of God's Spirit or is it the hard work of the people who support the elderly, listen to the lonely, welcome the newcomers, clean the toilets, vacuum the carpet, serve the coffee, invest their money, and sacrifice their time?

You can't unpick it. You can't pull it apart. The growth of a church is to do with you and not to do with you. It's to do with your effort, and at exactly the same time it's not your effort at all.

Closer reflection on Paul's writing reveals that this interwoven theme, simultaneously living in tune with the Spirit

---

6 For an excellent in-depth study, see James D. G. Dunn, *Theology of Paul the Apostle* (Edinburgh: T & T Clark, 2003), pp. 418–20.

of God and receiving the Spirit of God, are central to his whole framework of thought. 'Since we live by the Spirit, let us keep in step with the Spirit,' he tells the Galatians.[7] A passage in his first letter to the Corinthians illustrates perfectly the indissolubility of this relationship:

> I came to you in weakness with great fear and trembling. My message and my preaching were not with wise and persuasive words, but with a demonstration of the Spirit's power [operating through me], so that your faith might not rest on human wisdom, but on God's power.[8]

For Paul, although indwelt and energized by God's Spirit, living Christ's way is also a daily battle. If tradition is to be believed, he wrote his letter to the Ephesians during an imprisonment in Rome, around AD 62.[9] This would create a vivid backdrop for his words: 'For our struggle is not against flesh and blood, but against the rulers, against the authorities, against the powers of this dark world and against the spiritual forces of evil in the heavenly realms.'[10]

---

7 Galatians 5.25.

8 1 Corinthians 2.4–5.

9 He mentions this three times (3.1; 4.1; 6.20). Paul's authorship of Ephesians is disputed. If he is regarded as the author, the impersonal character of the letter, which lacks a personal greeting or any indication that its author has a personal relationship with its recipients, doesn't fit with the account in Acts of Paul staying for more than two years in Ephesus. See Peter T. O'Brien and D. A. Carson (eds), *The Letter to the Ephesians*, Pillar New Testament Commentary (Grand Rapids: W. B. Eerdmans, 1999), p. 5. It is for this reason that most scholars who still maintain Paul's authorship believe that it was a circular letter intended for many churches. For more, see Harold W. Attridge and Wayne A. Meeks (eds), *The HarperCollins Study Bible*, revised edn (New York: HarperCollins, 2006), pp. 1982–3. Some scholars believe that the text in our New Testament is simply the version that was delivered to the Ephesians.

10 Ephesians 6.12.

However frustrated Paul might have been with his individual jailers, he realizes that they are not to blame for his circumstances. The problem is not the 'flesh and blood' soldiers who stand guard and prevent him from leaving. They are simply obeying orders. The way Paul sees it, the real oppressors are 'the rulers', 'the authorities', 'the powers of this dark world' and 'the spiritual forces of evil' that sit behind them. Rather than his guards, it is the juggernaut of the imperial Roman system that has removed his freedom.

Paul understands that regimes and governments can develop cultures and values that, far from bringing salvation (liberty, freedom and well-being), become malevolent. Beyond the will of their members, there's a systemic oppressive spirituality, which can become bigger and more powerful than any of the individuals involved – sometimes including the leaders. For Paul, the integrated thinker, the lines between what we call 'politics' and 'religion' are non-existent.

In his book *The Grapes of Wrath*, John Steinbeck writes:

> The bank is something else than men. It happens that every man in a bank hates what the bank does, and yet the bank does it. The bank is something more than men, I tell you. It's the monster. Men made it, but they can't control it.[11]

The machine easily becomes the master. The creation becomes a monster. Institutions that at first are remarkably flexible and open-minded can gradually become terrible forces of destruction and death.

---

[11] John Steinbeck, *The Grapes of Wrath* (London: Penguin, 2002), p. 31.

Without ever minimizing its individual and personal aspects, Paul's words challenge all who read them to take the socio-political nature of evil seriously. At the same time as we work at the development of our own character, they call us to fight systematic and corporate evil with equal passion.

Walter Wink, who explores Paul's thought in his famous trilogy of books The Powers,[12] argues that in a world where God comes to judge evil, it is the fallen social, economic, religious, political and geopolitical structures, the 'powers' of our world, that must be transformed. Personal redemption cannot take place apart from the redemption of our social structures; our institutions, belief systems and cultural norms. Because these 'manifestations of power' always have an inner spirituality, any attempt to transform them without addressing the exploitation and control that sit behind them, as well as their outer forms, is doomed to failure. 'The Powers are good. The Powers are fallen. The Powers must be redeemed,' he says.[13]

'Faced with a world in rebellion, a world full of exploitation and wickedness, a good God must be a God of judgment,' writes Tom Wright.[14] Paul's answer is, yes, who would want to argue with that? Of course, the creator God will set the

---

[12] Walter Wink, *Naming the Powers: The language of power in the New Testament*; *Unmasking the Powers: The invisible forces that determine human existence*; *Engaging the Powers: Discernment and resistance in a world of domination* (Minneapolis: Fortress, 1984, 1986, 1992).

[13] Walter Wink, in *An Eerdmans Reader in Contemporary Political Theology*, ed. William T. Cavanaugh, Jeffrey W. Bailey and Craig Hovey (Grand Rapids: W. B. Eerdmans, 2011), p. 365.

[14] Tom Wright, *Surprised by Hope* (London: SPCK, 2007), p. 150.

world right. Justice will be done. Oppressive regimes will be overturned. God's promise of a new – renewed – earth is coming. None of this is simply a pipedream. The wolf will live with the lamb. Our social systems and institutions – including the Church – will be transformed. But, first, they too must face the refiner's fire. And the more that they, like us as individuals, are conformed to Christ in the here and now, the more that purging is already in the process of taking place.

Recently I was in a discussion with various local community groups, where the blame for the mind-numbing delays on a much-needed youth project were being laid, rather angrily, at the feet of the two local government officers who were present. But I know them both well, and although they couldn't say it, they were at least as frustrated as everyone else in the room. In truth, the real culprit behind the problem is the political system that produces what can be cold, heartless and sometimes dehumanizing policies.

Put starkly, what Paul is telling the Ephesian church is that right now God does not always get what God wants. This thought upsets many religious people because they claim that God is all-powerful; God can do anything, and to suggest otherwise is an affront to God.[15] But, the way I see it, not only does it marry up with the reality of the world as we encounter it, it fits with Paul's understanding. Paul recognizes that life is a 'struggle', simply because we live in

---

[15] Traditionally Christianity, along with the other two Abrahamic religions (those which trace their beginnings back to Abraham – Judaism and Islam), have attributed what is called omnipotence – 'unlimited power and control' – to God.

a world where God's will is clearly not yet done 'as it is in heaven'. It is this that we wrestle with each day of our lives.

Does God look down on the poverty and oppression of billions and – hearing their prayers and petitions – choose to turn away? No.

Does God listen to the desperate cry of the dispossessed, the forgotten, the abused, the bullied, the betrayed, the poor, the sick and the bereaved, but simply ignore or reject their plea? No.

The kingship of God – how the world would be if the God of love was in total control – is, at one and the same time, in pockets both already present and still a longed-for future hope in its completeness.

This 'now-and-not-yetness' of God's kingdom is what the theologians have often called 'inaugurated eschatology'. 'Eschatology' is the word for the part of theology which is concerned with the final events of history; the ultimate destiny of humanity. The term 'inaugurated' simply implies that what is coming has already begun; it has already been initiated. But, if we are going to use long terms, I much prefer the phrase 'collaborative eschatology' coined by Dominic Crossan. 'It is not that we are waiting for God, it is that God is waiting for us,' he writes.[16] Rather than waiting for God to do it, our task is to collaborate with God.

[16] John Dominic Crossan, 'Jesus and the Challenge of Collaborative Eschatology', in *The Historical Jesus: Five views*, ed. James K. Beilby and Paul R. Eddy (Downers Grove, IL: IVP, 2010), p. 125.

I contrast this with what I call 'spectator eschatology'. This comes in two versions. The first – a view still popular in many forms of Christianity even today – is that God somehow has the supernatural rescue of the earth all sorted while all we have to do is pray and twiddle our fingers. The second is a slightly modified version in which Christian hope is not about the transformation of the world at all, but instead only about individual salvation, whether in this life or in a life beyond death.

For Paul, Jesus' death and resurrection are nothing less than the inaugural moment of a worldwide revolutionary movement responsible for restoring, reconciling and renewing the whole of God's creation. And he knows that our lives are changed as we allow our small, flawed, personal micro-stories to be given a bigger, global, even cosmic context as we collaborate with God; a task which brings shape, meaning and hope to our journey through life. We are called to collaborate with God as we work to bring about his kingship right here; what Crossan describes as 'the Great Divine Clean-Up of the World'.[17]

Though we live 'East of Eden' we still bear the divine image. We are still God's representatives, in our working and business lives every bit as much as in our private lives. Our money, our time and all our other resources – both personal and professional – are tools, not toys. Our personal budgets and corporate annual accounts are simply the story of our ethics displayed in numbers. And, since we are already counted in, our task is to anticipate the future Day of the Lord in the way we live now. To possess

---

[17] Crossan, 'Jesus and the Challenge of Collaborative Eschatology', p. 109.

without becoming possessed. To work as God's representatives to tackle poverty, inequality and social injustice in
all its forms. To collaborate with God in the redemption of all
things. As Paul wrote:

> Finally, brothers and sisters, whatever is true, whatever is noble,
> whatever is right, whatever is pure, whatever is lovely, whatever
> is admirable – if anything is excellent or praiseworthy – think
> about such things. Whatever you have learned or received or
> heard from me, or seen in me – put it into practice. And the God
> of peace will be with you.[18]

If there are habits and behaviours that have no place in
the coming age, they are habits and behaviours that have
no place in our lives now, and no place in the businesses
and community activities over which we have influence or
control. Our personal code of ethics, our corporate investment manual, should reflect – indeed will always reflect –
who we really are and who we are becoming.

God might not always get what God wants, at least not
yet – but we pray and work for the day when he will.

Paul summed it up brilliantly: 'Let us live up to what we
have already attained.'[19]

We are all in. Now let's live like it!

---

[18] Philippians 4.8–9.
[19] Philippians 3.16.

Appendix

What did the Ancient Greeks think about the afterlife?

Homer's *Odyssey* tells the tale of Persephone (the goddess daughter of Zeus and queen of the underworld). The story begins with her abduction, at the direction of her father, by her uncle Hades, the lord of the dead. She is swept away, carried down to the underworld and forced to become Hades' wife. However, thanks to the efforts of her mother, Demeter, she is able to escape the darkness and return to the surface world for two-thirds of the year, resigned only to dwell with Hades for the remaining portion. So Persephone is associated with death and rebirth, through her yearly cycle of descending to the land of the dead and her joyous ascension to the world of the living. Odysseus, Orpheus and others were able to visit and subsequently leave the underworld.

There is fragmentary evidence (mainly from jewellery) that by the sixth century BC various groups, including the Orphic cult and the Pythagoreans (followers of the philosopher Pythagoras), had developed some kind of understanding of reincarnation or rebirth.

By the fourth century BC, in his book the *Republic*, Plato paints a picture of life after death into which he begins to build the concepts of punishment and reward, the possibility of rebirth/reincarnation and of the underworld having distinct good and bad places.

The *Republic* is a dialogue between Socrates (Plato's teacher) and others on justice, the city state and the 'just man'. In the final (tenth) book, which acts as a conclusion, Socrates recounts the myth of a man called Er who was killed in a battle.

Some days later, when his body was about to be cremated, Er sat up and told those around him about his journey through the afterlife. Initially, he and the other souls had arrived at an awe-inspiring place with openings that led either underground or up to the heavens and judges who told each soul which way they should go. At the same time, souls were returning through the openings, either telling of beautiful things if they came from the sky, or looking dirty and haggard and telling of awful experiences if they came back from the underworld, although it is explained that a few souls, guilty of particularly heinous crimes, were unable to return. After seven days, the returned souls set out on a journey, eventually arriving at 'the Spindle of Necessity', where they were required to choose their next life. Er noticed that those souls who had been in the heavens often made choices that gave them power in the next life, but which would often and unknowingly lead to pain and even atrocities, while those who had been in the underworld often chose a better life.

After choosing a life, the souls were assigned a guardian spirit, drank from the River of Forgetfulness, and fell asleep, at which point they were reborn into the life they had chosen.

It is equally interesting, however, that Aristotle, Plato's student, undoes all this. He believed that the human soul ceased to exist at death.

There was no life after death for anyone!

About Oasis

Oasis is a group of charities, founded by Steve Chalke, set up to pioneer models of sustainable, holistic local community transformation. Wherever we work we serve and respect all people whatever their gender, race, ethnic origin, religion, age, sexual orientation or physical and mental capability, through the pursuit of our two global goals:

- to build, and to help others build, strong inclusive communities where every person can find their place, flourish and achieve their God-given potential;
- to work with those who find themselves outside of healthy community to find their place once again.

We do all this through a wide variety of integrated, high-quality and diverse activities and partnerships. We deliver housing, education, healthcare, training, youth work, family support and many other community initiatives. Currently Oasis works in 42 local neighbourhoods in England and another 26 in other countries around the world – in Europe, Asia, Africa and North America. Our approach is always bespoke, tailored to each local community or people group that we work with.

Central to everything Oasis does is a commitment to a way of working that fosters a culture of inclusion, equality, open and healthy relationships, hope that change is possible and perseverance to keep going for the long haul.

Oasis has over five thousand staff, as well as many more thousands of volunteers. We are responsible for more than fifty schools, thirty thousand students, and numerous housing and health projects. Through working with local community members we are also involved in developing everything from foodbanks to debt advice centres, savings clubs to credit unions, local churches to city farms, community shops to breakfast clubs, children's centres to refugee housing, initiatives to combat human trafficking and sexual and gender-based violence to adult numeracy and literacy courses, libraries to football teams, partnerships with the NHS to employment initiatives and much more. Together we are building communities where everyone can thrive.

To find out more, or to discover how to get involved or support us, please visit:

<www.oasisuk.org> and <www.oasisglobal.org>.

Further reading

All the way from the most accessible to the most technical:

Brian Zahnd. *Sinners in the Hands of a Loving God: The scandalous truth of the very good news.* New York: Crown, 2017

Rob Bell. *Love Wins: At the heart of life's big questions.* HarperCollins, 2011

Mother Teresa. *Come Be My Light: The revealing private writings of the Nobel Peace Prize winner,* ed. Brian Kolodiejchuk. London: Ebury, 2008

Brigitte Kahl. *Galatians Re-imagined: Reading with the eyes of the vanquished.* Minneapolis: Augsburg Fortress, 2010

Diarmaid MacCulloch. *A History of Christianity: The first three thousand years.* London: Penguin, 2010

Walter Brueggemann. *The Bible Makes Sense,* revised edition. Cincinnati: St. Anthony Messenger Press, 2003

Karl Allan Kuhn. *Having Words with God: The Bible as conversation.* Minneapolis: Fortress Press, 2008

James D. G. Dunn. *The Theology of Paul the Apostle.* Grand Rapids: W. B. Eerdmans, 1998

Tony Jones. *Did God Kill Jesus?* San Francisco: HarperOne, 2015

Tom Wright. *Surprised by Hope.* London: SPCK, 2007

Miroslav Volf. *Exclusion & Embrace: A theological exploration of identity, otherness, and reconciliation.* Nashville: Abingdon, 1996

Anthony C. Thiselton. *New Horizons in Hermeneutics: The theory and practice of transforming biblical reading.* Grand Rapids: Zondervan, 1992

Paul Fiddes. *Past Event and Present Salvation: The Christian idea of atonement.* London: Darton, Longman, & Todd, 1989

Nicholas Ansell. *The Annihilation of Hell: Universal salvation and the redemption of time in the eschatology of Jürgen Moltmann.* Milton Keynes: Paternoster, 2013

N. T. Wright. *Paul and his Recent Interpreters: Some contemporary debates.* London: SPCK, 2015

We have misunderstood Paul, badly.

We have read his words through our own set of assumptions. We need to begin with Paul's world view, to see things the way he saw them.

What if 'original sin' was never part of Paul's thinking?

What if the idea that we are saved by faith in Christ, as Luther argued, was based on a mistranslation of Paul's words and a misunderstanding of his thinking?

Over the centuries, the Church has repeatedly failed to communicate, or even understand, the core of Paul's message. Although Paul has often been presented as the champion of exclusion, he was the very opposite. He was the great includer.

'Prepare to have your mind expanded and your spirit stretched.'
Lucy Winkett

'Pulsing and brimming and overflowing with life . . . This book is going to set so many people free.'
Rob Bell

'Accessible and readable . . . fascinating.'
Pauline Muir

Popular Theology
eBook available

ISBN 978-0-281-07940-7

9 780281 079407

spck.org.uk

@SPCKPublishing

/SPCKPublishing

@SPCK_Publishing

Steve Chalke MBE is a Baptist minister, the founder and leader of the Oasis Charitable Trust, and the author of more than fifty books.